Introduction to Education in the Community College

Mary E. Braselton, Ed.D.
Midland College

Kendall Hunt
publishing company

Cover image © 2010 Shutterstock, Inc.

The 13 competencies; technology application standards; Texas map showing regional headquarters and explanation from English Language Arts TEKs are used with permission. Copyright © 2010. Texas Education Agency. All Rights Reserved

Kendall Hunt
publishing company

www.kendallhunt.com
Send all inquiries to:
4050 Westmark Drive
Dubuque, IA 52004-1840

Copyright © 2010 by Mary E. Braselton

ISBN 978-0-7575-7644-7

Kendall Hunt Publishing Company has the exclusive rights to reproduce this work, to prepare derivative works from this work, to publicly distribute this work, to publicly perform this work and to publicly display this work.

All rights reserved. No part of this publication may be reproduced, stored in a retrieval system, or transmitted, in any form or by any means, electronic, mechanical, photocopying, recording, or otherwise, without the prior written permission of the copyright owner.

Printed in the United States of America
10 9 8 7 6 5 4 3 2 1

To Vivian Wristen Eubank, my mother and my first great teacher role model. She showed me through example that a professional teacher is one thing and one who teaches with passion is another. It is that precise combination of professionalism and passion—the art and science of teaching—which produces great teaching. That is what we all aspire to.

Foreword   vii
Preface   ix
Acknowledgments   xi
Introduction   xiii

INTRODUCTION TO THE TEACHING PROFESSION   1

LEARNING PLAN   2

WEB SEARCHES   4

THE HOT E-PORTFOLIO   10

COMPETENCY CHAPTERS   13

STANDARD 1

Designing Instruction and Assessment to Promote Student Learning   15

    Competency 1: Human Development   17
    Competency 2: Diversity   33
    Competency 3: Lesson Planning   53
    Competency 4: Learning Processes   73

STANDARD 2

Creating a Positive, Productive Classroom Environment   93

    Competency 5: Classroom Environment   95
    Competency 6: Classroom Management   109

STANDARD 3

Implementing Effective, Responsive Instruction and Assessment   129

    Competency 7: Communication   131
    Competency 8: Active Engagement   153
    Competency 9: Technology   173
    Competency 10: Planning for Performance, Achievement and Feedback   191

STANDARD 4
Fulfilling Professional Roles and Responsibilities 205
    Competency 11: Family Involvement 207
    Competency 12: Professional Knowledge and Skills 221
    Competency 13: Legal and Ethical Requirements 241

FINAL DIRECTIONS 263
    The Field Experience Guide 265

    How to Conduct a Classroom Observation 277

    The Reflective Teacher 279

    Writing an Educational Philosophy 280

    Educator Standards Web Search 281

    Web Searches 284

    Benjamin Bloom's Cognitive Taxonomy 287

    Scholar's Vocabulary Instructions 288

    Scholar's Vocabulary 289

    Answers to Practice Questions 293

Foreword

The close of the last century brought the growing recognition that something needed to change with teacher education. The rate at which beginning teachers left the profession with less than three years of work experience was escalating, and the demand for teachers was growing. Many factors influence the decision to leave the teaching profession, some of which are exogenous to the teaching profession, and some lie within the teaching profession.

One such factor was the progression of the courses taken in the pursuit of certification as a teacher. Typically, students did not take education courses until they were juniors and did not student teach until in the last semester. In other words, students were not exposed to the "real" profession until just before they graduated and went to work. As a result, many students did not know what they were getting until they were in it. After having invested time and money in a college degree, many went on into teaching but some did not; of those who did, some discovered they liked it but many others did not.

The determination was made that students needed to be exposed to the teaching profession earlier in the postsecondary experience. In 2004 the Texas Higher Education Coordinating Board convened an advisory committee to create an Associate of Arts degree in Teaching. The committee, made up of representatives from both four-and two-year schools met to devise a fully transferable associate degree that would introduce students to the teaching profession at the lower division level of college. One of the key results of the effort was the development of two new courses: Education 1301: Introduction to the Teaching Professions and Education 2301: Introduction to Special Populations. Both courses embed substantial field experience to make sure that students are introduced not only to the teaching profession theoretically, but also practically. This textbook is designed to address the topics found in the first course.

Rex C. Peebles, PhD
Vice President of Instruction
TheCB Advisory Committee Member
Midland College

Preface

BOOK DESIGN

The organizational design of this book mirrors the content of the State-mandated Pedagogy and Professional Development Standards. This design meets the Texas State Board of Education mandate to incorporate the Pedagogy and Professional Responsibilities (PPR) competencies insofar as possible into the Introduction to the Teaching Profession (EDUC 1301) course. The book is divided into sections: Introduction to the Profession, 13 Competency Chapters, and Final Directions.

INTRODUCTION TO THE PROFESSION

Because each state has similar but different requirements for teacher certification, it is important for students to understand the community college relationship to becoming a teacher in Texas, so Dr. Rex Peebles, Vice-President of Instruction at Midland College, has written the Foreword explaining that relationship.

The front matter of this book includes **web searches** intended to introduce students to the professional resources of their chosen profession. The web searches include information on how to obtain certification as well as how to find information on the Texas Education Agency, the State Board for Educator Certification, and the Coordinating Board web sites.

This book is also designed with the final examination in mind: a **HOT ePortfolio,** the HOT standing for *higher-order thinking*. An introduction to portfolio assessment is given for portfolio construction emphasizing authentic experience. The performance design of the HOT ePortfolio enables each student to showcase the proficiency not only with technology but also with each of the 13 competencies. Even though each of the competencies is studied topically, it becomes clear that all of the competencies are integrated in the completed ePortfolio. The ePortfolio is performance-based and allows the student to demonstrate both the art and science of teaching through authentic experience.

COMPETENCY CHAPTERS

This book is divided into 13 chapters each of which is devoted to one of the 13 competencies listed in the State Standards. Breaking from a traditional textbook model, the content of each chapter is presented in a **lesson plan** format to model for students a basic 9-step lesson plan ending with a multiple-choice assessment.

Within each lesson plan, students will find objectives, lesson foci, models, assignments, and suggestions for additional artifacts for the ePortfolio.

FINAL DIRECTIONS

The State of Texas requires a 16-hour **field experience** component which all students much complete in order to pass the course. This book includes a workable field experience design for most independent school districts in Texas.

The end of the book features an **Interactive Glossary** which students will be encouraged to complete as they work with each competency. This Interactive Glossary serves as a reinforcement strategy for learning educational jargon and, ultimately, as a study guide for the TExES.

Also included in the end matter are the pages from the TExES Preparation Manual for test 160, EC-12. These pages provide guides for the scope of each competency and serve as a permanent reference for students.

Acknowledgments

I gratefully acknowledge Kay Humes, former colleague and friend, whose creativity is exceeded only by her energy.

I also acknowledge Dr. Will Morris, Dean of Social and Behavioral Sciences and Education, and Dr. Rex Peebles, Vice President of Instruction, at Midland College. Both men understand the need for quality educators and the struggles of the systems which prepare them and employ them. Their support is invaluable and provides an incredible working environment.

I also gratefully acknowledge those in my learning community: Dr. Margaret Wade, Dean of Science at Midland College, who said, "My faculty wants to meet with you to discuss pedagogy!" and Dr. Teri Gilmour, Faculty Senate President, who organized a group of faculty members by saying, "Let's meet at Murray's Deli to discuss online teaching!"

Introduction

Introduction to the Profession

> "By learning you will teach;
> by teaching you will understand." *Latin Proverb*

Interestingly enough, if you want to become a teacher in the State of Texas, you do not get a degree in education. In fact, Texas colleges and universities do not offer education degrees, but all traditional teacher candidates must graduate through an approved teacher education program from an accredited college or university. That means your "major" must be in an academic area like English, Science, Social Studies, or Mathematics. In addition to those content classes, you will take a "block" of courses which train you in pedagogy (teaching) and in professional responsibilities. These courses are highly regulated and supervised by the State of Texas and the degree-granting institution.

This book has been especially developed for the student at the community college who wishes to obtain a teaching degree. The route to certification by way of the community college is very simple: graduate with the Associate of Arts in Teaching (AAT), then transfer to a four-year institution to earn a baccalaureate degree. The four-year institution help the student complete teacher certification requirements.

At the end of the training, each student must pass state-designed competency exams (TExES) before the State issues certification. Most students will take a minimum of two tests: one in the content area, such as mathematics, and one in pedagogy and professional development. This textbook is designed with the Pedagogy and Professional Development (PPR) examination in mind.

Design of This Book

The State of Texas mandates that the **Associate of Arts in Teaching (AAT)** "course content should be aligned as applicable with State Board for Educator Certification Pedagogy and Professional Responsibilities standards"; therefore, the purpose for this book is to prepare students for the university preparation through chapters which align with the PPR.

The Associate of Arts in Teaching

The community college's involvement in the teacher certification process is relatively new. In 2003, the State of Texas predicted severe shortages in teachers to staff the classrooms of Texas schools.

Teacher Job Outlook

The Texas Workforce Commission (as quoted on the State Board of Education web site) indicated that "Texas will need over 82,000 new teachers by 2008. The Bureau of Labor Statistics projects teaching as one of the fastest growing occupations over the next 5–10 years and beyond, with demand and growth continuing to increase. The average teacher salary in Texas is $38,857. Special programs and incentives are available to help people become and remain teachers." Therefore, the challenge to the Coordinating Board was how to interest more students in becoming teachers? One of the creative and brilliant answers was to open up a new recruiting and training avenue for community college students who were thinking about teaching as a career—the AAT. In reality, the AAT consists of the "core curriculum" of the college and two courses in education: EDUC 1301: An Introduction to the Teaching Profession, and EDUC 2301, An Introduction to Special Populations. When taken in conjunction with the AAT, both courses transfer to the university and are accounted for in the student's degree plan leading to graduation.

Although there are teaching positions in all areas and levels of public education in Texas, there are some teaching areas which have been designated as "High Needs Areas": They are mathematics, science, bilingual education, special education, foreign languages, and technology applications. This means that the demand is greater than the supply of teachers. However, the demand will also depend upon the area of the state in which you apply for a job.

Why AAT? Its Mission

The mission of an education program at the community college is to provide pre-service courses rich in content that will help students assess their interest in a teaching career. This experience provides one of the strengths of community college preparation for teaching. At the university, students do not take a course in education until the junior year, and occasionally, students wind up in student teaching only to determine that they do not want to teach. To enhance the community college experience, THECB has determined that each of the two courses will require students to complete 16 hours of field-based experiences in P-12 schools. Students will observe and assist in Pre-Kindergarten through high school classrooms in order to determine which level they want to teach.

The AAT allows students to *try on* education in foundational courses by getting field experience hours in actual classrooms and participating in designing lesson plans and completing short teaching assignments. Some students seek even more opportunities to teach in programs such as Junior Achievement and public library reading programs, and literacy programs. While *trying* on education as a career, students learn a great deal about the State-designed competencies which all teachers must master before becoming certified.

Financial Assistance

With new attention focused on teacher shortages, financial assistance may be available to help you reach your goal. You can find a comprehensive list of possible funding sources on the SBOE web site. Some possibilities include: Teach for Texas: grants; Certified Educational Aide Exemption Program: tuition exemptions; Teach for America: cash awards to apply to student loans; Troops to Teachers: military veterans can transition to the classroom; Teacher Loan Forgiveness: Money is available for teachers in high-needs fields; Grow Your Own Programs: many ISDs provide monetary incentives for employees; Grants: THECB provides resources for teachers on their web site, G.I. Bill Benefits: reimbursement for some costs. Other resources may be available at your own schools, too.

Your first assignment in this book will be to visit the SBEC web site to learn a little more about how to become a teacher in Texas.

Introduction to the Teaching Profession

Learning Plan
Web Searches
The HOT ePortfolio

LEARNING PLAN

Learning Plan for Education 1301 and 2301

LEARNING PLAN: A Learning Plan is a document which plans "learning" over an extended period of time. In the case of the Associate of Arts in Teaching (AAT), your extended learning will take place over two semesters. The plan involves two education courses required for completion of the AAT: EDUC 1301 and EDUC 2301. Your learning plan encompasses the State Standards for Pedagogy and Professional Responsibilities (PPR) and the corollary 13 Competencies which not only directs your learning but also allows you to demonstrate skill proficiency as you develop into a novice teacher. The applied knowledge of the competencies forms the basis for a criterion-referenced examination known as the Texas Examination of Essential Skills: TExES.

The entire document is found on the State Board for Educator Certification (SBEC)/Texas Education Agency (TEA) web site: *http://www.texes.ets.org/texes/prepMaterials/*.

The following Learning Plan forms the curriculum for EDUC 1301: Introduction to the Teaching Profession, and EDUC 2301: Introduction to Special Populations. Preservice teachers should adopt the curriculum as a personal learning plan and set personal achievement benchmarks accordingly. In EDUC 1301, students apply these competencies to teaching in the regular classroom; in EDUC 2301, students apply these same competencies to teaching special populations.

Components of YOUR Learning Plan

1. THE COMPETENCY CHART (see page 3)

    As you can see from the Competency Chart, the four Domains/Standards are broken into 13 competencies (001–013). Each of these competencies can and will be broken into more specific topics and referred to in each education preparation course you take. The following link provides the document source for the competencies: 160 Pedagogy and Professional Responsibilities EC-12.

2. LANGUAGE ARTS

    Reading, writing, listening, and speaking form the basis for teaching, so teachers are expected to master all four of these language arts. This component of your learning plan involves close reading for different purposes as well as comprehending what is read, the ability to write lesson plans and reflect upon your learning, listen and follow instructions, and finally, make professional presentations to peers and others as opportunities arise. Ultimately, students are expected to integrate the many skills a teacher must possess.

3. THE ELECTRONIC PORTFOLIO

    Ultimately, as you master each of the competencies, you will produce concrete artifacts which demonstrate your learning. Your product (artifact) will demonstrate the level of progress toward your learning goal of mastering the Pedagogy and Professional Responsibility (PPR) competencies. By documenting your learning in the electronic portfolio, you will begin to integrate the competencies in ways that require synthesis and evaluation (higher-order thinking skills).

Directions for the Electronic Portfolio are given separately.

Test Framework for Field 100, 110, 130: Pedagogy and Professional Responsibilities EC–6, 4–8, 8–12

Domain/Standard	Competency
1: Designing Instruction and Assessment to Promote Student Learning	001: The teacher understands **human developmental processes** and applies this knowledge to plan instruction and ongoing assessment that motivate students and are responsive to their developmental characteristics and needs.
	002: The teacher understands student **diversity** and knows how to plan learning experiences and design assessments that are responsive to differences among students and that promote all students' learning.
	003: The teacher understands procedures for **designing effective and coherent instruction and assessment** based on appropriate learning goals and objectives.
	004: The teacher understands **learning processes** and factors that impact student learning and demonstrates this knowledge by planning effective, **engaging instruction** and appropriate assessments.
2: Creating a Positive, Productive Classroom Environment	005: The teacher knows how to establish a **classroom climate** that fosters learning, equity, and excellence and uses this knowledge to create a **physical and emotional environment** that is safe and productive.
	006: The teacher understands strategies for creating an organized and productive learning environment and for **managing student behavior**.
3: Implementing Effective, Responsive Instruction and Assessment	007: The teacher understands and applies principles and strategies for **communicating** effectively in varied teaching and learning contexts.
	008: The teacher provides appropriate instruction that **actively engages** students in the learning process.
	009: The teacher incorporates the effective use of **technology** to plan, organize, deliver, and evaluate instruction for all students.
	010: The teacher **monitors student performance** and achievement; provides students with timely, high-quality **feedback**; and responds flexibly to promote learning for all students.
4: Fulfilling Professional Roles and Responsibilities	011: The teacher understands the importance of **family involvement** in children's education and knows how to interact and communicate effectively with families.
	012: The teacher enhances **professional knowledge** and skills by effectively interacting with other members of the educational community and participating in various types of professional activities.
	013: The teacher understands and adheres to **legal and ethical requirements** for educators and is knowledgeable of the structure of education in Texas.

4 Introduction to the Teaching Profession

WEB SEARCHES

Web Search: Why Teach?

In this web search, you will be introduced to the State Board for Educator Certification web site and several other web sites. These web sites contain information that is critical to your future planning as you work toward certification.

Access the State Board for Educator Certification (SBEC) at this web site:
http://www.sbec.state.tx.us/SBECOnline/default.asp

1. In the left-hand column, click "State Board for Educator Certification." Click "Educator Certification." In the left-hand column, click "Certification Information." Click "Certification Information Home." Then click "Becoming a classroom teacher in Texas." What are three basic requirements for becoming a teacher in Texas?

    1.

    2.

    3.

2. If you are already certified, how do you become certified in another area?

3. Click on "Resources to Help Pay for Educator Preparation" and research one area which might apply to you and describe how you might obtain funding under this program.

4. Return to the home page and in the left-hand column, click on the "Fingerprinting" link. Who will be required to undergo a national criminal history background check in Texas? What is the cost associated with this check? Who pays for fingerprinting?

5. Return to the home page and in the left-hand column, click on the "Certification Laws and Rules" link.

    Click on "State Board for Educator Certification—Administrative Rules."

    Click on "Texas Administrative Code—Currently in Effect."

    Click on Chapter 230 "Professional Educator Preparation and Certification."

    Click on Chapter S "Educational Aide Certificate."

    Click on each of these links—"230.553," "230.554," and "230.555"—to discover the rules for being a certified aide in public schools. Which one of these levels do you qualify for when you obtain the AAT? Describe your credentials here.

6. Click on the following link: http://www.usca.edu/essays/vol102004/thompson.pdf

   List the 12 characteristics of highly-qualified teachers.

   1.
   2.
   3.
   4.
   5.
   6.
   7.
   8.
   9.
   10.
   11.
   12.

7. Click on this link: http://www.tasanet.org/files/PDFs/gr/2008/08qualitystudy.pdf produced by the Association of Texas Professional Educators (ATPE). Page 5 of this report documents four important findings. What are they?

   1.
   2.
   3.
   4.

8. Google "Teacher Salaries in Texas 2008" and click on the top link: "Becoming a Teacher in Texas/Teacher Certification in Texas." How does the salary in the city you hope to teach in compare with the mean salary in Texas? For how many days do you work to get this salary?

9. Now that you have completed some general informational areas of the career in teaching, write a brief 11-sentence reflection based on the most important things you have learned.

6 Introduction to the Teaching Profession

Web Search for Locating PPR Standards and Competencies

This web search will familiarize you with the State Board for Educator Certification web site. Go to *http://www.sbec.state.tx.us/*

- Click on "Testing/Accountability."
- Click on "Educator Testing."
- Click on "Study Guides & Preparation Manual."
- Click on "TExES"—Texas Examinations of Educator Standards.
- Scroll down to test 160–Pedagogy and Professional Responsibilities EC-12.
- Begin reading on page 6 and scroll through page 16.

Fill in the following chart with Domains/Standards and Competencies.

Domain/Standard	Competency	Key Words

This information will help you form an organizational basis for foundations in education courses. The curriculum for foundations courses (community college and university) is taken from these sources.

Introduction to the Teaching Profession 7

Educator Standards Web Search

The Texas Educator Standards define the knowledge and behaviors that all teachers should have before they enter a classroom as a lead teacher. Although there are only four Standards, each standard is divided into sub-areas of competency which preservice teachers are expected to define, learn, and execute as a matter of habit.

1. Click on this link to find the State Board for Educator Certification (SBEC):

    http://www.sbec.state.tx.us

This is the home page for SBEC. This web site can be overwhelming, but your tenacity will enable you to find information which will help you understand who determines what classroom teachers should know, what they should know, and how individuals certify to be teachers among many other topics.

- In the left-hand column, click on "Testing/Accountability."
- Click on "Educator Testing."
- Click on "Educator Standards."
- Click on "Approved New Educator Standards."
- SCROLL down to "Pedagogy and Professional Responsibilities."
- Select **one of the five** "Pedagogy and Professional Responsibilities Standards" categories and click on it.

Category Selected: _____

Type Standard #1: _____

_____

Type Standard #2: _____

_____

Type Standard #3: _____

_____

Type Standard #4: _____

_____

After reading through the Standards, noting the columns below, "What Teachers Know" and "What Teachers Can Do," type one example of "What Teachers Know" and "What Teachers Can Do" from each of the four Standards.

8 Introduction to the Teaching Profession

	What Teachers Know	**What Teachers Can Do**
Standard #1		
Standard #2		
Standard #3		
Standard #4		

- Return to the SBEC home page and in the left-hand column, click "State Board for Educator Certification."
- Click on "Educator Certification."
- In the left-hand column, click on "Certification Information."
- Click on "Certification Information Home."
- Click on "Becoming a classroom teacher in Texas."

Type your answers to each of the following questions.

1. What are three basic requirements for becoming a teacher in Texas?

    1.

    2.

    3.

- Return to the home page and in the left-hand column, click on "Educator Certification."
- In the left-hand column, click on "Career and Technical Education."
- Click on "Specific Requirements for Standard Career and Technical Education Certificates Based on Experience and Preparation in Skill Areas."
- Click on "approved educator preparation program."

2. Name the five "Certification Routes."

    1.

    2.

    3.

    4.

    5.

3. Find the region these four universities are in:
   - Sul Ross University is in which region?   Answer: _____
   - Texas Tech University is in which region?   Answer: _____
   - UT Tyler is in which region?   Answer: _____
   - _____ is in which region?   Answer: _____
     (you choose)

4. Click on any college or university. Identify: _____

Write a brief paragraph discussing what you learned about the teacher certification program at that university. Pay particular attention to program entrance requirements.

THE HOT E-PORTFOLIO

A widely-used form of authentic assessment is the course/subject portfolio. To practice this form of assessment and gain knowledge that will assist you in the preparation of a professional portfolio, you will create an electronic portfolio (EP) documenting your mastery of the thirteen competencies of the Pedagogy and Professional Responsibilities (PPR) for Texas teachers.

Students will create this portfolio in the EDUC 1301 course with a minimum of one entry per competency and continue to document growth in your EDUC 2301 class with one additional entry. At the end of EDUC 2301, the resulting portfolio will demonstrate your understanding of the PPR standards with a minimum of two original entries for each competency.

The portfolio will contain representative work samples selected from a variety of course assignments and individual research. These work samples will demonstrate how much you have learned and the progress you have made in understanding the PPR standards.

Basic Considerations: The ePortfolio

- will be created with Microsoft Office PowerPoint 2007.
    - will **not** be created using the same rules as a presentation.
    - Reference *Save Our Slides* by William Earnest, Kendall Hunt.
- should present your knowledge and skills related to the PPR standards.
- should stand on its own documenting original products and artifacts.
- will feature your technology skills.
    - hyperlink slides and sections;
    - insert clip art, photos, sounds, music, video, scans, graphic organizers; and
    - scan field experience documentation forms.
- will be presented during a student-led conference using a CDRW. If you are in an online course, you must follow the directions of your professor.
- links must work. (It is a good idea to use the CD on a computer you did not use to create the portfolio to be sure all of the links work. Put all links in a folder with the title "links").

Artifacts considerations: Following are some suggestions for types of artifacts you could use to create your portfolio:

Reflections	Creative writings	Essays
Interviews	Inventories	Journal entries
Learning Styles assessments	Letters	Observations and comments
Photographs	Poetry	Posters
Problem statements & solutions	Reader-response logs	Recorded commentary
Reports	Reviews	Self-assessment checklists
Short stories	Surveys	Video-taped performances
Presentations	Awards	Closed Captioning
Interactive Glossary	Training Certificates	Original Case Studies
Photographs	Affidavits	Q-Notes
References	Bibliographies	Technology Experience
Tutoring Experience	Classroom Arrangements	Neighborhood Scans
Principal Interviews	Organization Activity	
Professional Organization memberships	Comments on Netiquette	

http://www.albion.com/netiquette/corerules.html

Additional Hints for a Successful Presentation:

- Check the room's lighting.
- Cue the slide show (double-check files).
- Check other multimedia and hypermedia issues.
- Check the sound level.
- Check links to the Internet, etc.
- Push one button to start the presentation.

IMPORTANT: When creating the CD for presentation, use a Package-to-CD function. This function will make a copy of all links, so the presentation will work just like your thumb drive.

Technology Considerations for the Two Courses:

- Formative Technology required in EDUC 1301: Basic PPT with hyperlinks and images
- Summative Technology required in EDUC 2301: Use TIVA (text, images, video, and audio)

Competency Chapters

Standard		Range of Competencies
1	Designing Instruction and Assessment to Promote Student Learning	001–004
2	Creating a Positive, Productive Classroom Environment	005–006
3	Implementing Effective, Responsive Instruction and Assessment	007–010
4	Fulfilling Professional Roles and Responsibilities	011–013

Standard 1

Designing Instruction and Assessment to Promote Student Learning

Competency 1: Human Development
Competency 2: Diversity
Competency 3: Lesson Planning
Competency 4: Learning Processes

Competency 1

Human Development

LESSON PLAN FOR COMPETENCY 1

STATE STANDARDS: STANDARD 1, COMPETENCY 1

Competency 001: The teacher understands **human developmental processes** and applies this knowledge to plan instruction and ongoing assessment that motivate students and are responsive to their developmental characteristics and needs.

STATE TEACHER PROFICIENCIES

The State of Texas provides a bulleted list of proficiencies that each teacher should master in preservice training. This first competency list for human development is much longer than those that follow for subsequent competencies. The bolded words within this list of proficiencies may be used as words for the Scholar's Vocabulary. (See Appendices for details on the Scholar's Vocabulary.)

Competency 001

The teacher understands human developmental processes and applies this knowledge to plan instruction and ongoing assessment that motivate students and are responsive to their developmental characteristics and needs.

The beginning teacher:

- Knows the typical **stages** of **cognitive,** social, physical, and emotional development of students in early childhood through grade 12.
- Recognizes the wide range of individual developmental differences that characterizes students in early childhood through grade 12 and the **implications** of this developmental variation for **instructional planning.**
- Analyzes ways in which developmental characteristics of students in early childhood through grade 12 impact learning and performance, and applies knowledge of students' developmental characteristics and needs to plan effective learning experiences and **assessments.**
- Demonstrates an understanding of physical changes that occur in early childhood through **adolescence,** factors that affect students' physical growth and health (e.g., nutrition, sleep, prenatal exposure to drugs, abuse), and ways in which physical development impacts development in other **domains** (i.e., cognitive, social, emotional).
- Recognizes factors affecting the social and emotional development of students in early childhood through adolescence (e.g., lack of affection and attention, parental divorce, homelessness), and knows that students' social and emotional development impacts their development in other domains (i.e., cognitive, physical).
- Uses knowledge of cognitive changes in students in early childhood through adolescence (e.g., from an emphasis on **concrete thinking** to the **emergence and refinement** of abstract thinking and reasoning, increased ability to engage in reflective thinking, increased focus on the world beyond the school setting) to plan developmentally appropriate instruction and assessment that promote learning and development.
- Understands that development in any one domain (i.e., cognitive, social, physical, emotional) impacts development in other domains.
- Recognizes signs of **developmental delays** or **impairments** in students in early childhood through grade 4.
- Knows the stages of **play development** (i.e., from solitary to cooperative) and the important role of play in young children's learning and development.
- Uses knowledge of the developmental characteristics and needs of students in early childhood through grade 4 to plan meaningful, integrated, and active learning and play experiences that promote the development of the whole child.
- Recognizes that positive and productive learning environments involve creating a **culture** of high academic expectations, **equity** throughout the **learning community,** and developmental responsiveness.
- Recognizes the importance of helping students in early childhood through grade 12 learn and apply life skills (e.g., decision-making skills, organizational skills, goal-setting skills, self-direction, workplace skills).
- Knows the **rationale** for appropriate middle-level education and how middle-level schools are structured to address the characteristics and needs of young adolescents.
- Recognizes typical challenges for students during later childhood, adolescence, and young adulthood (e.g., **self-image,** physical appearance, eating disorders, feelings of **rebelliousness, identity formation,** educational and career decisions) and effective ways to help students address these challenges.
- Understands ways in which student involvement in risky behaviors (e.g., drug and alcohol use, gang involvement) impacts development and learning.
- Demonstrates knowledge of the importance of **peers,** peer acceptance, and **conformity** to peer group norms and expectations for adolescents, and understands the significance of peer-related issues for teaching and learning.

TEACHING OBJECTIVES

At the end of the lesson, the student should be able to:

✦ Demonstrate comprehension of human development as connected to specific age groups;
✦ Describe two major theorists/theories connected to human development;
✦ Demonstrate comprehension of the terms associated with human development;
✦ Create a lesson which demonstrates understanding of the Zone of Proximal Development;
✦ Understand extrinsic and intrinsic motivation which influences both group and individual behavior and learning and can apply this understanding to planning lessons; and
✦ Explain how motivation relates to self-esteem issues.

C1 KEY WORDS: HUMAN DEVELOPMENT

Terms associated with human development

Abstract	Schema	Self-Esteem
Concrete	Readiness	Zone of Proximal Development
Cognitive	Adolescence	Developmentally Appropriate
Physical	Gender	Multiple Intelligences
Moral	Behavioral	Psychological

INTRODUCTION/FOCUS

> A recent *Jay Leno Show* provided a prime example of teaching that was developmentally incorrect. As a lark, a guest comedienne "taught" a group of kindergarteners, "Because," she explained to the audience, "Anyone can teach, right?" She *instructed* the five-year-olds as though they were adults, and the amusement arose from the camera focused on their tiny, confused faces. The laughing audience could see that the serious children wanted to follow her line of thinking, but they could not process her banter and abstract innuendo because they were not adults.
>
> The audience laughed and laughed. At the end of the interaction, she asked the children if they could tell her something they had learned. The same, painful looks appeared on their faces as the children tried to think of responses. They genuinely did not want to hurt her feelings not understanding, of course, that they were the "butt" of her joke; they simply had no learning to report.
>
> Of course, the comedic sketch was designed for laughs, but when teachers teach lessons that are developmentally incorrect, it is no laughing matter.
>
> *Jay Leno Show,* **November 6, 2009. NBC.**

This comedienne did not forget about assessment. Periodically, she pointedly asked "Okay?" or "Right?" at the end of many rapid-fire sentences, but, like many conversational habits, she gave no wait time for her tiny audience to respond. Instead the camera panned to the children whose confused eyes and distorted facial expressions kept the audience roaring.

TRANSITION: Neither the *lesson* nor the informal assessment were appropriate or valid, and, at the end of the day, no learning took place. Real teachers need to know a great deal about human development—what IS appropriate instruction and how do you know when to teach what and how much is too much?

Physical growth in children does not necessarily follow a pattern no more than does their social growth, emotional growth, and cognitive development. It is because of these developmental stages that children go through in their own time, that teachers must become aware of the diversity within one single classroom. The main divisions for development seem to fall within preschool, primary and elementary school, middle school, and high school. Remember that all schools do not divide "age/grade levels" in the same ways, so making sweeping statements about developmental characteristics is a dangerous practice.

By studying the proficiencies for Competency 1, students will learn something about human development as it relates to the teacher's knowledge and role in the classroom.

INSTRUCTIONAL INPUT AND GUIDED PRACTICE

What we need to know about human development

The Instructional Input in this lesson plan will contain *guided practice* in the form of questions placed throughout the chapter. References to web sites will also serve as guided practice as you research topics to gain further knowledge and information and application.

QUESTION
Why is it important for teachers to have a good understanding of human developmental processes?

Answer: Some children begin kindergarten knowing how to read; many others do not. Some children begin first grade with math concepts beginning to form; many other have never heard of mathematics. As children enter junior high school, they are beginning puberty—some of them mature much more quickly than others. The ones who do not mature as rapidly worry constantly about why they are not "like" everyone else. Eventually, students enter high school with much different interests and abilities: some seem to be natural athletes and some seem to be natural klutzes. All of the described changes involve a natural, normal process called human development. Teachers must study human development to learn the "stages" children go through and at what "ages" these changes are likely to occur. The State of Texas mandates that future teachers study human development. The mandate is in the form of the competency statement: "The teacher understands **human developmental** processes and applies this knowledge to **plan instruction** and ongoing **assessment** that **motivate** students and are responsive to their developmental characteristics and needs."

BEGIN AT THE BEGINNING

Introduction to Human Development

Human development is an ongoing process starting at conception and ending at death. Social scientists study human development in terms of the *social, psychological, cognitive, physical* and *moral development* of human beings. Because humans develop at different rates, each of these areas of study is pertinent to the educator in the 21st Century. While teachers may not know the scientific terms for why a child is developmentally lagging or developmentally advanced, teachers should know enough about human development to identify the type of developmental diversity and to obtain the necessary support to help the child advance his learning.

You will gain basic knowledge for teachers through the following discussion of five well-known individuals in human development research: Abraham Maslow, Jean Piaget, Erik Erikson, Lev Vyotsky, and Laurence Kohlberg.

Human Development Theorists

The following outline lists areas of study associated with human development:

The Stages of Development vary by theorist, but generally, teachers specialize in Early Childhood (K–6); Middle School (4–8); or high school (9–12). Yet, within each of these categories, a tremendous diversity exists in child development.

> **PARENTAL DILEMMA**
>
> Start a "late birthday" child in the first grade or "hold the child back" a year? The dilemma rests on the child's developmental stage.

1. The Preschool Child (3, 4, 5, 6 years)
2. The Primary-Aged Child (6, 7, 8, 9, 10, 11 years)
3. The Middle School Child (11, 12, 13, 14 years)
4. The High School Student (14, 15, 16, 17 years)

> **ADMINISTRATIVE DILEMMAS**
>
> Should 9th graders be in the same school as high schoolers? Should elementary schools be further divided between Elementary and Middle? Should certain grade levels be on campuses by themselves? All of these school organizational models exist in Texas, and usually, they reflect the thinking of the public.

The following theorists have studied human development in each of the areas mentioned above: **social, psychological, cognitive, physical,** and **moral development.** The lesson which follows will focus on Jean Piaget and Lev Vygotsky's developmental theories, while Abraham Maslow's Hierarchy of Needs is included in the discussion because his research elaborates basic human needs that develop from the most basic survival to the point of enrichment. You should know something about all of these theorists even though this text does not cover all of them in depth.

Social theories describe how children become natural observers or participants in society. **Cognitive theories** describe how the brain develops and functions. **Physical theories** describe how the body develops. **Emotional and psychological theories** describe how the feelings develop. Finally, **moral development theories** describe how and when a child learns right from wrong.

Theorists and Associated Theories

1. **Abraham Maslow** (Hierarchy of Needs)
2. **Jean Piaget** (Cognitive Development)
3. John Watson and B. F. Skinner (Behavioral Theorists)
    a. Ivan Pavlov
4. **Erik Erikson** (Personality/Psychosocial Development)
5. William James (Attention)
6. Howard Gardner (Multiple Intelligences)
7. Charles Spearman (g Intelligence)
8. **Lev Vygotsky** (Social Nature of Learning)
9. **Laurence Kohlberg** (Moral Development)
10. Carol Gilligan (Moral Development; gender)

Following are some brief descriptions of a few of these theorists; others will be described in subsequent competency lessons.

Beginning with Abraham Maslow, a noted social scientist, students can begin to relate to the human condition in general. When preservice teachers understand Maslow's Hierarchy of Needs, they begin to see that children at all ages must have basic needs met before learning can take place.

Abraham Maslow

Abraham Maslow's Hierarchy of Needs appears in many forms, but most normally in a simple pyramid. The basic needs of the human being are on the bottom, and as the human being grows and develops, obstacles notwithstanding, he has the potential to develop to the highest form of self-actualization. Maslow also thought that some education might be a hindrance to that development if it took place without taking into account the child's emotional condition. This web site (*www.abraham-maslow.com/*) contains several links which develop the concepts of basic needs and provides ways by which education can enhance human development.

Several years ago, I heard a distinguished speaker address the age-old issue of **nature vs nurture** as it relates to a child's capacity for and progress through education. He said that the problem comes down to two issues: Are you who you are because you can't help it—it's an accident of birth? (nature). Or, are you the sum total of your life's experiences? (nurture). The speaker said he could make a strong argument on the side of nurture. If nurture IS, in fact, more important than nature, just think of the impact that teachers have upon their students since students are with teachers many more hours a day than with their parents. Many (most?) of the memorable experiences students have ARE composed of the sum total of their school experiences. Something to think about!

DEVELOPING AS A TEACHER

How does Maslow's Hierarchy of Needs involve a teacher? How does the teacher make a difference within this hierarchy?

Find one web site/group which considers the question of nature vs nurture. Briefly consider the nature vs nurture argument. What is your belief about what/which is more important?

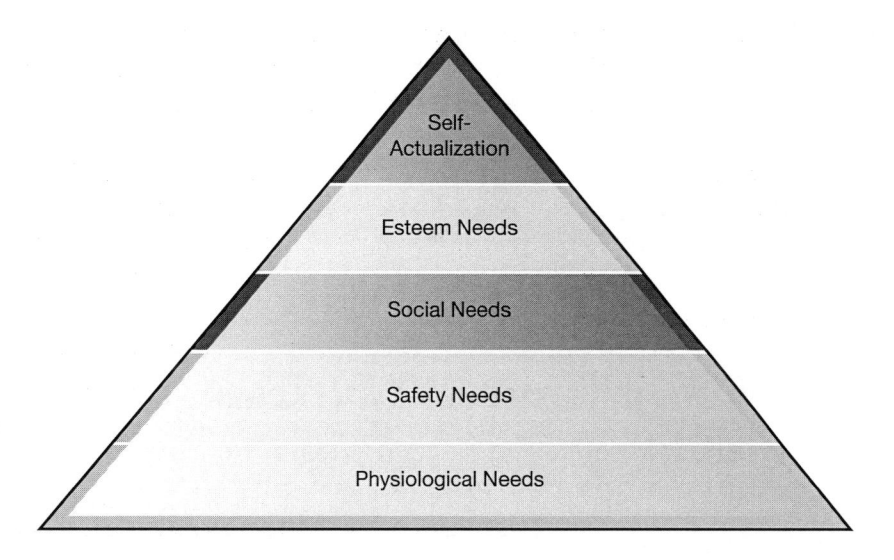

```
           Self-
        Actualization

         Esteem Needs

         Social Needs

         Safety Needs

       Physiological Needs
```

Love and food and water form the base of Maslow's pyramid and provide the basic level of needs that an individual has. If he is deprived of love and food, or physiological needs, he will die quickly. Once survival is assured, an individual needs to be safe (safety needs). After safety, an individual is capable of reaching out for social reassurance (social needs) and then, he wants to feel validated (esteem needs). The adult who meets all of these needs or has all of these needs met stands a good chance of becoming a elf-actualized person—one capable of altruistic acts.

Similarly, human *wants* seem to be universal: All human beings want to be happy, to feel important, to experience love, and to have a variety of life experiences.

That people have needs to thrive is what this chart explains. The alert classroom teacher knows the student who does not have all of the basic survival needs met will probably be hungry and/or sleepy in class. Until these needs are met, educational needs are probably never going to occur. While this competency focuses on development, the second Standard focuses on classroom environment and the safety needs of students. Once the school is assured that students are physiologically taken care of, the education process can begin.

More information can be found at this web site:

http://honolulu.hawaii.edu/intranet/committees/FacDevCom/guidebk/teachtip/maslow.htm

Jean Piaget

Jean Piaget systematically observed (clinical method) children from birth through adolescence. He was particularly interested in how children constructed and organized ideas and concepts. He called these **cognitive structures** or **schemata**. He determined that development emerges from action.

Behavioral schemata includes behavior which explores and responds to stimuli in the environment. **Symbolic schemata** begins with the second year when children begin to think about objects, events, and experiences. At this time children begin to represent objects without needing to "touch." An example would be "da-da" for daddy. **Operational schemata** begins by the first grade when children are able to perform logical operations or mental activities on objects or events which lead to logical outcomes. For example, a first grader can use large Legos® to build a house.

Best known as the Stages of Cognitive Development, Piaget's theory divides child development into four stages: Sensori-Motor Stage, Pre-operational Stage, Concrete Operational Stage, Formal Operations Stage.

Explanations for each of these stages can be accessed on multiple web sites, but this one from Purdue University has a comprehensive explanation of the theory and many added features including a research study on how many students at which ages have actually reached each stage. Note that this site includes a Formal Operational Stage 2 which encompasses graduate students.

http://education.calumet.purdue.edu/vockell/EdPsyBook/Edpsy4/edpsy4_stages.htm

Piaget concluded that schools should emphasize cooperative decision-making and problem solving, and nurture moral development by requiring students to work out common rules based on fairness.

> **DEVELOPING AS A TEACHER**
>
> Describe Piaget's method for developing his cognitive and moral development theories? Do you think this method might have led to some weaknesses in the theory? If so, what are they?

Erik Erikson

Erik Erikson is most associated with the term *identity*. One's identity is best defined as one's feeling of well-being or self comfort. If an individual seems comfortable with his *lot in life*, his body, and level of recognition, he is thought to be normal and happy. This theory seems vague and would be difficult to replicate. For example, words such as *normal* and *happy* are very difficult to define and certainly difficult to quantify. Some vocabulary and related terms with this theorist are: identity, gender, occupation, androgyny, stereotypes, epigenetic principle, psychosocial crisis, and the eight stages of psychosocial development.

Lev Vygotsky

Best known for his theory on the social nature of learning, **Lev Vygotsky** said that children exist within a social context made up of parents, friends, relatives, siblings, teachers and peers. They communicate, stimulate, and learn from each other. To facilitate that learning, Vygotsky emphasizes group or cooperative learning. This style of learning is featured in the following web site where there is an interactive traditional classroom which *transforms* into a model that Vygotsky would endorse. The web site also includes four additional links to terms important to this theory.

http://coe.sdsu.edu/eet/articles/sdtheory/index.htm

Constructivism, taught both as a learning strategy/teaching method and a theory, is also connected to Vygotsky's theory. See this web site for an explanation of constructivism and the Zone of Proximal Development. Note particularly the graphic of ZPD which is a clear example of how one picture is worth a thousand words.

http://www.learningandteaching.info/learning/constructivism.htm

Zone of Proximal Development

Lev Vygotsky is perhaps best known as contributing to the research of social communication humans enjoy. He also described something called the Zone of Proximal Development, shortened to ZPD. The easiest way to understand this theory is to study this diagram. Sometimes, I call ZPD the *Three Bears* approach to teaching/learning where, like the beds Goldilocks attempted to nap in, one was too soft, one was too hard, but one was just right!

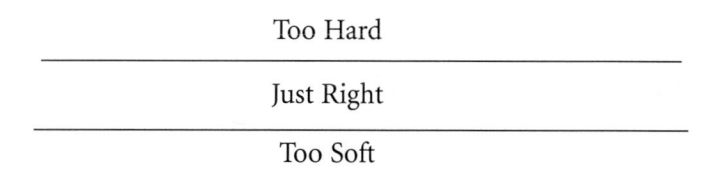

Too Hard
Just Right
Too Soft

What the Three Bears Model means is that children have a certain cognitive developmental level. When the teacher makes the lesson too difficult (too hard), children give up. When the teacher makes the lesson too easy (too soft), children misbehave and find other, more interesting things to do. The challenge is to make the lesson "just right" so that all children will be challenged to learn.

TEACHER DILEMMA

You have a 4th grade class of 21 students. Seven students are very, very bright, seven are average, and seven perform below standard. You are going to teach a science lesson on Maslow's Hierarchy of Needs. How do you accommodate each child's learning level in one classroom?

More information can be found about ZPD at *www.learnnc.org/reference/1892*

Laurence Kohlberg

Laurence Kohlberg introduced the *Just Community* to the classroom. He wrote about three levels of moral reasoning: preconventional morality, conventional morality, and postconventional morality. Simply explained, Kohlberg brought teacher and students together to settle problems and to make rules on a one person:one vote basis. This idea has merit (akin to the democratic theory of classroom management), but it also has some problems. For example, schools must agree to let students have time and the power to make their decisions.

Kohlberg's theory includes the Six Stages of Development. More about Kohlberg can be accessed at *http://faculty.plts.edu/gpence/html/kohlberg.htm*. Of particular interest in this article are the moral dilemmas which Kohlberg presents.

What is your response to this dilemma? Argue the point with a friend, then turn to the web site to find out what Kohlberg thought: http://faculty.plts.edu/gpence/html/kohlberg.htm

As you can see, this lesson only briefly covers five of the list of well-known human development theorists. These theorists are given credit the world over for studying the human condition and attempting to describe it in such ways that norms can be established. The result of their efforts has produced credible research which helps many understand the human condition. Perhaps no career needs this understanding more than teaching (unless it is parenting). Below are a few critical terms to understand about development.

Motivation

The term *motivation* is something of an oxymoron in that social scientists have developed definitions for two types (perhaps more) of motivation and named them *extrinsic and intrinsic*. When we say things like "He was *born* motivated" or "She's a real go-getter" we are referring to someone who excels at a given task without prodding by a teacher or a parent. We also say things like "He won't do anything unless I give him something!" meaning that the individual does not move off of *dead center* without being compensated in some way.

> **TEACHER DILEMMA**
>
> I can remember asking my junior English students to complete a certain task or to ask for volunteers to help with a task and, often, the response was, "What are you going to give me?" Just last week, a college student said, "If you offer students extra credit, they will probably come to the student professional organization meeting!" One wonders when students develop intrinsic motivation—learn for the sake of learning.

All of these statements and behaviors refer to extrinsic (rewarded) and intrinsic (innate) motivation.

> **TEACHER DILEMMA**
>
> If you offer students "something" in return for learning, do you actually increase their internal motivation? In fact, the question becomes "Do students learn more when given rewards?" Furthermore, does gifting in return for performance validating students as knowers? If you believe that everyone can learn, do you believe everyone can learn without being given extrinsic prompts?

Motivation is an ongoing problem for teachers who sincerely wish that their students learn without gifts.

> **STUDENT DILEMMAS**
>
> - What is your personal motivation to succeed in your educational goals?
> - What is your motivation to teach?
> - Do you respond more to extrinsic prompts or do you just want to learn?
> - Should schools be concerned with the morality of intrinsic motivation?

INDEPENDENT PRACTICE AND MODELING (HOMEWORK)

1. **Scholar's Vocabulary:** Using the state-produced list of proficiencies preservice teachers should have related to Competency 1, highlight terms you wish to place in your interactive glossary. You should have a minimum of 5 terms from C1. (See model in the Appendices.)
2. **Reflective Writing:** Using the 11-sentence model in the appendices, write a reflection on Competency 1.
3. **Piaget and the Comics:**
    a. Assignment: Review the web sites in the **Input** section of the Lesson Plan above.

    b. Be sure you understand the four stages of Jean Piaget's theory of cognitive development. You may wish to do more outside research on Piaget via the Internet.

    c. Keeping Piaget's four-part chart handy, start perusing the daily comics to find one cartoon which absolutely exemplifies each Stage of Development Piaget elaborates. This part of the assignment requires you to evaluate/identify a visual representation of the concept.

    d. You will have a total of four cartoons which appear in this order:
      1. Sensori-Motor
      2. Pre-operational Stage
      3. Concrete Operational Stage
      4. Formal Operations Stage

    e. Clip/scan each cartoon you have chosen into a Word document. While you can find good cartoons online, be aware that many are copyright-protected. If you do use a copyrighted cartoon, reference its source in your work. Provide the web source for each cartoon.

    f. Underneath each cartoon write a brief paragraph explaining the stage of development (Piaget) and how you connect THIS cartoon to the stage. This part of the assignment requires you to synthesize the information you have read and understood and requires you to reproduce it in another form.
      1. Stage of Development
      2. Explain the cartoon and its connection to the stage of development.

    g. **Modeling/Example:** The cartoon "ZITS" is an excellent model because Zits, the main adolescent character, has typical teenage angst. Other good cartoons are "Family Circle" and "Dennis the Menace" because the young ones in these scenarios often have trouble with being literal versus being abstract. Many other applicable cartoons exist, of course, so have fun reading the comics for this higher-order thinking activity.

Competency 1   Human Development

4. **Abstract Thinking:**

    The following assignment requires you to understand Vygotsky's theory on the zone of proximal development (ZPD). This theory focuses on the developmental understanding of your students: "low," "moderate," or "high." Concrete learners require lots of motivating and explanations while more abstract learners grasp ideas quickly and are likely to proceed without a lot of instruction.

    a. Study the following chart which will enable you to prepare a lesson which will help you assess learning for each developmental stage of your students.
    b. Develop ONE question based on ONE TEKS (go to the TEA web site and find a set of TEKS in the area you wish to teach). This question might be anything that you would want your students to know about this particular TEKS objective.

    Example: What are the implications of the behavioral objectives?

    Jay Gatsby wrote in his journal in the book *The Great Gatsby* (Be sure to reference the TEKS grade level).

    c. Then, apply each of the "low," "moderate," and "high" to this question. For example, how would a "low abstract student" respond to this question? Etc.
    d. Write your responses in a chart modeled after the one below.

Levels of Abstract Thinking

Low	Moderate	High
Confused about the problem	Can define the problem	Can think of the problem from many perspectives
Doesn't know what can be done	Can think of one or two possible responses to the problem	Can generate many alternative plans
"Show me"	Has trouble thinking through a comprehensive plan	Can choose a plan and think through each step
Has one or two habitual responses to problems		

Source: *Developmental supervision,* Glickman

LEVELS OF ABSTRACT THINKING

CLOSURE/FOLLOW-UP

While the lesson above only covers a fraction of what there is to learn about human development, it does focus on several important concepts that all teachers need to understand and keep in mind for every lesson they prepare.

1. Children do not develop socially, cognitively, morally, or physically at the same rate;
2. Children's learning is enabled or hampered by the teacher's lesson preparation;
3. Teachers must remain observant about each student's learning;
4. Teachers must plan for assessment of learning as they prepare lessons. Assessment is ongoing.

ASSESSMENT

Ask yourself whether you have mastered these objectives.

+ **Objective 1:** Demonstrate comprehension of human development as connected to specific age groups (Cartoon Assignment).
+ **Objective 2:** Describe the major theorists/theories connected to human development (Input; Research).
+ **Objective 3:** Demonstrate comprehension of the terms associated with human development (Word Wall and C1 Assignment).
+ **Objective 4:** Explain the *Three Bears* approach to teaching/learning.
+ **Objective 5:** Explain how you would motivate a "low-abstract" learner to try harder.

PRACTICE QUESTIONS

Now assess your learning by answering these questions. Answers are given in the Appendices.

1. At which stage does a child develop new schemes, but he still cannot think logically?
   a. sensorimotor
   b. preoperational
   c. concrete operational
   d. both a & c

2. The formal operational stage covers which age groups?
   a. birth to two
   b. seven to eleven years
   c. eleven/twelve years
   d. eleven years & older

3. Which stage develops schemas primarily through sense and motor activities?
   a. formal stage
   b. preoperational stage
   c. sensorimotor stage
   d. all of the above

30   Competency 1   Human Development

4. A person who can form a hypothesis prior to discovery is most likely in which age range?
    a. eleven years and older
    b. seven to eleven years
    c. birth to two years
    d. two to seven years

5. A person who learns best from using a V-Tech Reader is most likely in which stage of development?
    a. formal
    b. sensorimotor
    c. preoperational
    d. concrete operational

6. Valerie Paschenko's daughter is running a temperature of 103° and is frantically trying to get to the pharmacy to get medicine before it closes. She exceeds the speed limit by 20 mph and in her worried state drives erratically. The daughter, Suzi, is very upset—not only is she feeling very bad, her mother is speeding. According to Piaget:
    a. The child is a typical twelve-year-old demonstrating the stage of moral relativism;
    b. The child is an eight-year-old in the stage of morality of cooperation;
    c. The child is a typical six-year-old in the stage of morality of constraint; or
    d. The child is undisciplined and her screaming causes his mother to have a rear-end collision.

7. Of the following examples, which one does not represent Vygotsky's Theory of Social Development?
    a. Allison's older brother, John, teaches her a song to help her remember the fifty states;
    b. Ramona and Stuart work together to understand their chemistry homework;
    c. A fifth grade class taking a field trip to Fort Davis to learn about early Texas settlement from a State Park Ranger;
    d. Tyrone, studying alone at his desk, is trying to make sense of multiplication tables.

8. Elvis, a sixteen-year-old boy, proceeded through a traffic light that had just turned red, or *pink* as he described it to his friends later. Officer Lorenzo saw the young man speed up and dart through the light just as he reached the intersection, so the officer turned on his lights and proceeded to pull Elvis over. While pulling to the curb, Elvis was trying desperately to think of a reason that would justify his breaking the law. Elvis believes…
    a. the officer will consider his reasons and not give him a ticket (moral relativism);
    b. that the rules are bendable and the officer will give him a "warning";
    c. behavior is wrong or right, regardless of the reason;
    d. his father is going to be furious if he gets a ticket.

9. Middle schoolers who get along at school commonly have thee characteristics. Which one does not fit?
    a. They think positively
    b. They intentionally start conflicts
    c. They take responsibility
    d. They make good/best friends

10. One way teachers can encourage middle schoolers to improve self-esteem is to encourage them to:
    a. Put down others
    b. Start conflicts
    c. Be yourself
    c. Try hard to fit in

CAREER PLANNING

It is possible to get specialized advanced degrees in human development. When this competency is introduced into teacher education, either in a course like EDUC 1301 or EDUC 2301, or even an Educational Psychology class, students get a superficial acquaintance with the theories and theorists associated with each type of development. If you are interested in the content of this competency, continue to study educational psychology and after a certain number of years in the classroom and advanced studies, a teacher can become a school counselor or a licensed professional counselor (LPC).

SUGGESTIONS FOR ADDITIONAL ASSIGNMENTS

Even if you decide not to do any of these extra assignments for your ePortfolio, read through these assignments and try to respond verbally with appropriate answers.

1. Write a short essay describing your motivation for teaching a certain age-level child; be sure to include your experience with that age-level.

2. Write reflective essays describing one or more effective schools you observe during your required observations:
   a. Take pictures of school and/or class mission.
      Be sure to get permission to photograph children.
   b. Compare missions in several elementary schools.
      These will either be posted on classroom walls or published in the faculty handbook.
   c. Compare missions across several grade levels.

3. Interview the school secretary and ask him/her to help you construct a list of all the personnel that works in an elementary school.
   a. Create a chart among all the schools you observe in and compare personnel across the levels.
   b. Describe those who are hired specifically to assist with developmental issues (what are their titles, job descriptions, duties?).

4. Interview several "people on the street" and ask for definitions of a school: i.e., "What is a school?".
   a. Log the answers of several people and write a reflection about how the answers differ, or how they are the same.
   b. Compare answers among school personnel and people on the street.

5. Sit in the teacher workroom (with permission) and observe the verbal and nonverbal behavior. Take notes and write a reflection comparing behaviors (no names—schools or people) to your ideal of teachers and the reality of what is said/behavior.

6. Human developmental levels: match a cartoon strip with the developmental levels of each grade level you observe. Explain the connection between the cartoon and the observation.

7. Create a developmental cartoon strip for the stages of one of the following theorists. Be sure to identify whether you are working on social, cognitive, or moral or ethical development.
   a. Piaget
   b. Kohlberg
   c. Erikson

8. In your classroom observations, describe in detail how a teacher integrates the learning taxonomies: cognitive, affective, and psychomotor.

9. Should schools be concerned with the moral development of children? How might a teacher (of any age level or discipline) approach moral development?

10. Research each of Erikson's Eight Stages of Psychosocial Development on the web and give concrete examples of real people in each stage. As you look for real examples, you may consider, for example, the infant who does NOT have a "loving, trusting relationship" with the caregiver. Synthesize your findings and relate to the teacher's predicament of teaching more than the curriculum.

11. Write a moral dilemma utilizing "Heinz Steals the Drug" as a model. Write arguments for and against each side.

12. Think about the friends you have today. Have they all matured at the same rate? How do you define *mature*?

13. All classroom teachers have a philosophy (stated or unstated) integral to the way they manage their classrooms. Observe one teacher's management techniques over time and explain what the teacher's philosophy is through your observation. Is their classroom management style effective? Why or why not? Describe briefly the management style and evaluate.

14. Create a table which allows you to compare/contrast the four theorists: Piaget, Erikson, Kohlberg, and Vygotsky.

15. What makes the middle school years so volatile?

16. Make a comparison chart utilizing the general characteristics for each of these age levels: elementary school, middle school, and high school.

Competency 2

Diversity

LESSON PLAN FOR COMPETENCY 2

STATE STANDARDS: STANDARD 1, COMPETENCY 2

Competency 002: The teacher understands student **diversity** and knows how to plan learning experiences and design assessments that are responsive to differences among students and that promote all students' learning.

STATE TEACHER PROFICIENCIES

Competency 002

The teacher understands student diversity and knows how to plan learning experiences and design assessments that are responsive to differences among students and that promote all students' learning.

The beginning teacher:

- Demonstrates knowledge of students with **diverse personal and social characteristics** (e.g., those related to **ethnicity, gender, language background, exceptionality**) and the significance of student diversity for teaching, learning, and assessment.
- **Accepts and respects students** with diverse backgrounds and needs.
- Knows how to **use diversity** in the classroom and the community **to enrich** all students' learning experiences.
- Knows **strategies** for enhancing one's own understanding of students' diverse backgrounds and needs.
- Knows how to **plan and adapt lessons** to address students' varied backgrounds, skills, interests, and learning needs, including the needs of English language learners and students with **disabilities.**
- Understands **cultural and socioeconomic differences** (including differential access to technology) and knows how to plan instruction that is responsive to cultural and socioeconomic differences among students.
- Understands the **instructional significance** of varied **student learning needs and preferences.**

TEACHING OBJECTIVES

At the end of the lesson, the student should be able to:

- Identify terms associated with at-risk and diversity;
- Identify a personal learning style;
- Explain the teacher/learner connection to learning styles;
- Explain the rationales behind grouping;
- Draw connections between high expectations and student performance;
- Identify characteristics of special groups of students;
- Debate theories of inclusion (mainstreaming) and exclusive grouping.

C2 KEY WORDS: DIVERSITY

The following terms are often associated with diversity. Create your own glossary of these terms locating at least one good web site for each term and defining each term from that web site.

Pygmalion Effect	Self-fulfilling Prophecy	Hawthorne Effect
Teacher Expectations	Stereotyping	Labeling
Culture	Multiculturalism	Ethnocentrism
Cultural Pluralism	Ethnicity	Identity
Discrimination	Racism	Immigration
Acculturation	Learning Styles	Minority
Multiple Intelligences	Age	Disadvantaged
SES	Family	Learning Style
At-Risk	Grouping	

INTRODUCTION/FOCUS

"Diversity in the classroom is a microcosm of the macrocosm."

Dr. Braselton

The quote above simply means that each classroom has a variety of youngsters—they vary in size, maturity, ethnicity, family background, interests, and so on in infinitesimal ways. The smallness of the classroom (microcosm) is representative of the largeness of the world (macrocosm).

> Demonstration:
>
> Bring enough apples to class for every one (or every two) students to have one. Apples should be as many different sizes, shapes, and varieties as you can find. Distribute the apples to the class and have students describe their apples to each other and/or to the class. Once satisfied that all differences have been covered, take out a knife and a cutting board, and laying the apple crossways, cut through the apple. You will expose a star-shaped figure within the center of the apple.
>
> The point is that each child is different in a variety of unique ways; it is the teacher's responsibility to find the "star quality" in each student.

TRANSITION: This demonstration shows us that, like the apples in this demonstration, students are very different. In fact, most people know instinctively that they are different from other people from a very early age. Most people also think they are unique—that there is something different about them from all other people. Those differences among a sea of students provide a great deal of anxiety in some teachers. That is why preservice teachers study the many types of physical, social, emotional, and cognitive developmental diversity found in Competency 1: Human Development.

> **The relevant question is, then, what are we to learn about diversity that will prepare us for the classroom?**

INSTRUCTIONAL INPUT AND GUIDED PRACTICE

What we need to know about diversity

The Instructional Input in this lesson plan will contain *guided practice* in the form of questions placed throughout the chapter. References to web sites will also serve as guided practice as you research topics to gain further knowledge and information and application.

BEGIN AT THE BEGINNING

Introduction to Diversity

This chapter focuses on the diversity of student learning: special groups of students including special education (inclusion), grouping, learning styles, high expectations and performance, and multiculturalism. While the topic of diversity is much, much larger than these few topics, the beginning teacher needs to learn about the broad nature of diversity and how to turn points of diversity into strengths.

When the term *diversity* is introduced, most students think of cultural diversity, but in reality, it is much more than culture. Teachers can expect to have a wide variety of students who not only differ in culture, but they also differ in abilities, talents, and backgrounds. Some other reasons students may be thought of as diverse include patterns of immigration and special education identification. Other factors that diversify students include normal variations in physical, social, emotional, and cognitive development as you learned in Chapter 1.

> **QUESTION**
> Why is it important for teachers to have a good understanding of human diversity?
>
> *Answer:* Most every human being thinks of himself or herself as unique in a few or even a lot of ways. Sometimes that self-distinction of difference serves as a point of superiority and translates into "*my individual differences* make me *better* than or *less* than others who do not have my same characteristics." Those characteristics can be cultural, academic, social, or even based on beauty or popularity. While all of those characteristics are important to the discussion of diversity, the subject of *diversity* in the classroom, however, is more about learning and how diversity affects the learning process. Just as children do not look alike, all children do not learn alike. The astute teacher learns to identify points of diversity in ways that result in meaningful learning for all students.

At-Risk Terminology

An important part of diversity is identifying the at-risk child. Many terms are associated with at-risk, but here are the major ones:

At-risk	Urban communities	Inner-city
Appearance	Expectations	Culture
Social promotion	Language	Retaining a grade
Values	High-stakes testing	Communities
Retention (drop-out)	Family structures	SES
Educationally disadvantaged	Reading ability	Slow learners
Behavior	Handicapping conditions	Attendance
Gifted	Boredom	Minority
"Late" birth dates	Attention problems	Single-parent families
First generation	Relocating schools	Compensatory education

As you can see, many of these are common terms that are studied in other chapters, but in Chapter 2, each term should be placed in the context of diversity. For instance, the term *relocating schools* refers to children who move/migrate from one area of the state(s) to another. They lose friends and may be slow to adjust in a new environment. Therefore, these students are *at risk* of failure. Obviously, the social milieu in which migration takes place has psychological and developmental implications for the child involved.

The following chart taken from the TEA web site describes how the state identifies at-risk students:

At-Risk/State Compensatory Education

Identification of At-Risk Students

Section 29.081 of the Texas Education code defines state criteria used to identify students at risk of dropping out of school. A student at risk of dropping out of school includes each student who is under 21 years of age and who:

- is in prekindergarten, kindergarten, or grade 1, 2, or 3, and did not perform satisfactorily on a readiness test or assessment instrument administered during the current school year.

- is in grade 7, 8, 9, 10, 11, or 12, and did not maintain an average equivalent to 70 on a scale of 100 in two or more subjects in the foundation curriculum during a semester in the preceding or current school year, or is not maintaining such an average in two or more subjects in the foundation curriculum in the current semester.
- was not advanced from one grade level to the next for one or more school years.
- did not perform satisfactorily on an assessment instrument administered to the student under Subchapter B, Chapter 39, and who has not in the previous or current school year subsequently performed on that instrument or another appropriate instrument at a level equal to at least 110 percent of the level of satisfactory performance on that instrument.
- is pregnant or is a parent.
- has been placed in an alternative education program in accordance with Section 37.006 during the preceding or current school year.
- has been expelled in accordance with Section 37.007 during the preceding or current school year.
- is currently on parole, probation, deferred prosecution, or other conditional release.
- was previously reported through the Public Education Information Management System (PEIMS) to have dropped out of school.
- is a student of limited English proficiency, as defined by Section 29.052.
- is in the custody or care of the Department of Protective and Regulatory Services or has, during the current school year, been referred to the department by a school official, officer of the juvenile court, or law enforcement official.
- is homeless, as defined by the McKinney-Vento Homeless Education Assistance Improvement Act of 2001, Section 725.
- resided in the preceding school year or resides in the current school year in a residential placement facility in the district, including a detention facility, substance abuse treatment facility, emergency shelter, psychiatric hospital, halfway house, or foster group home.

House Bill 1691 of the 78th Legislature also amended Section 42.152 of the Texas Education Code to allow charges to the state compensatory education allotment [in proportion to the percentage of students that meet the criteria in Section 29.081(d) or (g)] for programs that serve students who are enrolled in an accelerated reading program under Section 28.006(g) or who are enrolled in a program for treatment of students who have dyslexia or a related disorder as required by Section 38.003.

In addition, a district may also approve local criteria to be used for identifying at-risk students. Students identified using local criteria are limited to 10 percent of the number of the district's previous year's students that were identified using state criteria. Students identified as being at risk using local criteria are not reported in PEIMS.

GROUPING

Confronted with such a wide array of diversity among all students, schools have long studied how best to group students for optimal learning. Some believe that all gifted and talented and honors students should be separated from the mainstream and taught independently. Others believe that schools should group students heterogeneously.

In general, how do educators handle variability and diversity in students? Historically, students have been ability-grouped by virtue of a standardized test. This is a common practice today with some variations: between-class ability grouping or within-class ability grouping.

38 Competency 2 Diversity

Between-class ability grouping refers to the practice of ability-grouping students for certain studies such as English and/or mathematics. That means that *advanced* students are placed in classes with other *advanced* students. This also means that low-achieving students are placed with other low-achieving students. Research abounds on the positive and negative results of this type of grouping. These students are *homogeneously* grouped. When students are randomly placed into physical education or history classes, they are *heterogeneously* grouped.

In years past, children were often put into reading groups labeled "Bluebirds," "Redbirds," and "Canaries." Every child knew before too much time passed that the difference among the groups was ability: Bluebirds were smart, Redbirds were learning, and Canaries were struggling! Separating students into honors, advanced, standard, and developmental groups is the same thing today—students of similar ability are grouped together and taught the same way.

Within-class ability grouping is still a common practice in elementary classrooms particularly in reading groups—much like the "Bluebirds" and "Canaries" of yesteryear.

What all of this grouping leads to is a practice called *tracking*. Tracked students seem to fall into a certain level track and continue in that track throughout their school years. Some liken this practice to that of other countries whose systems divide students among a workforce track or the college-bound track. Americans have a fondness for freedom of choice, however, so our educational culture has a tendency to want students to break out of a low-performing track and move to higher-performing tracks. That may be one reason so much emphasis is placed on teaching competency and continuous testing.

QUESTIONS
Do you believe students should be ability-grouped? Why or why not?
Should schools practice grouping? Why or why not? Give specific examples.
Do you believe one method of grouping is superior to others? If so, why?

PARENT QUESTIONS
Do you believe students should be ability-grouped? Why or why not?
Should schools practice grouping? Why or why not? Give specific examples.

SPECIAL EDUCATION

Special groups of students: Certainly everyone knows that special groups of students need extra time, attention, and even modified instruction to succeed. Today, many special needs students are included (inclusion) within the traditional classroom.

QUESTIONS
How will you handle inclusion within your classroom?
What are some possible modifications you will be expected to make?

Some terms to know about a few special groups of students:

   English Language Learners (ELLs)
   Gifted and Talented (GT)
   Limited English Proficient Students (LEPS)

English as a Second Language (ESL)
Bilingual
Individualized Education Plan
94-142, Section 504, IDEA

Since the Civil Rights Era of the 1950s, the federal government has been involved in making sure that these special groups of students get an equitable education. The Elementary and Secondary Education Act (ESEA), Individuals with Disabilities Education Act (IDEA), and Public Law 94-142 or Education of All Handicapped Children Act are just a few of the important legislative acts that govern special education.

What these laws have attempted to create is equity of educational opportunity for all students in the least restrictive environment regardless of the disability. Thus, mainstream teachers must learn to work with support teams to learn how to teach all students in their classrooms.

You will study characteristics of these diverse groups and how to make modifications in another course before completing your certification requirements.

What you will come to realize upon studying about students who have disabilities is that what is good teaching for these groups is also good teaching for all students.

It is appropriate to speak of *stereotyping* of students before introducing teacher expectations. Stereotyping often leads people to have preconceived ideas about who can perform academically and who cannot. Stereotyping is the labeling of a student as having characteristics of an entire group. Prejudices and negative effects can occur as a result of stereotyping an individual. Today, high school students often speak of the "kickers," "stoners," "in crowd," "freaks," "nerds," or "Goths" as just a few of a myriad of labels attached to groups of students.

For some reason, humans like to laugh at groups of people. For instance, we laugh at blonde jokes, lawyer jokes, fishermen jokes, jock jokes, and mother-in-law jokes. While we would not laugh at handicapping conditions, we still have a tendency to lump children into groups of ability. That tendency is changing with our own education, so we must emphasize that teachers cannot afford to predetermine what a child can do or cannot do.

TEACHER EXPECTATIONS

Following that train of thought, teachers must have high expectations for all children. The Effective Schools Research of the 1980s introduced educators to the notion that teachers must have high expectations for all students regardless of ability because the unmistakable result is higher-achieving students. The **Pygmalion Effect** or **Self-fulfilling Prophecy,** is a common term associated with teacher beliefs. If you believe a child will fail, he probably will; but if you believe he will succeed, he will probably exceed your expectations. Research has long connected a teacher's high expectations to student achievement.

This term is taken from the 1913 play, *Pygmalion,* by George Bernard Shaw and more recently the book's adaptation into the best-selling musical, *My Fair Lady.* The play(s) describe an arrogant professor of phonetics who takes a common flower girl off the streets of London and makes a bet that he can turn her into a lady. You must see the video or play to learn the outcome, but suffice it to say, it is positive.

The **Hawthorne Effect** comes from a study based on teacher expectations and student performance. In this study, students were identified as very intelligent (even though they weren't) to the teachers who would be teaching them. As a result of the label "very intelligent" the teachers treated the students very differently and, when tested, the students scored above national norms!

Conversely, a group of students identified as less capable were treated differently by the teachers, and these students scored below national norms. The conclusion from the Hawthorne study was that teacher expectation is as important as student background and ability. Teachers must have high expectations for all students and constantly reinforce the need for student performance.

LEARNING STYLES

> **QUESTIONS**
> How will you accommodate different learning styles in your classroom?
>
> **Answer:** This topic is discussed more fully in Chapter 4, but for now, learning styles describes an individual's favored way of learning. Since all learning takes place through the senses, teachers categorize children as visual, hands-on, or auditory learners. The important point to understand about each of these learning styles is that teachers have to design lessons (Chapter 3) using a variety of strategies that appeal to all learning styles.
>
> What is your preferred learning style? To answer this question, go to one of these web sites to take an online learning style preference inventory.
>
> www.learning-styles-online.com/inventory/
> www.usd.edu/trio/tut/ts/stylest.html
>
> Several learning style inventories can easily be found online, so take more than one to inform yourself about the differences and implications of different learning styles.

> **QUESTION**
> What is the connection between a teacher's preferred learning style and a student's preferred learning style?

DIFFERENTIATED INSTRUCTION

Designing lessons for all types of learners leads teachers to *differentiate* instruction. Differentiated Instruction (DI) is a process of planning that recognizes individuals are highly diverse and, as such, should be taught with varying instructional approaches.

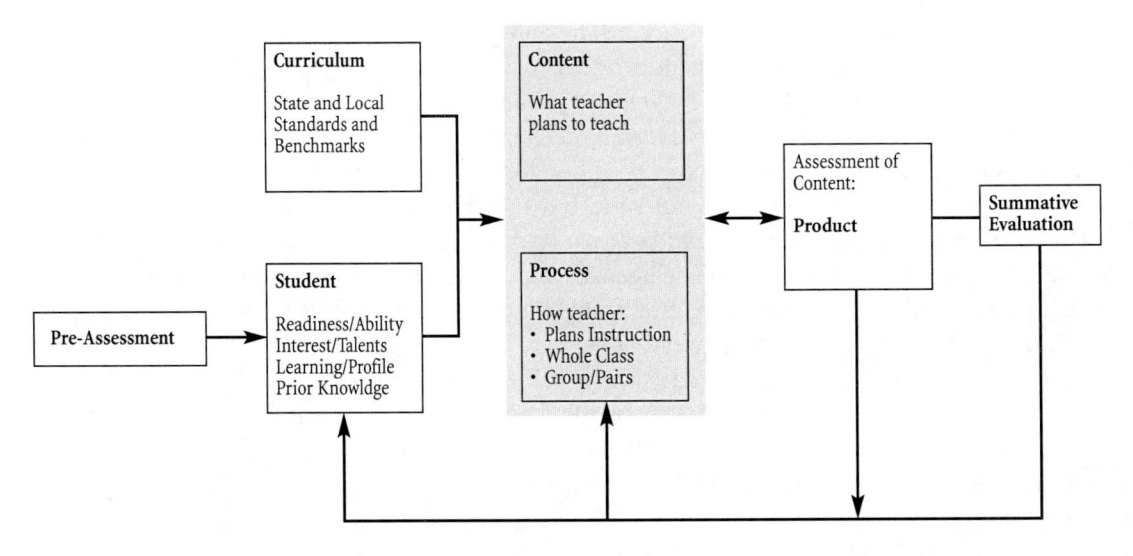

Adapted from *http://www.cast.org/publications/ncac/ncac_diffinstructudl.html*

By reviewing this figure of the planning process for differentiated instruction, the teacher preassesses students recognizing that the skills they bring to the classroom each day are variable. The teacher takes the mandated curriculum and plans a lesson utilizing various strategies that address learning style, group preferences, choices in assignments, etc.

This web site *http://www.cast.org/publications/ncac/ncac_diffinstructudl.html* offers information on the process of differentiated instruction.

Once you understand the model for DI, you will need to work with the process section of planning. The following figure shows a model of a planning pyramid that is useful in planning for differentiated instruction.

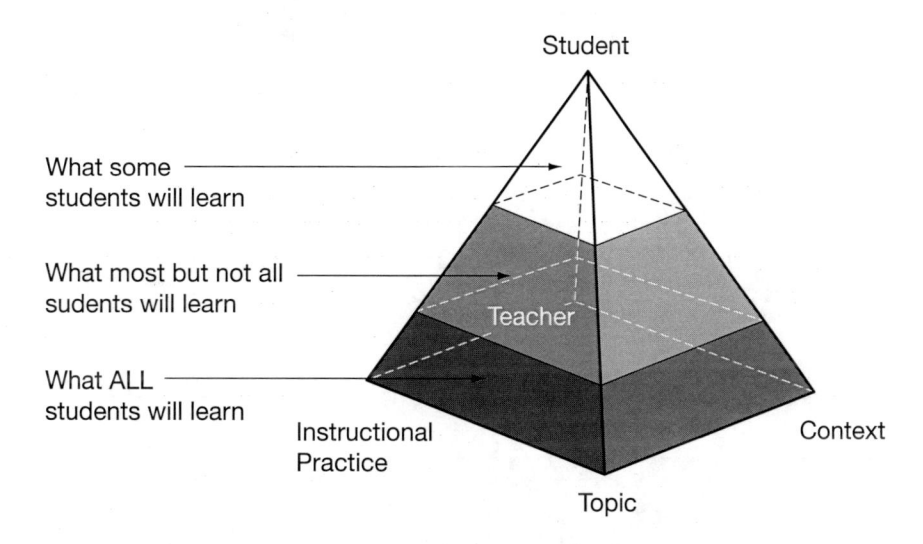

Adapted from *http://www.teachervision.fen.com/tv/printables/0865863393_31.pdf* 2-17-10 "free printables"

To plan differentiated instruction, teachers can refer to the following graphic to understand better what types of instruction are most effective. While disclaimers exist as to the validity of this model, one can self-assess his own learning preferences and generalize to the preferences of students.

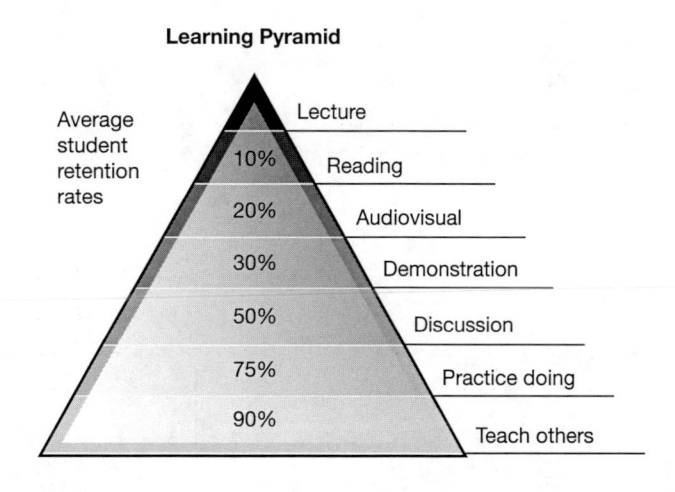

Learning Pyramid

Average student retention rates:
- 10% Lecture
- 20% Reading / Audiovisual
- 30% Demonstration
- 50% Discussion
- 75% Practice doing
- 90% Teach others

Adapted from *http://pegasus.cc.ucf.edu/~tbayston/eme6313/learning_pyramid.jpg*

From Schumm, Jeanne Shay, Vaughn, Sharon and Leavell, Alexandra G. (1994, May) Planning Pyramid: A framework for planning for diverse student needs during content area instruction. *The Reading Teacher,* 47(8), 608–615.

OTHER LEARNING THEORIES

Multiple Intelligences: One of the most interesting theories to advance into mainstream thinking is Howard Gardner's Theory of Multiple Intelligences. This theory takes a very rational look at human intelligence.

> **QUESTIONS**
> Have you ever felt *stupid* in a classroom? I was in my mother's advanced ninth grade English classroom, and I know I felt like something was wrong with me because I could not understand what a thesis sentence was. I also felt *stupid* in my Algebra class, which I took in the eighth grade. "Why," I thought, "do we have to use symbols? Why don't we just use numbers?"
>
> *Answer:* Most everyone can relate to one or the other of those statements. Gardner attempts to explain that everyone has native intelligence in one or more of the areas that he identifies as multiple intelligences: verbal-linguistic, mathematical-logical, spatial, bodily-kinesthetic, musical, interpersonal, intrapersonal, and naturalist. He has strong inclinations toward a couple of other areas, but for our purposes, these eight areas will suffice.

Howard Gardner attaches characteristics to each of his multiple intelligences.

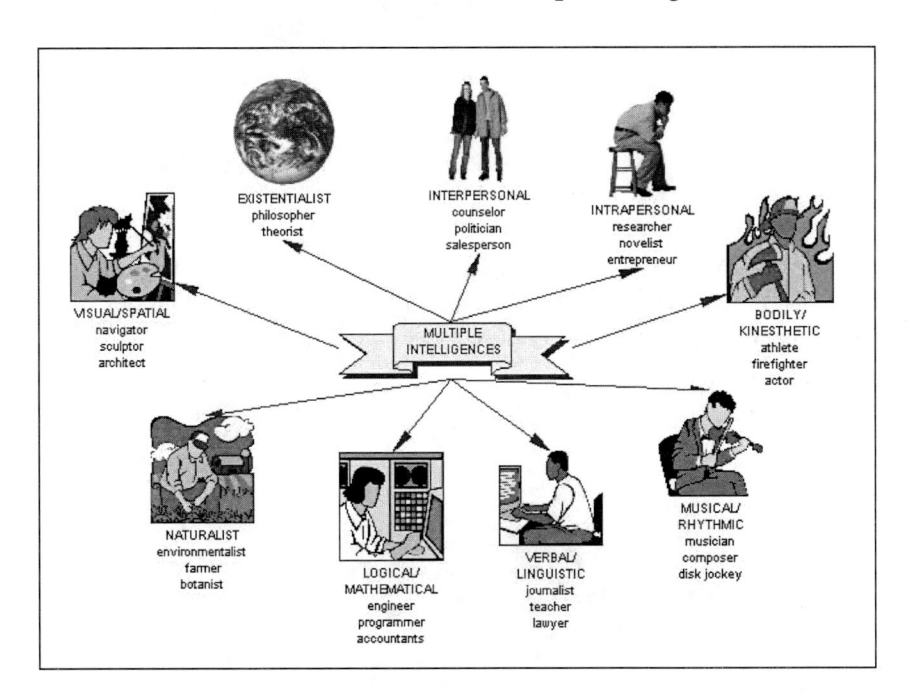

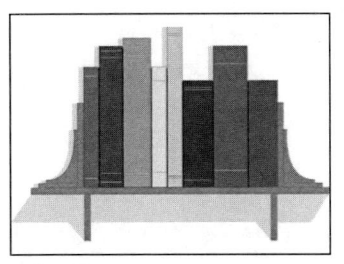

MULTIPLE INTELLIGENCES

- EXISTENTIALIST — philosopher, theorist
- INTERPERSONAL — counselor, politician, salesperson
- INTRAPERSONAL — researcher, novelist, entrepreneur
- VISUAL/SPATIAL — navigator, sculptor, architect
- BODILY/KINESTHETIC — athlete, firefighter, actor
- NATURALIST — environmentalist, farmer, botanist
- LOGICAL/MATHEMATICAL — engineer, programmer, accountants
- VERBAL/LINGUISTIC — journalist, teacher, lawyer
- MUSICAL/RHYTHMIC — musician, composer, disk jockey

Verbal—Linguistic
- Reading
- Writing
- Tell stories
- Talk
- Memorize
- Work at puzzles

Math—Logic
- Math
- Reasoning
- Logic
- Problem-solving
- Patterns

Competency 2 Diversity 43

Spatial
- Reading
- Maps
- Charts
- Drawing
- Mazes
- Puzzles
- Imaging things
- Visualization

Bodily—Kinesthetic
- Athletics
- Dancing
- Acting
- Crafts
- Using tools

Naturalist
- Understanding nature
- Making distinctions
- Identifying flora and fauna

Musical
- Singing
- Picking up sounds
- Remembering melodies
- Rythms

Personal
- Understanding people
- Leading
- Organizing
- Communicating
- Resolving conflicts
- Selling

Intrapersonal
- Understanding self
- Recognizing strengths and weaknesses
- Setting goals

After reviewing the different types of intelligences according to Gardner, check off all the ways you believe you are *intelligent* according to this theory.

Learn more about Howard Gardner at *www.howardgardner.com*.

Now that you have had a brief introduction to the competency on diversity, it is time to apply your knowledge of Competency 2, Diversity, provided by the State of Texas in Standard 1.

INDEPENDENT PRACTICE AND MODELING (HOMEWORK)

1. **Scholar's Vocabulary:** Using the TEXAS PPR state-produced list of proficiencies preservice teachers should master related to Competency 2, highlight terms you wish to place in your interactive glossary. You should have a minimum of five terms from C2.

2. **Reflective Writing:** Complete your reflective writing assignment for Competency 2 by using the eleven-sentence model.

3. **Learning Style Inventories:** This competency includes understanding your own learning preferences. Some research finds that teachers have a tendency to teach the way they like to learn. If you teach only one way to the exclusion of others, you may lose diverse learners along the way.

Locate at least one "learning style inventory" (Google the term and choose from a list of inventories). Take at least one inventory (two to see if they match) and discuss your learning preferences. This understanding is important because teachers have a tendency to plan lessons that play into their own learning preferences.

Evaluate your findings of one or two learning inventories that you take to discover something of your own learning style. Write a brief essay detailing how preference for your own learning style might be detrimental to other students in the class.

4. Examine a public school textbook during one of your observations. Do the writers/publishers include diverse cultures? Learning activities? Or evidence that diversity is acceptable?

EVALUATION/INDEPENDENT PRACTICE

Diversity Essay

The following "wheel" contains several spokes upon which you are to document your personal types of diversity. You should have a minimum of five personal "diversities," but you may insert more if you wish.

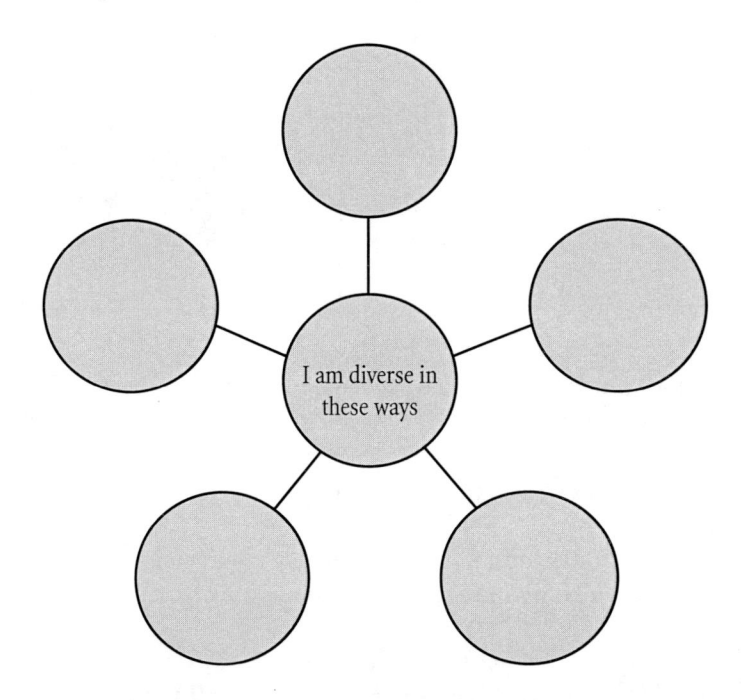

(Diagram: central circle labeled "I am diverse in these ways" with five spokes radiating to empty circles)

Diversity Essay Assignment

1. My Own Kind of Diversity

   As we interact with others, we often notice how they are "different" from us. We have internal speech that speaks to us and says things like, "Whoa, that person surely has blue hair!" or "What a nice (sweet, sexy, tall, well-dressed) person that is!" The following writing assignment is intended to help the student reflect upon his/her individual diversity. What do you think others might notice about you as being diverse?

   a. Expand your research beyond this text to discover how you are diverse by conducting online research to give you ideas.

b. Using these resources, define *diversity* to the best of your ability (one paragraph; be sure to use footnotes for researched information).
c. Then, using the Diversity Graphic Organizer that you have filled out, write two more paragraphs detailing how you are diverse.
d. This essay should not be more than two double-spaced pages.

2. Write a brief essay detailing at least one way you are intelligent according to Howard Gardner's theory of multiple intelligences. Offer specific analysis on why you believe you have a particular intelligence.

3. Respond to the following three questions (3Qs) that focus on your learning about diversity.

   Q1: What new terms did I learn about diversity that I did not already know?
   Q2: What topics in the Instructional Input do I need to research more?
   Q3: How will I use this knowledge in the future?

4. Write and present a sample lesson utilizing the planning pyramid (see figure and web site that follow) and multiple intelligences to "differentiate" instruction. You may pick any grade level and any subject you wish. To find the Texas Essential Knowledge and Skills, go to the TEA web site: www.tea.state.tx.us
   a. In the left-hand column, click on "Curriculum."
   b. Click on "Curriculum Standards/TEKS."
   c. Click on "Texas Essential Knowledge and Skills."
   d. Scroll down and pick a grade level or subject area of interest.
   e. Identify and include the text of the TEKS you wish to use.

An example of the Texas Essential Knowledge and Skills follows. Always document the TEKS by number and wording.

113.6. Social Studies, Grade 4

(b) Knowledge and skills

   (2) History. The student understands the causes and effects of European exploration and colonization of Texas and the Western Hemisphere. The student is expected to:

   (C) Explain when, where, and why the Spanish established Catholic missions in Texas

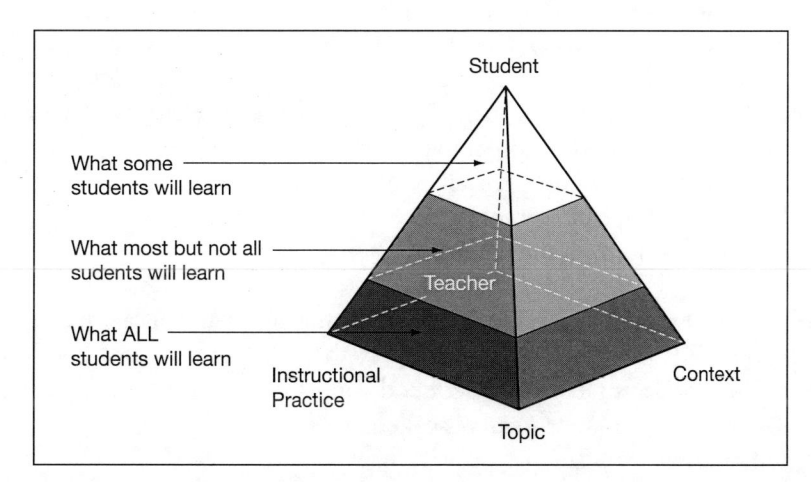

Accessed at *http://www.teachervision.fen.com/tv/printables/0865863393_31.pdf* 2-17-10 "free printables"

Plan to teach an eight- to ten-minute portion of the lesson using a minimum of two of the multiple intelligences.

CLOSURE/FOLLOW-UP

Diversity is a very broad topic, yet one that teachers need to be able to define in manageable terms. It seems that each "type" of diversity requires teachers to make judgment calls in some form or another; so in the interest of fairness and objectivity, teachers must be informed. Diversity is an ongoing study for teachers.

ASSESSMENT

Ask yourself whether you have mastered these objectives.

- **Objective 1:** Can I identify terms associated with at-risk and diversity?
- **Objective 2:** Do I know my personal learning style?
- **Objective 3:** Define the teacher/learner connection to learning styles.
- **Objective 4:** What are the rationales behind the different types of grouping?
- **Objective 5:** What are the connections between high expectations and student performance?
- **Objective 6:** What are the characteristics of special groups of students?
- **Objective 7:** What are some of the multiple beliefs regarding theories of inclusion (mainstreaming) and exclusive grouping, and am I able to verbalize the major belief systems?

PRACTICE QUESTIONS

Now, assess your learning by answering these questions. The answers are given in the Appendices.

1. The youngest of four children, Natasha, is a fourth grader at her community school, George Washington Elementary. Whenever the teacher presents any math concept, Natasha begins to panic and struggle. Immediately, her hand goes up, and she asks her teacher, Mrs. Phillips, for help. Natasha doesn't even try to work the problem on her own. The reason for Natasha's behavior is that she is:
   a. the youngest of four children.
   b. lazy and unmotivated.
   c. learning disabled.
   d. a product of gender training.

2. When the physical education teacher, Coach Garza, structures games and activities in the gym, he always lines the girls up in one line and the boys up in the other line to compete against each other. He believes that this gender division will make the girls try harder. This plan is probably detrimental because:
   a. it allows for no positive interaction between genders.
   b. boys are physically stronger, but girls are more intellectual.
   c. boys will always win the contests easily.
   d. girls are too dependent upon the teacher.

3. Students who have high IQs are often placed in International Baccalaureate, Honors, or Gifted and Talented programs, and their teachers often expect them to perform at a high level of competency. The teacher expectancy of these students, consequently, most often produces positive results. This occurrence of positive expectations for these students is called:
   a. The Pygmalion Effect
   b. The Hawthorne Effect
   c. Gardner's Assessment
   d. The IDEA Comparison

4. Multiculturalism allows a positive integration of various ethnic cultures into the classroom. Many methods exist for the teacher to create a positive multicultural environment. Which of the following examples potentially provides that environment?
   a. Celebrating various Chinese holidays
   b. Reserving library books about African tribal cultures
   c. Studying the life of an Eskimo family
   d. All of the above

5. Is it necessary to separate into different classrooms students who are diagnosed with mental retardation and students who are not?
   a. Yes, because the students who have mental retardation will be at different learning levels than children with normal intelligence.
   b. No, this would be a case of discrimination because you would be discriminating against the students with disabilities in denying them equal access to learning.
   c. Yes, you would need to separate the students so you could focus on the special education students' needs, but time should be set aside for interaction with other students.
   d. There is not enough information given to answer this question.

6. Juan is suffering academically in Mr. Fallon's Earth Science class because of his limited English vocabulary. He does better when the teacher places the students into groups and allows them to work cooperatively. What type of grouping model is Mr. Fallon using?
   a. Between-class grouping
   b. Parallel grouping
   c. Within-class grouping
   d. Similar grouping

7. Mrs. Kennedy teaches a sophomore-level science class. The next unit is on atoms, but she is skeptical that the students are ready to move forward as a group since few of her students have excellent grades thus far. Those with low grades are reluctant to participate in class discussion or even in lab work. In order to motivate these distant learners she should:
   I. Send notes home with her students to give their parents.
   II. Teach the atom unit using overheads with activities to relate to the space program.
   II. Assess each student to decide which learning style may be most effective.

   a. I and III
   b. II
   c. II and I
   d. II and III

8. Mr. Jones has an elementary class of seventeen first-grade students. During the math lesson, some of his students have difficulty keeping up with the majority of the class. In order to provide for these children he should:
   a. have an aide tutor these children while the rest take a play break.
   b. group them by ability and spend adequate time with each group.
   c. allow the faster-learning children to watch a movie while he works with the slower ones inside the same classroom.
   d. nothing, just keep encouraging students to catch up.

9. Mrs. Thomas, a fourth-grade teacher, is having some discipline problems with a student, Johnny, in her classroom. She noticed that some of his classmates were picking on him and calling him names during recess and before class. She reprimanded the students that were guilty of saying and doing these hurtful things; however, Johnny continued to misbehave in class. When it was time to do seat work Johnny would tell her that he was stupid and did not know how to do the work. What should Mrs. Thomas do to help build up Johnny's self-esteem and still keep him under control?
    a. Contact Johnny's parents and let them make suggestions about how they would like to see him disciplined.
    b. Make those students who were rude to Johnny stand in front of the class and apologize to him.
    c. Mrs. Thomas can walk around the class more and let Johnny know that he is doing a good job.
    d. Mrs. Thomas could let Johnny be her helper for a day or a week.

10. I am a new White history teacher at a predominantly Black school. The students tell me that February is Black History Month and traditionally, the history department plans a full month of activities. Unfortunately, the only Black person I know of is Martin Luther King, Jr. What should I do to show students I care? I'm not so sure a whole month should be devoted to Black History.
    a. Compromise and teach one lesson about Martin Luther King, Jr.
    b. Tell the students that the curriculum does not include Black history.
    c. Ask the history chairman about my responsibilities.
    d. Spend time researching Black historians and include Black History Month into my lesson plans.

CAREER PLANNING

Students who continue to study diversity can major in sociology or psychology, bilingual education or English as a Second Language, special education, or gifted and talented. Graduate degrees are available in all of these areas, and public schools encourage employment in these areas as many are identified as high needs—meaning there are not enough applicants to fill available positions. Public schools value college graduates who have an understanding of diversity.

MATERIALS NEEDED

Apples, knife, Internet

SUGGESTIONS FOR ADDITIONAL ASSIGNMENTS

Choose one or more of these activities to demonstrate your understanding and proficiency with the competency.

1. Name or list some of the many ways humans are diverse.
   a. Draw an umbrella over the list. The umbrella symbolizes the inclusiveness of diversity.

   b. Create a second umbrella and label the umbrella "me."

   c. Now name all the ways you are diverse.
   d. The final step(s) might be to "pair and share" by networking with someone else in the class discussing the ways you are different as well as honest reactions to that diversity.
   e. Write a reflective essay elaborating on your diversity.

2. America is made up of diverse people. In fact, Americans are fond of saying "Everyone came from somewhere!" Perhaps one of the most awesome freedoms Americans enjoy is the protected right to celebrate diversity. Find out why America enjoys this freedom. Research the following social institutions, and analyze the reason(s) that Americans are safe from persecution because of their diversity.
   a. Political freedom
   b. Religious freedom
   c. Social freedom
   d. Educational freedom

3. Any typical classroom features multiple kinds of diversity. Suppose your classroom enjoys students who are Hispanic, gifted, musically talented, and Goth-inspired. Taking each of these individuals or groups, describe how a teacher might use that diversity to the *advantage* of the entire class.

4. Read a book on diversity or multiculturalism. In an essay, bullet the main ideas, and write a one-page personal experience with one of the bulleted ideas.

   Suggested books:

   Building a House for Diversity by Marjorie Woodruff
   Teaching from a Multicultural Perspective by Helen Roberts
   Developing Multicultural Educators by Jana Noel

50 Competency 2 Diversity

5. You have planned a reading lesson for third graders, most of whom can read on grade level. One student, however, reads at the 2.2 (second grade, second month) grade level.
    a. Select a paragraph from a third-grade reader;
    b. Perform a readability test on the paragraph by using the web site below;
    c. Determine whether the reading lesson is appropriate for the 2.2-level reader;
    d. Document your findings; and
    e. Tell whether you were surprised or not.

    Readability Formula web site: On this web site you can insert your paragraph and it will calculate the readability for you.

    http://www.readabilityformulas.com/free-readability-formula-assessment.php

    Other web sites:

    http://www.renlearn.com/ar/atossummary.htm

    Click on "Using Readability Levels to Guide Students to Books."

    After reading this article and after applying at least one readability formula, write a substantive reflection indicating your thoughts on the findings of your research.

6. Interview an assistant principal or an SOS Counselor (crisis intervention). Suggested questions:
    a. Identify the "groups" of students within a high school population you are observing. You may get answers such as "head bangers," "gangs," "Goths," "kickers," "Preppies," etc.
    b. At what age do adolescents begin to identify with different groups and why, in their opinions, these groups exist?
    c. What kind of management, dropout, absenteeism, etc., problems occur within these groups?
    d. What program(s) does the school have in place to work with these students?

7. Interview a grade-level counselor. Ask for (anonymous) examples of students who fall through the cracks and the reasons for failure. Suggested questions:
    a. What is the dropout rate at this school?
    b. At what age do students drop out?
    c. Why do they drop out?
    d. How does diversity connect with the dropout problem?
    e. How is the school addressing the dropout problem?

8. View a movie such as *The Blind Side,* and identify and discuss the at-risk factors that plagued "Big Mike."
    a. In questioning Michael about his Ole Miss decision, the NCAA official tells Michael that "other families might want to 'take in' promising athletes to populate their favorite football teams." Did this statement catch you off guard?
    b. Do you believe this situation might possibly result in the "worry" the NCAA had about Michael and Ole Miss?

9. Compare the education of the leaders of two cultural minorities in a "Q" chart. Include names of leaders of movements, dates, and circumstances. What impact do/did these leaders have on minority education today?

"Q" What is the question?	"A" What is the answer?
EX1: Who was Medgar Evers?	He was...; he was educated
	.....

10. You are a young Afghani student who lives in Afghanistan. Write a letter to President Obama telling him how you feel/what you think about U.S. involvement in the war citing at least three reasons for support of your position. Address the letter to President Barak Obama, 1600 Pennsylvania Avenue, Washington DC 20500.

11. **Who Am I?** List twenty adjectives or phrases that describe the kind of person you think you are. Use this chart to help you organize your thoughts:

I AM...

1.

2.

...

20.

This list usually becomes very personal and more difficult to write after the first few items. After you complete the list, respond to these questions: Was this list difficult to write? Why? Do you think your friends would write the same things about you that you wrote on your list? Which of these items make you truly diverse?

Once you have completed the list and answered the questions, imagine what each child in a classroom would write, and write a brief paragraph explaining your thoughts on diversity and student expectations.

12. View the movie/video *Sean's Story: A Lesson in Life* produced by Films for the Humanities and Sciences (#5299). This is the story of a child with Down's Syndrome who was part of a legal battle over inclusion. After watching *Sean's Story,* type a one- to two-page opinion paper on inclusion. Before beginning to write your paper, think about the following issues:
    - Should all students, regardless of disability, be in a regular classroom setting? (full inclusion)
    - What factors should be considered when making decisions about "least restrictive environment"?
    - How does inclusion affect the classroom teacher and other students in the class?
    - What are the benefits of inclusion to the affected student and to the parent?

When you begin writing the paper, you should clearly state the extent to which you believe inclusion should be practiced. Convince the reader that you really believe what you are writing!

Films for the Humanities & Sciences, PO Box 2053, Princeton, NJ 08543
www.films.com

13. View the movie *My Fair Lady,* and describe the results of Professor Higgins' positive expectations in the transformation of Liza Doolittle from a common flower girl into a lady.

14. Read the following article, which explains and models the Learning Pyramid. This template exists to help teachers differentiate instruction in meaningful ways.

    Review the following article: Schumm, J.S., S. Vaughn, & J. Harris. 1997. "Pyramid Power for Collaborative Planning." *Teaching Exceptional Children, 26(6), 62-66.*

    Document your learning in a bulleted list.

15. During one of your class observations, ask a counselor or principal what the ethnic ratios are for this school (you can also access the AEIS Report online for any school). Compare the campus ratios to the district ratios.

16. Develop a glossary of special education acronyms.

17. Examine a blank sample IEP from any campus. Ask if you can attend an ARD meeting (Admissions, Review, Dismissal) understanding that permission may not be given. What information is the regular classroom teacher responsible for on this form? What district or campus resources will be available to help teachers?

18. Read this indispensible book for a thorough understanding of the at-risk factor of poverty: Payne, Ruby K. 2005. *A framework for understanding poverty,* 4th ed. Highlands, TX: aha! Process, Inc.

Competency 3

Lesson Planning

LESSON PLAN FOR COMPETENCY 3

STATE STANDARDS: STANDARD 1, COMPETENCY 3

Competency 003: The teacher understands procedures for **designing** effective and coherent **instruction** and **assessment** based on appropriate learning goals and objectives.

STATE TEACHER PROFICIENCIES

Competency 003

The teacher understands procedures for designing effective and coherent instruction and assessment based on appropriate learning goals and objectives.

The beginning teacher:

- Understands the significance of the **Texas Essential Knowledge and Skills** (TEKS) and of prerequisite knowledge and skills in determining instructional goals and objectives.
- Uses appropriate criteria to evaluate the appropriateness of **learning goals** and **objectives** (e.g., clarity; relevance; significance; age-appropriateness; ability to be assessed; responsiveness to students' current skills and knowledge, background, needs, and interests; **alignment** with **campus and district goals**).
- Uses assessment to **analyze students' strengths** and needs, evaluate **teacher effectiveness,** and guide **instructional planning** for individuals and groups.
- Understands the connection between various components of the Texas statewide assessment program, the TEKS, and instruction, and analyzes data from state and other assessment tools using **common statistical measures** to help identify students' strengths and needs.
- Demonstrates knowledge of various types of **materials and resources** (including technological resources and resources outside the school) that may be used to enhance student learning and **engagement,** and evaluates the appropriateness of specific materials and resources for use in particular situations, to address specific purposes, and to meet varied student needs.
- **Plans lessons** and **structures units** so that activities progress in a logical **sequence** and support stated **instructional goals.**
- Plans learning experiences that provide students with **developmentally appropriate** opportunities to explore content from integrated and varied perspectives (e.g., by presenting **thematic units** that incorporate different disciplines, providing intradisciplinary and interdisciplinary instruction, designing instruction that enables students to work **cooperatively,** providing **multicultural** learning experiences, prompting students to consider ideas from multiple viewpoints, encouraging students' application of knowledge and skills to the world beyond the school).
- **Allocates time appropriately** within lessons and units, including providing adequate opportunities for students to engage in **reflection, self-assessment, and closure.**

TEACHING OBJECTIVES

At the end of the lesson, the student should be able to:

- Define curriculum and instruction;
- Differentiate teacher-centered instruction from learner-centered instruction;
- Demonstrate a learner-centered lesson featuring cooperative learning;
- Memorize and recall Benjamin Bloom's six-word cognitive taxonomy;
- Construct higher-order thinking questions based on Benjamin Bloom's Cognitive taxonomy;
- Construct teaching objectives based on the taxonomy;
  - ◇ Differentiate between general and specific objectives;
- Create original lesson plans using the 9-step lesson planning model;
- Know and explain all steps of the lesson plan model.

ESSON PLANNING 55

C3 KEY WORDS: LESSON PLANNING

Terms associated with lesson planning

Madeline Hunter	Lesson Cycle	Writing Objectives
Gagne's 9 Events of Instruction	Benjamin Bloom	Curriculum
Taxonomies of Objectives	Writing Objectives	Co-curricular
Cognitive	Types of Instruction	Extracurricular
Types of Assessment	Scope and Sequence	Didactic
Teacher-Centered	Learner-Centered	Birdwalking
Core Curriculum	Scope and Sequence	Constructivism
Cooperative Learning	Collaborative Learning	

INTRODUCTION/FOCUS

"If you don't know where you are going, you might wind up someplace else."

Yogi Berra

Yogi Berra's quote is applicable to lesson planning. Teachers who do not set teaching objectives often *birdwalk! Birdwalking* is a term that is often attributed to teachers who are easily distracted and "walk" from one subject to another without ever reaching the point! Have you ever had a teacher who was easily led off track? That was probably a teacher that students laughed at behind his/her back and periodically designated fellow students to introduce a topic that would get him/her off track. Going off track won't happen if teachers plan effectively.

TRANSITION: Both Berra's quote and the term *birdwalking* lead to the topic and main idea for Competency 3: Lesson Planning.

"If you fail to plan, you plan to fail!" Everyone has undoubtedly heard this adage before. This adage is particularly important to the career of teaching. When a teacher doesn't plan, all kinds of things happen: he may talk about all kinds of different subjects (birdwalking), he may have discipline problems, or he "talks to" students as opposed to "teaching" them. Planning is critical to students' learning.

INSTRUCTIONAL INPUT AND GUIDED PRACTICE

What we need to know about lesson planning

The Instructional Input in this lesson plan will contain *guided practice* in the form of questions placed throughout the chapter. References to web sites will also serve as guided practice as you research topics to gain further knowledge and information and application.

BEGIN AT THE BEGINNING

Introduction to Lesson Planning

The reason birdwalking occurs is that teachers do not set appropriate or clearly understandable objectives for each lesson. Beginning teachers learn how to avoid birdwalking and how to accomplish real learning by using Benjamin Bloom's Cognitive Taxonomy and following a structured lesson planning format. By learning Blooms's Cognitive Taxonomy early in their educational careers, and by learning Madeline Hunter's lesson cycle, teachers can use it to plan lessons understanding that a failure to set good learning objectives results in little or no learning.

> **Where do I begin? "Begin at the beginning and go," said the king in** *Alice in Wonderland.*
>
> **What is curriculum? Where does it come from? How do I know what I will teach?**

Introduction to Curriculum and Instruction

Two important terms that must be differentiated are *curriculum* and *instruction*.
Curriculum is defined in various ways. It is essentially the "what" of daily teaching.

- the planned subject-matter content and skills to be presented to students; or
- all of the experiences students encounter, whether planned or unplanned (co-curricular or extracurricular).

For our purposes when we speak of curriculum, we speak of the Texas Essential Knowledge and Skills (TEKS)—or that "subject-matter content" that will be presented to students and that will be tested by the Texas Assessment of Knowledge and Skills (TAKS).

Instruction also has several definitions. Instruction is associated with the "how," or methods that a teacher uses to present curriculum. Instructional methods include the myriad of strategies that teachers use to appeal to students to motivate them to learn.

In short, the curriculum is set by the State of Texas, and in essence the State dictates what will be taught in the TEKS. The TEKS have been carefully constructed to scaffold (or build upon) from one year to the next. That is why children must "master" one grade level before moving to the next. Good teachers instinctively know how to take the State curriculum and translate it into creative lessons through their instruction. The State does not tell teachers "how" to teach.

The following quote, taken from the first page of the Texas Education Agency web site/curriculum, clarifies the State's role in curriculum:

> Curriculum and instructional materials are integral parts of a public school system. The State Board of Education periodically updates the state's curriculum standards called the Texas Essential Knowledge and Skills (TEKS). Textbooks and other instructional materials are then written for children based on those standards. More than 48 million textbooks are distributed by the Texas Education Agency to Texas public school students each year.
>
> *http://www.tea.state.tx.us.*

What is clear from the curriculum, however, is that instruction should be **student-centered** rather than **teacher-centered.** What these two terms mean is simply that students must be the first consideration when planning instruction. That means a student's developmental stage, his diversity, and his preferred learning style must be taken into account. Conversely, those of us of a certain age laughingly refer to teacher-centered instruction as "my way or the highway." In other words, the old-fashioned way of delivering knowledge and testing what the teacher thought he taught is no longer the preferred method of instruction. Read more about student-centered instruction and teacher-centered instruction later in the chapter.

Core Curriculum

As college students, you are probably quite aware of the core curriculum. When you entered college, you were given a core list of classes that you have to take before you can graduate. Those of you who have filed degree plans have checked off the "core" classes you have taken in readiness for graduation. In public school, when we refer to *core curriculum*, we refer primarily to the four academic content areas:

- English/language arts/reading (also referred to as "literacy")
- History/social studies/geography
- Mathematics
- Science

Texas Essential Knowledge and Skills

Otherwise known as the TEKS, the State of Texas has a scaffolded set of teaching objectives that form the curriculum for most academic areas in public school today. Following you will see an example of the TEKS.

Sample Explanation Taken from English Language Arts (TEKS)

1) The English Language Arts and Reading Texas Essential Knowledge and Skills (TEKS) are organized into the following strands: Reading, where students read and understand a wide variety of literary and informational texts; Writing, where students compose a variety of written texts with a clear controlling idea, coherent organization, and sufficient detail; Research, where students are expected to know how to locate a range of relevant sources and evaluate, synthesize, and present ideas and information; Listening and Speaking, where students listen and respond to the ideas of others while contributing their own ideas in conversations and in groups; and Oral and Written Conventions, where students learn how to use the oral and written conventions of the English language in speaking and writing. The standards are cumulative—students will continue to address earlier standards as needed while they attend to standards for their grade. In sixth grade, students will engage in activities that build on their prior knowledge and skills in order to strengthen their reading, writing, and oral language skills. Students should read and write on a daily basis.

http://ritter.tea.state.tx.us/rules/tac/chapter110/ch110a.html

---

Sometimes, schools combine some or all of these classes and teach **interdisciplinary thematic units (ITUs)**. The purpose of ITU is to demonstrate that all learning is connected. The term *interdisciplinary* becomes very relevant when you are choosing a specific area of education to specialize in.

If you are going to obtain an interdisciplinary (or generalist) degree, let's say to teach grades 4–8, the 4–8 generalist degree will enable you to teach all four of the core content areas: ELA, Math, Science, and Social Studies. If you take a "composite" degree for secondary, you may teach all four sciences, or Government, History, Economics, and Geography. Sometimes, English majors get a composite in English, Speech, and Journalism. Discuss options with your academic advisor.

Co-Curricular and Extracurricular

Generally, clubs and athletics have commonly been referred to as *extracurricular*. That is because they are considered separate from the academic learning of the regular school day.

However, in exemplary education many activities are significant components of the total educational program and are *co-curricular* rather than extracurricular.

Co-Curricular means that regardless of whether they occur before, during, or after school, the activities are essential to the whole curriculum (intramurals, study skills, and advisement).

Scope and Sequence

To learn what the Scope and Sequence of a discipline includes, refer to the TEKS once more. By looking at a given set of TEKS, say third-grade math, you will see a certain number of skills that third graders must master. That is the scope of what you will teach. The sequence is the order in which you will teach it.

> **TEACHER DILEMMA**
>
> Whether for a school year, a semester, six weeks, or one week, when planning the scope of the curriculum you should decide what is to be accomplished in that period of time.
>
> The State Curriculum (i.e., TEKS): you can examine the major document that helps guide you in selecting the content of your curriculum.
>
> Standards: Listed state by state, discipline by discipline, you can compare Texas with other states at the following web site:
>
> *http://www.statestandards.com*

Now that you know what curriculum is and where it comes from, you need to know how to use it. Following is a sample from the eighth grade English Language Arts TEKS posted on the TEA web site:

---

b) Knowledge and skills.

(1) Listening/speaking/purposes. The student listens actively and purposefully in a variety of settings. The student is expected to:

(A) determine the purposes for listening, such as to gain information, to solve problems, or to enjoy and appreciate (4–8);

(B) eliminate barriers to effective listening (4–8);

(C) understand the major ideas and supporting evidence in spoken messages (4–8); and

(D) listen to learn by taking notes, organizing, and summarizing spoken ideas (6–8).

This paragraph from the eighth grade ELA TEKS, shows that eighth graders should become good listeners because listening is a skill needed throughout life. These TEKS (c) also say that eighth graders should "understand the major ideas and supporting evidence in spoken messages" among many, many other things. That statement is clearly stressing that students need to learn how to think critically, so they need to use higher-order learning skills (HOTS), and Benjamin Bloom is the vehicle by which teachers plan for that kind of thinking.

Teacher-Centered Instruction vs. Student-Centered Instruction

Now that you understand what curriculum is and where it comes from, it is important to understand that instruction, or the *way teachers teach,* can be simplistically divided into two methods: **teacher-centered instruction** and **student-centered instruction.**

Also known as **didactic instruction,** teacher-centered instruction usually involves lecturing to students. The teacher expects students to sit quietly and take notes on the lecture and at some point, through lecture notes and reading in a textbook, respond to questions about the lesson.

In recent years, educators have discovered that the way most children learn best is through hands-on experiences. One theory, **Constructivist Learning Theory,** is dedicated to the idea that students need to *construct* their own learning experiences for them to have lasting effect. I liken this theory to the bricklayer who carefully places one row of brick upon another. Eventually, the laborer will have a complete wall.

Some classroom curriculum is well adapted to hands on; for example, a science class conducts experiments while a history class studying the Civil War has a harder time creating "hands-on" experiences for students. A physical education course in basketball is certainly hands on, while an English class lesson involving reading a novel is not.

Types of student-centered instruction include **collaborative or cooperative learning.** Such lessons require students to work together to discover the *truths* of the materials they are supposed to learn. Another type of lesson that falls into the student-centered category is **discovery learning,** wherein a student *discovers* for himself the truths to be learned. This method is likened to the *Aha* or *Eureka* moment students feel when they finally understand a concept.

Understanding and Writing Objectives

Objectives are usually divided into three taxonomies (or classifications): **cognitive, affective,** and **psychomotor.** Academics will write most objectives in the cognitive domain. However, when teachers wish to include values as outcomes of lessons, the affective domain serves as a model.

Example: The learner will appreciate the opera *Carmen* after seeing it performed on stage.

Likewise, if the teacher wishes to involve movement (as in sports or acting) or manipulation (as in mathematics or music), the psychomotor domain provides a model for writing those objectives.

Example: The learner will demonstrate a triple axel with a smooth landing.

Writing Objectives

The objective that governs the lesson may be likened to the thesis that governs the public speech and the freshman English paper. Normally, the objective begins with the phrase: "The student will . . ." The word that follows is an active verb and the remainder of the sentence provides the substance to complete the sentence. Writing objectives by this pattern follows the research of **Mager.**

Example: "The student will write objectives reflecting Mager's pattern."

Gronlund, on the other hand, provides another way to write objectives. He suggests a general objective that can then be broken into many smaller step-like objectives. Such objectives are very good for planning a six-week unit or a semester's work. For example, if you are teaching a six-week unit on the American Dream exemplified in American Literature, the objectives might begin:

The student will appreciate the social, economic, and literary ramifications of the American Dream by:
1. Reading *The Great Gatsby;*
    a. monitored by daily tests and
    b. a six-week examination.

2. Researching the political period that gave rise to the American Dream;
   a. produce a five-page report on the era and
   b. deliver an oral report on the research.
3. Preparing a notebook filled with media references to the American Dream;
   a. clip ten magazine articles/news stories/advertisements and
   b. evaluate each notebook entry for social worth.

Gronlund's approach includes specific ways to measure the outcome of the objective; for example, a grading matrix may be provided to focus the grading.

Writing objectives takes practice. Even the most experienced of teachers have difficulty writing clear objectives all the time. One way to increase your expertise in this area is through studying Benjamin Bloom's Cognitive Taxonomy.

Higher-Order Thinking Skills (HOTS) and Benjamin Bloom

Benjamin Bloom created a way to think about learning. Beginning with knowledge, we are able to progress to much higher levels of thinking. This hierarchy of thinking/learning is constructed in such a way that teachers can construct learning objectives, teach to those objectives, and assess what has been taught/learned.

The following graphic is a learning tool to help teachers remember where to put emphasis on questions and objectives. Use this web site or the chart in the appendices to fill in the blanks:

http://www.nwlink.com/~Donclark/hrd/bloom.html

LOTS OF HOTS

K

C

A

_____

A

S

E

Above the line is *LOTS* or Lower-Order Thinking Skills, and below the line is *HOTS* or Higher-Order Thinking Skills. Use this graphic/acronym to help remember the six-word chart: Knowledge, Comprehension, Application, Analysis, Synthesis, and Evaluation (KCAASE).

See the chart of Benjamin Bloom's Cognitive Taxonomy of Thinking in the Appendices. You will see this chart (many forms of it) throughout your teaching career. Some companies have even marketed spiral, cardboard covered flip charts for teacher's ease of use.

Accessed at: http://www.mentoringminds.com/taks-flip-charts.php

RESOURCE

Note the active verbs that are provided to help the teacher create goals and objectives that can be measured at each level. Be aware that if you do an online search on Benjamin Bloom, you will find numerous charts outlining these same terms. Use any/all that you are comfortable with.

WRITING EDUCATIONAL OBJECTIVES

The State of Texas has already written educational objectives in the form of the TEKS or general objectives. You already saw a sample of eighth grade ELA objectives. Once you access the TEKS, and copy those into your lesson plan, you will still have to write your own "teacher objectives," which are more specific and related to the specific topic/lesson you intend to teach. Your teacher objectives take the formal TEKS and rephrase them into the exact points using the exact short story or textbook from which you want to teach. Reading the TEKS and writing teacher objectives is difficult for the beginner, but by utilizing the information that follows, you can get a good start on learning how to write educational objectives.

The best, most important, objectives are "measurable objectives" or specific objectives. That means simply that when you write an objective, you must write it in a way that you can actually measure the amount of learning a student has accomplished. Normally, when teachers "test" over a subject, they use the results to measure learning, but if the test doesn't test what is taught (a weak objective), then the results are likely to be disappointing for both the teacher and the student. When you learn to write good, measurable objectives, you will have the basis for setting your grading policy.

The guidelines for writing measurable objectives are rather standard and include these three parts: the knowledge to be learned, the conditions under which it is to be learned, and the criteria for assessing learning. Often these three parts are written in the form of a table:

The knowledge to be learned (the teacher's teaching objective)	The conditions under which student learning is to take place	The criteria for assessing student learning (specific, measureable objective)
My objective for you: The teacher will be able to write learning objectives.	How will you do this? The student accesses Benjamin Bloom's Taxonomy of Cognitive Learning and practices lower- to higher-order thinking questions from an online web site or from the appendices.	How will I assess it? The student will be able to write learning objectives for all six levels of Bloom's Cognitive Taxonomy without error.

Examples of objectives that can be measured are:

Describe seven out of ten electrical hazards when installing a home wiring system.
Students will describe the two most important functions of the electoral college.
Create a five-part plan to evacuate the physical education building in case of threat.

Now that you have some knowledge about writing teaching objectives, writing the lesson plan is important.

WRITING A LESSON PLAN (LP)

Madeline Hunter (former Professor of Education at UCLA) set the standard for lesson planning. While her template is not the only format that teachers use, it is the standard for lesson planning that beginning education students learn. Be advised that different teachers (schools) use different approaches to preparing a lesson.

The lesson planning process usually follows a guide that is called the *lesson* cycle. The basic parts of the lesson cycle are:

> State Objective (TEKS)
> Teaching Objective (teacher objective)
> Anticipatory Set/Focus (Introduction)
> > Transition (usually stating the learning objective)
> Instructional Input (the lesson)
> Modeling the Information
> Checking for Understanding
> Guided Practice
> Independent Practice (homework)
> Closure
> Assessment

REFLECTION

You may hear experienced teachers say "You don't need to write all that out in a lesson plan!" Keep in mind that once you become experienced, you will not need to write lengthy LPs; but until that time comes, you will benefit (and so will your students) by putting in the planning time. This is just one instance where you must learn to crawl before you can run. See the Appendices to retrieve a lesson planning template.

The idea behind writing an LP is to make sure teachers are teaching what they say they are teaching or what the TEKS say they should be teaching. More importantly, with a plan, students know what is being taught and know what they are to learn. Research shows that students who have teachers who teach using good teaching objectives learn more.

Mastery Learning

Madeline Hunter created a step method for writing lesson plans that is associated with mastery learning. The concept of mastery learning as an instructional method presumes that all children can learn if they are provided the appropriate conditions. If children do not master a specific concept, they do not advance to another learning objective until they demonstrate proficiency with the first one. In a way, the State of Texas has adopted mastery learning because if a student doesn't master the work given at a certain grade level, he or she may not progress to the next grade level.

To help teachers with planning, a planning guide for the lesson cycle provides a consistent model for teachers to design lessons that focus on teaching objectives. The cycle begins with the anticipatory set, which is the focus for the day. It is also called the lesson *set* or the *introduction*. Toward the end of the introduction, the teacher should emphasize the learning objective with a good transitional statement. That statement is the stated *objective* or the *purpose* for the lesson. Research informs us that students (or adults for that matter) who know what they are supposed to learn do much better when told what they are to learn in advance.

The next part of the cycle is the *input* or the instructional part of the plan. This is where the actual planning part takes place. Included within the instructional input can be *guided practice* where the teacher watches carefully while students work with the new knowledge. Teachers interject many types of teaching strategies into the lesson part of the cycle. *Modeling* is another important part of the instructional input. Good teachers always try to *model* the information/product they want students to reproduce and remember. Teachers can use *think-alouds* to model while they work on the board or the overhead. The fifth part of the cycle is *checking for understanding*. The watchful teacher monitors and adjusts instruction by watching for students who do not understand. Teachers use discussion, questioning, informal assessment, or green/red cards held up by students to determine who understands and who does not.

The sixth and seventh parts of the cycle are the *guided practice* and the *independent practice*. Guided practice is done under the watchful eyes of the teacher while independent practice is homework or independent study by each student. While *closure* can occur at several points throughout the lesson, it usually ends the instructional period. It is only effective if students do it in response to what is learned. Finally, closure may be done in conjunction with assessment or evaluation. Students can be held responsible for their learning through exit slips, 2Qs, 1-2-3 Go!, or other such quick responses at the end of the period. Students must turn in a response before leaving the room.

Now that you have the basics for writing a lesson plan, you will need still more knowledge about how to plan a student-centered lesson. Types of instruction and teaching strategies are included in Chapter 8, Competency 8.

INSTRUCTIONAL INPUT

1. **Scholar's Vocabulary:** Using the TEXAS PPR, State-produced list of proficiencies, preservice teachers should master related to Competency 3, highlight terms you wish to place in your interactive glossary. You should have a minimum of five terms from C3.

2. **Reflective Writing:** Complete the reflective writing using the eleven-sentence template. Upload this essay into the ePortfolio.

3. **Discovering Differences in Learning Groups:** Research and note as many differences as you can between cooperative (collaborative) learning groups and traditional classroom learning. (Some answers will be given at the end of the chapter.)

Cooperative Learning Groups	Traditional Learning
1.	1.
2.	2.
3.	3.
4.	4.
5.	5.
6.	6.
7.	7.
8.	8.
9.	9.
10.	10.

INDEPENDENT PRACTICE AND MODELING (HOMEWORK)

1. **Objectives:** Using any of the topics that follow, write six questions—one at each level of Bloom's Cognitive Taxonomy. Pretend these six questions are **test questions** over the same topic. TOPICS: Baking bread, basketball, libraries, newspapers/magazines, or vocabulary (see the model at the end of the lesson).

   Next, using the information in the "input" on "Writing Educational Objectives," turn these same questions into **objectives for teaching** a lesson on the same topic. When you finish this assignment, you will have twelve objectives. Be sure to label "test questions" and "teaching objectives" and label each level of Bloom's Cognitive Taxonomy (KCAASE).

2. **Lesson Plan:** Research/choose any TEKS for any grade level and any subject and create an original lesson plan following the 9-part lesson plan model.

   Caution:
   - Be sure to create all documents needed for handouts and tests.
   - Be sure your teacher objectives can be measured.

3. **Poster Plan:** This assignment is for an entire class. Each student should use the same Lesson Plan in Assignment 2. Recreate the plan by enlarging the font, cutting and pasting the essential parts (9) of the plan onto a poster board, labeling the parts, and preparing all support materials for the plan and attaching them in some way to the poster. (Put your name on the back.) Be sure to include enough information that a substitute teacher could follow through with it successfully.

POSTER PLAN

Failing to plan is planning to

f
a
i
l

Andrew Carnegie

Select specific Texas Essential Knowledge and Skills (TEKS) from the Texas Education Agency (TEA) web site to create a lesson plan (LP) using the nine parts of the following lesson plan cycle as described previously. The completed poster plan will be evaluated by classmates using a scoring rubric provided by the instructor (at the end of the chapter). Clearly mark at the top of the poster what subject/grade level the LP is designed for.
9-Part Lesson Plan Cycle:

1. Objectives (both TEKS/teacher)
2. Anticipatory Set (focus)
   Transition (state purpose)
3. Instructional Input
4. Modeling
5. Checking for Understanding
6. Guided Practice
7. Independent Practice (homework)
8. Closure
9. Assessment

Use the grading matrix at the end of this chapter to assess each poster plan represented in the class. Average each student's scores, place the average in the appropriate blank, then rank the posters in order from first through last place (no ties).

When everyone has completed the averaging and ranking, all students should be asked to *stand beside* the poster that they chose for the first-place ranking. Select students should explain why they selected that poster. Ask students to then go to their second-place poster, etc., until this point has been made. Normally the majority of students will congregate around the first two or three posters interchangeably. The point is that quality planning can be determined even by inexperienced lesson plan writers. The instructor should take this opportunity to critique plans.

Follow-up assignments for the Poster Plan might involve writing a critique that would be helpful for a fellow student, or working in groups to re-do posters.

Be sure to take photos of students with their posters for the e-Portfolio.

CLOSURE/FOLLOW-UP

The lesson you have just completed is one of the most important lessons in all of teaching. Yes, you need to understand children's developmental stages, and yes, you need to understand how diverse all children are, but you need the basic understanding that there is no substitute for planning lessons that meet the needs of children. Toward that end, the State of Texas has gone to great lengths of time and expense to create the Texas Essential Knowledge and Skills so that all children will learn similar things at similar ages. Your role in planning is primary and essential, and the more practice you have at planning, the better the job you will do in the classroom. The more experience you have at this level of preparation, the easier the job will be AND the less time it will take once you get there.

Hopefully, you are beginning to see that all competencies are intricately connected—you design a lesson based on the age level (maturity level) of your students (C1 & C2); the lesson begins with teaching objectives at some level of BB's Cognitive Taxonomy; the lesson (along with informal assessment) adheres to the objective; finally, the formal assessment "tests" what the teacher-set objectives state.

ASSESSMENT

Ask yourself whether you have mastered these objectives.

- **Objective 1:** Differentiate between curriculum and instruction. Tell where to locate curriculum for the schools in the State of Texas.
- **Objective 2:** Differentiate teacher-centered instruction from student-centered instruction.
- **Objective 3:** Did you memorize and can you recall Benjamin Bloom's six-word cognitive taxonomy?
- **Objective 4:** Construct higher-order thinking questions based on the taxonomy using analysis, evaluation, and synthesis.
- **Objective 5:** Can you construct teaching objectives based on the taxonomy?
  - ◇ Differentiate between general and specific objectives and tell the purpose for each.
- **Objective 6:** Can you create original lesson plans using the 9-step model?
- **Objective 7:** Do you know and can you explain all steps of the lesson plan model?

PRACTICE QUESTIONS

Now assess your learning by answering these questions. Answers are given in the Appendices.

1. Mr. Gonzalez stands in front of his fourth-period science class lecturing them over the information in their Science lesson taken directly from Chapter 5 of their textbook. The seventh-grade students are not required to answer any questions; they are just required to sit, listen, and take in all of the information the teacher is giving them. He suggests that they take notes on the lesson. What type of presentation method is this?
   a. Inductive presentation method
   b. Deductive presentation method
   c. Cooperative presentation method
   d. Teacher-centered lesson

2. On the other hand, Mr. Smyth is a very exciting Science teacher. He knows how to incorporate effective lecture techniques into every lesson. He gets the students to think, be observant, interpret data, and express human values about the content. The students really like his "playing dumb" role sometimes, because he asks them questions that they know he knows the answer to, but he asks them in such a funny way that hands fly up to match wits with him. What teaching method does Mr. Smith use?
   a. Deductive teaching method
   b. Traditional teaching method
   c. Discovery teaching method
   d. Collaborative teaching method

3. Mrs. Templeton also is very exciting and interesting to listen to. Her students show excitement when they come in the classroom door. Yesterday, she taught a difficult class on longitude and latitude. To catch their attention, she used a Pilates ball and a tennis ball to teach this lesson. She taught by asking discovery questions about how the students would explain to someone where they were in the wilderness without a map. Mrs. Templeton asked carefully designed, specific questions in order to bring the students to the correct conclusion. What type of lecture is this?
   a. Traditional lecture
   b. Guided discovery learning lecture
   c. Jigsaw lecture
   d. Elaborative questioning lecture

4. Mrs. Mears presents a problem to the class and the students have to explore alternative points of view and find acceptable solutions to the problem. What type of lecture style is this?
   a. Comparative lecture
   b. Formal oral essay
   c. Provocative lecture
   d. Problem-centered lecture

5. Mrs. Reynolds plays vocabulary games such as vocabulary bingo, vocabulary concentration, and vocabulary hunt on the computer with her class. What is Mrs. Reynolds trying to do with all of these vocabulary games?
   a. Develop students' vocabulary
   b. Have fun and learn words
   c. Pass the time productively
   d. Make sure her students like her

6. Mrs. Kincade is a great lecturer. She knows the material, and she knows how to relate it to every situation. She always has a personal story to relate in all of her lectures. Her students learn a lot and remember a lot through hearing her relevant stories. This is an example of what teaching method?
   a. Set induction with anecdotes
   b. Ice breakers to put students at ease
   c. Storytelling tales that have a point
   d. Grabbers and stabbers to gain compliance

7. Mrs. Reynolds always asks her students these five questions about lessons read or studied: 1) What do you see? Notice? Observe? 2) How are these alike? How are they different? 3) Why? 4) What would happen if . . .? 5) How do you know? These questions are designed to get the class to think about what they are reading or studying. This is an example of what type of strategy?
   a. Advanced organizers or graphic organizers
   b. Critical-thinking skills incorporating HOTS
   c. Note taking in two-column note format
   d. Evaluations of critical issues in the lessons

8. Mrs. Campbell has her students calculate the area of their Geometry classroom to help them understand the concept of area in math. This is an example of:
   a. Learner-centered instruction
   b. Cooperative instruction
   c. Collaborative instruction
   d. Jigsaw instruction

9. Principal Frederick has named a site-based committee to rewrite the teaching objectives for senior English. He is determined that all of the senior-level teachers adhere to the same objectives and that all objectives should be measurable. In naming Mariana Dushek to chair the committee, he has specifically told her to begin writing the measurable objectives in group. He wants which model for writing objectives?
   a. Benjamin Bloom's Taxonomy Model
   b. Frederick Chopin's measurements for children
   c. Madeline Hunter's Lesson Objectives
   d. Gronlund's Model for Writing Objectives

10. In the LOTS of HOTS model, this is an example of synthesis:
    a. Potatoes can be made into potato bread.
    b. Potatoes can be dug from the ground.
    c. Potatoes can be tossed when hot.
    d. Potatoes can be used in a hands-on study of the Irish Depression.

CAREER PLANNING

Students who like the study of academic content often get a graduate degree in curriculum and instruction. School districts have district-wide C&I positions. You could become a Director of Secondary Education or Director of Elementary Education or a Curriculum Specialist in districts large enough to have these support positions.

MATERIALS NEEDED

Internet; 9-Part Lesson Plan template; grading matrix for the Poster Plan.

SUGGESTIONS FOR ADDITIONAL ASSIGNMENTS

The following activities are intended to help preservice teachers as they learn how to design instruction.

1. Web Search for TEKS:

   Ever since high-stakes testing came into being several years ago, the State-mandated objectives for learning have become more and more specific and have become incremental building one grade upon the next. In fact, many teachers are extremely dissatisfied with the mandates in place often saying that there is no more room for creativity—just time for teaching "to the test." A close examination of the TEKS, however, shows that there is a great deal of repetition and reinforcement from grade level to grade level. Beginning with the first grade, follow a few TEKS from one grade to the next to discover for yourself how much reinforcement takes place from one grade level to the next.

2. Support this statement: "The State tells teachers *what* to teach, but it does not tell teachers *how* to teach." How does a new teacher determine age-appropriateness of teaching goals when the State writes objectives by grade level?

3. Research site-based teams and reflect upon how such teams might impact your future employment.

4. Assessment: As part of a lesson plan you write and present, give classmates a test; analyze the test; or visit with a professor and ask that professor what types of analysis s/he does on tests before assigning final grades.

5. Select a "Reading" test from the State's released tests. You should be alert to the types of questions asked, how they are formatted, and reflect upon how you would teach a student to pass this test.

6. Create a table and do a comparison chart comparing or contrasting lesson planning templates: Madeline Hunter's LP, Gagne's 9 Events of Instruction, and one other lesson planning model of your choice.

   Answer the following questions: Describe the similarities and differences among the three models. Will you need all parts of the LP each day? Why or why not?

7. Advanced challenge: Create an interdisciplinary lesson on the topic of multiculturalism. You may design this lesson in one of the following manners:
   a. Point: counterpoint (debate format in which you are allowed to play the Devil's Advocate); or
   b. Team teaching; History/American Literature
      i. In this model, you will assume the role of lead English or History teacher and allow space/time/material for the secondary lesson to be integrated. (You must insert the secondary person's objectives.)

8. Create a lesson or review a lesson you have done and estimate how much time it will take to teach each section. Create an LP template featuring a time column.

9. Describe one teacher's verbal approach in making learning objectives clear to students. What does she say that makes her learning objectives clear?

10. Examine a teacher's tests. Ask for the teaching objectives included in that test. Do the tests match the objectives taught? Are the objectives clearly stated either in lesson plans or in study guides? How do the students know what to study for the tests?

11. (a) Describe some ways to get students to learn while you are taking care of other business. (b) Discuss ways to check students' understanding of the material.

MODEL FOR TEST QUESTIONS

Bloom's Taxonomy
Assessment Questions for Grade 11

Knowledge Level: List three observations about the appearance of bacon.

a. _____

b. _____

c. _____

Comprehension Level: Explain where bacon comes from.

Application Level: What are some examples of how we can use bacon?

Analysis Level: Compare and contrast bacon and T-bone steak.

Synthesis Level: Invent an original use for bacon. For example, create a recipe.

Evaluation Level: Discuss in approximately five sentences what breakfast would be like without bacon.

Suggested answers for "Discovering Differences in Learning Groups" found above

Cooperative Learning Groups	Traditional Learning
1. learning together	1. learn by oneself
2. no one person has to have all the answers	2. has to have all the answers
3. verbalization promotes learning	3. often done alone, silently
4. interpersonal supports	4. intrapersonal dependence
5. interpersonal skills practice	5. no chance for social skills interaction
6. promotes interdependence	6. promotes self-reliance
7. when one learns, all learn	7. one learns, fails alone
8. face-to-face, immediate feedback	8. no feedback
9. rewarded for group products	9. rewarded for personal effort
10.	10.

GRADING MATRIX FOR POSTER PLANS

#	Focus	TEKS/Obj	Input	Model	CFU	Guided	Independent	Assess	Closure	AVE	Rank
1											
2											
3											
4											
5											
6											
7											
8											
9											
10											
11											
12											
13											
14											
15											
16											
17											
18											
19											
20											

√ ++ = 100; √ + = 95; √ = 80; √ - = 70; √ - - = 50   Mark each column and total the #s.

9-PART LESSON PLAN TEMPLATE

1. TEKS Objective (documented exactly from the TEA web site).

2. Teaching/Learning Objective(s) (TEKS rewritten to reflect what the teacher intends to teach)

3. Anticipatory Set (must be interesting)

    a. Transition (connection between set and input)

4. Instructional Input (This is the lesson; it may include guided practice)

5. Modeling (the teacher models the desired behavior)

6. Guided Practice (this is work the students do with the teacher's assistance)

7. Independent Practice (homework)

8. Closure (only effective if students do it)

9. Assessment (may be informal/formal; provide samples)

Competency 4

Learning Processes

LESSON PLAN FOR COMPETENCY 4

STATE STANDARDS: STANDARD 1, COMPETENCY 4

Competency 004: The teacher understands **learning processes** and factors that impact student learning and demonstrates this knowledge by planning effective, engaging instruction and appropriate assessments.

STATE TEACHER PROFICIENCIES

Competency 004

The teacher understands learning processes and factors that impact student learning and demonstrates this knowledge by planning effective, engaging instruction and appropriate assessments.

The beginning teacher:

- Understands the role of **learning theory** in the instructional process and uses **instructional strategies** and appropriate **technologies** to facilitate student learning (e.g., connecting new information and ideas to prior knowledge, making learning meaningful and **relevant** to students).
- Understands that young children think **concretely** and rely primarily on **motor and sensory** input and **direct experience** for development of skills and knowledge, and uses this understanding to plan effective, developmentally appropriate learning experiences and assessments.
- Understands that the middle-level years are a **transitional stage** in which students may exhibit characteristics of both older and younger children, and that these are critical years for developing important skills and attitudes (e.g., working and getting along with others, appreciating **diversity,** making a commitment to continued schooling).
- Recognizes how characteristics of students at different developmental levels (e.g., limited **attention span** and need for physical activity and **movement** for younger children; importance of **peers, search for identity, questioning of values,** and exploration of long-term **career and life goals** for older students) impact teaching and learning.
- Applies knowledge of the implications for learning and instruction of the range of **thinking abilities** found among students in any one grade level and students' increasing ability over time to engage in **abstract thinking** and **reasoning.**
- Stimulates **reflection, critical thinking,** and **inquiry** among students (e.g., supports the concept of play as a valid vehicle for young children's learning; provides opportunities for young children to **manipulate** materials and to **test ideas** and **hypotheses;** engages students in structured, **hands-on problem-solving** activities that are challenging; encourages **exploration** and **risk-taking;** creates a **learning community** that promotes positive contributions, effective communication, and the respectful exchange of ideas).
- Enhances learning for students by providing **age-appropriate instruction** that encourages the use and refinement of **higher-order thinking skills** (e.g., prompting students to explore ideas from diverse perspectives; structuring active learning experiences involving cooperative learning, problem solving, **open-ended questioning,** and inquiry; promoting students' development of **research skills**).
- Teaches, models, and **monitors organizational** and **time-management skills** at an age-appropriate level (e.g., establishing regular places for classroom toys and materials for young children, keeping related materials together, using **organizational tools,** using effective strategies for locating information and organizing information systematically).
- Teaches, models, and monitors age-appropriate **study skills** (e.g., using **graphic organizers, outlining, note-taking, summarizing, test-taking**), and structures research projects appropriately (e.g., teaches students the steps in research, establishes checkpoints during research projects, helps students use **time-management tools**).
- Analyzes ways in which teacher behaviors (e.g., **teacher expectations, student grouping practices, teacher-student interactions**) impact student learning, and plans instruction and assessment that minimize the effects of negative factors and enhance all students' learning.
- Analyzes ways in which factors in the home and community (e.g., parent expectations, availability of **community resources, community problems**) impact student learning, and plans instruction and assessment with awareness of social and cultural factors to enhance all students' learning.

- Understands the importance of **self-directed learning** and plans instruction and assessment that promote students' motivation and their sense of **ownership** of and **responsibility** for their own learning.
- Analyzes ways in which various teacher roles (e.g., **facilitator, lecturer**) and student roles (e.g., **active learner, observer, group participant**) impact student learning.
- Incorporates students' different approaches to learning (e.g., **auditory, visual, tactile, kinesthetic**) into instructional practices.

TEACHING OBJECTIVES

At the end of the lesson, the student should be able to:

- Identify several learning theories
- Recall major theorists presented in previous chapters and scaffold new theorists to make connections between the theory, theorist, and how learning occurs
  ◇ Benjamin Bloom's Cognitive Taxonomy (C3)
  ◇ Jean Piaget: Piagetian Theory (C1)
  ◇ Edgar Dale: Dale's Cone of Learning (C3)
  ◇ Howard Gardner's Theory of Multiple Intelligences (C2)
  ◇ Laurence Kohlberg's Theory of Moral Development (C1)
  ◇ Nature vs. Nurture theories
  ◇ Albert Bandura's Social Learning Theory
  ◇ Robert Sternberg's Triarchic Theory of Intelligence
- Expand knowledge of lesson planning to include teaching strategies for presentation of information
  ◇ Robert Gagne: Gagne's Nine Events of Instruction (C3) http://ide.ed.psu.edu/id
  ◇ Madeline Hunter: Lesson Cycle (See C3)
  ◇ Mager/Gronlund: Writing Objectives (See C3)
  ◇ Scaffolding
  ◇ Hands-on problem solving
  ◇ Questioning techniques
- Compare different approaches to the lecture
- Analyze personal thinking skills
- Create charts to improve organizational skills
  ◇ Time-management skills

C4 KEY WORDS: LEARNING PROCESSES

Terms associated with learning processes

Brain-Based Learning	Thinking Skills	Creative Thinking
Scaffolding	Instructional Style	Metacognition
Think Alouds	Pedagogy	Learning Styles
Social Learning Theory	Triarchic Theory of Intelligence	Wait Time
Intelligence	Motivation	Schema Theory
Glickman's Chart	Attention Span	

Strategies: Rehearsal, Organization, Elaboration
Specific Approaches: Constructivist, Questioning, Manipulatives, Cooperative

INTRODUCTION/FOCUS

I've heard preservice teachers say many times, "I don't want to be a run-of-the-mill teacher. My classes are going to be interesting and fun—not like those I had in school." (See the graphic of Benjamin Bloom's Cognitive Taxonomy labeled "boring" and "cool" at the end of this lesson plan.) "Fun, not boring" is at once a commendable goal, but it indicts all teachers and their teaching methods at some time in any career. In response I say, "Then, what are you going to do that's so different?"

College students do not yet have the answer for that question, but what this competency does is give the students some tools for making that teaching objective and lesson interesting and *fun*. (Personal Note: I do not believe that all teaching and all learning is fun.)

TRANSITION: If the personal goal is to make fun and interesting lessons, then students need to own a large personal repertoire of teaching strategies. This competency addresses the teacher's personal teaching style (for that will dictate the way you like to teach) with a particular emphasis on the lecture as a common teaching method; teaching/learning strategies for a variety of learners; thinking about thinking; and a review of applicable theorists.

INSTRUCTIONAL INPUT AND GUIDED PRACTICE

What we should know about learning processes

The Instructional Input in this lesson plan will contain *guided practice* in the form of questions placed throughout the chapter. References to web sites will also serve as guided practice as you research topics to gain further knowledge and information and application.

BEGIN AT THE BEGINNING

Introduction to Learning Theories

Every teacher should know something about learning theory. This lesson presents a few of the most quoted theorists, but you should know that there are many, many more theorists who research how learning occurs. The theorists presented in this lesson deal primarily with the application of learning as we perceive it to take place in the classroom.

> **QUESTION**
> How does learning occur anyway?
>
> *Answer:* Exactly how learning occurs is a mystery. Even with the most sophisticated research on the human brain today, the final frontiers of how connections between information and knowledge occur remains a mystery. Research does indicate certain parts of the brain "fire up" with certain stimuli, and the explanations of "what happens" are both complex and fascinating. Wouldn't it be wonderful if we could find that "stimuli" for each and every student every day?

What we do know about learning is pretty well limited to the following:

- Hemisphericity: left brain, right brain
- Larks and Owls
- Learning Styles
- Multiple Intelligences
- Stress Studies
- Information Processing Theory
- Layered Curriculum depends upon Bloom's Cognitive Taxonomy

A few other things that are important for teachers to know include:

- The brain is 80 percent water.
- The brightest babies are born to mothers who eat high protein diets and have low stress during pregnancy.
- It is believed that the chemicals in carbonated drinks affect synapses negatively, whereas water increases synapses/dendrites.
- Brain food includes meat, cheese, eggs, liver, nuts, fresh fruits, water.
- Sleep is critical.
    - The very young and adolescents need more sleep than older individuals.
    - You cannot learn if you are sleep-deprived.
    - Things learned during the day are processed during deep REM sleep.
    - Research shows the importance of sleep to "cement" new knowledge into the brain. A Harvard Medical School study shows that certain types of learning (discrimination) were hindered when students were sleep-deprived right after learning. Even when later allowed to catch up on the deprived sleep, their test performance did not improve. Learning and sleep go hand in hand. *(Stickgold, R., et. al. 2000. Nature Neuroscience, 3(12) 1237–1238.)*
    - Brain Chemicals play a large role in learning

In the meantime, teachers should learn all they can about learning theory and theorists.

> In previous chapters, you have studied theories attributed to Benjamin Bloom, Jean Piaget, Edgar Dale, Howard Gardner, and Laurence Kohlberg. **Bloom** developed a cognitive taxonomy that classifies types of learning. Teachers use this taxonomy to design learning objectives. **Piaget,** on the other hand, worked with the ages of children. He developed a system to describe learning capability by four age classifications.
>
> **Dale** contributed interesting research on the ways students receive information and remember it. Others have produced similar charts to Dale's, but some say that no evidence exists to confirm its validity; still, when one combines a favored learning style with this chart, it is common to find common understanding.
>
> **Gardner** suggests that individuals have different talents and skills. This theory resonates with everyone, because most recognize that they have individual talents that others do not have. Idiomatically, it takes all of us in all of our glorious diversity to create an interesting world.

Finally, **Kohlberg** researched the moral development of children. This research coincides with Piaget's theory of development suggesting that morality is learned behavior and develops as the child grows.

These theorists provide a context for scaffolding new knowledge about how learning occurs.

In 1976, Benjamin Bloom (Bloom's Taxonomy) wrote that students' account for learning.

Cognitive Characteristics = 50%

Quality Teaching = 25%

Affective Characteristics = 25%

Bloom, Benjamin. 1976. Human characteristics and school learning. *New York: McGraw-Hill.*

If this quote represents truth about learning, then fifty percent of an individual's capacity to learn is based upon his or her native intelligence. Twenty-five percent of an individual's capacity to learn rests upon quality teaching, and the last twenty-five percent is attributed to a child's affective characteristics or his motivation to learn.

Quality teaching and motivation compose the two variables in Bloom's model of learning. That means that teachers must know all they can know about teaching and learning and about increasing students' motivation or else stand by and watch students fall far short of their potential. Even if one disputes the percentage attributed to a teacher's affect upon any given student, most would agree that teachers do make a difference every day in every classroom.

To study this competency, how learning occurs, it is important to study learning theory and theorists, pedagogical techniques, lesson planning, and thinking.

Two Theories about Cognitive Characteristics: Nature vs. Nurture

Several years ago, Dr. Russell Long, then President of West Texas A&M University, delivered an address to a group of educators. A former teacher himself, Dr. Long said "*this problem* of nature vs nurture comes down to two parts: are you who you are because you can't help it—it's an accident of birth? Or, are you the sum total of your life's experiences?" Dr. Long continued to say he could make a strong argument on the side of nurture. If nurture is more important than nature, just think of the impact teachers have upon their students since students are with teachers many more hours a day than with their parents. "Many, if not most, of the experiences students have ARE the sum total of their school experiences. Something to think about!"

Cognitive characteristics attributed to human beings include the *entity theory* and the *incremental theory*. The entity theory is also called the *Doctrine of Native Intelligence* and is the *nature* part of the debate. This doctrine by definition says that children are born with a set intelligence. It is the educational community's job then to create an environment whereby all children can development that native intelligence to the maximum extent possible. This doctrine sets in place a hierarchical structure where children are taught at their perceived level of ability. It assumes that people are not equal.

> **QUESTIONS**
> It is easy to identify the major problem with this type of thinking—how are students tested so they can be ability-grouped? Can intelligence be measured? If so, why do poor, at-risk, and minority students get lower scores on intelligence tests than their upper-class peers?
>
> *Answer:* Many social psychologists say "yes," intelligence can be measured. They believe that results of such tests accurately reflect the conditions of society. Others who say *yes* believe that some score poorly because they did have lower intelligence (low intelligence = poor = lower intelligence). Other psychologists agree that intelligence tests are accurate and differences in performance among certain groups are to be expected.
>
> Still others say "no" that intelligence cannot be tested. These folks believe in the concept of inherited intelligence, but believe such tests are biased. Their hope is to create an intelligence test free of cultural bias.

On the other hand, many social psychologists reject the notion of inherited intelligence. These folks are at the center of the nature vs. nurture debate and tout the *incremental theory* of intelligence. They believe that given a level playing field, the innate intelligence of these children will emerge equal to those who are deemed intelligent at birth. These researchers acknowledge that at-risk, poor, minority students are at the heart of the issue but see their very social inequality as the heart of the low scores. By addressing social inequality through compensatory education (Chapter 1 and Early Childhood programs, etc.), the culture of poverty can be broken.

Motivation

Two types of motivation are normally addressed when speaking about motivation, and popular psychology relates both to the theories of intelligence although those connections have not been validated through research to date.

Extrinsic motivation involves encouraging students to learn by giving tangible rewards such as candy or tokens. Some say superfluous rewards (everyone wins) create an environment of expectation and entitlement.

On the other hand, intrinsic motivation is apparent in some individuals who sincerely work and learn because they want to. These students thrive on completing assignments and often do more than the teacher expects.

Obviously, the better type of motivation is intrinsic, but the biggest question involving motivation is "Can one teach intrinsic motivation?" What educators do to encourage and facilitate internal desire is to create an inviting classroom environment and develop invitational delivery methods. Research does show that nothing in the environment will sustain motivation for great lengths of time, so the educator must continually encourage learners through a variety of means to work harder and smarter.

The Nature of Learning for Teachers

The following two figures demonstrate the nature of learning for teachers. The first chart demonstrates what a "Student Teacher's Brain" looks like where everything is compartmentalized. Note the "lesson plans" on the left. In Chapter 3, the preservice teacher learned facts about lesson plan guides and writing objectives. This preservice teacher may even pass a stringent test on all of those objectives presented in Chapter 3.

However, making the transition from classroom learning to developing a lesson and presenting it in the classroom are two entirely different things. Note the next two sections: classroom management and classroom presentation. The best-planned lesson must be presented in the classroom context with students making noise, asking questions, demanding make-up work, and turning in late (or early) work. The teacher must also find creative (fun?) ways to present the lesson, which will enthrall all the students and keep them on task at the same time.

80 Competency 4 Learning Processes

The preservice teacher remembers doing observations where the expert teachers they observed made it look easy.

A Student Teacher's Brain

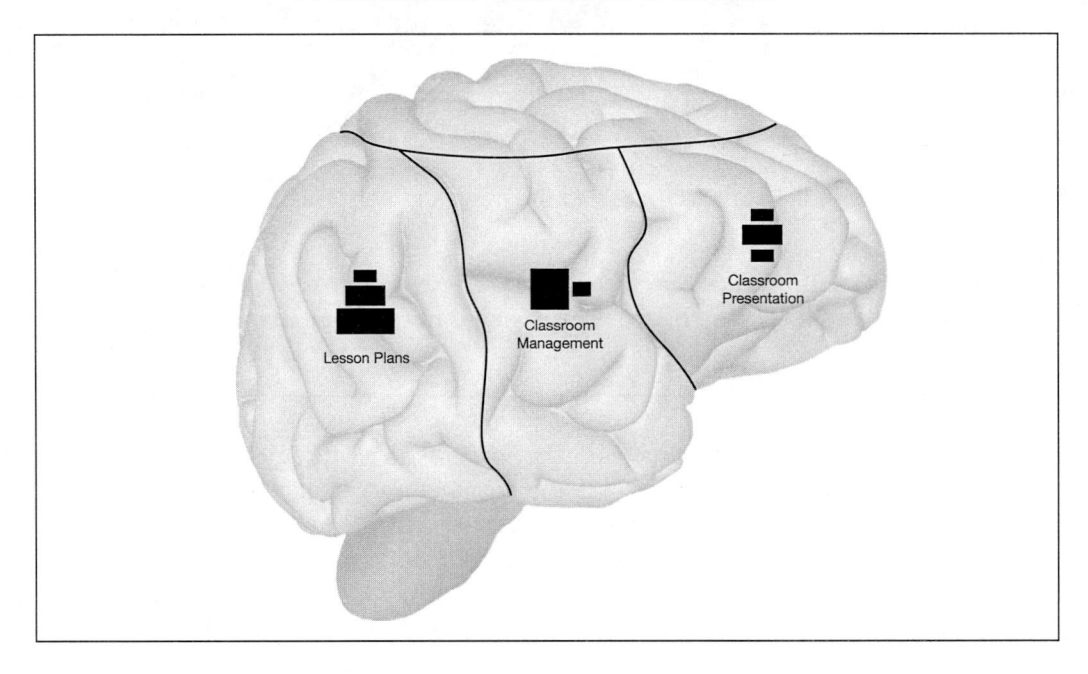

Lesson Plans · Classroom Management · Classroom Presentation

The second graphic reveals the Mentor Teacher's Brain, where all of the teacher functions float seamlessly about the brain. No divisions exist among all the functions.

A Mentor Teacher's Brain

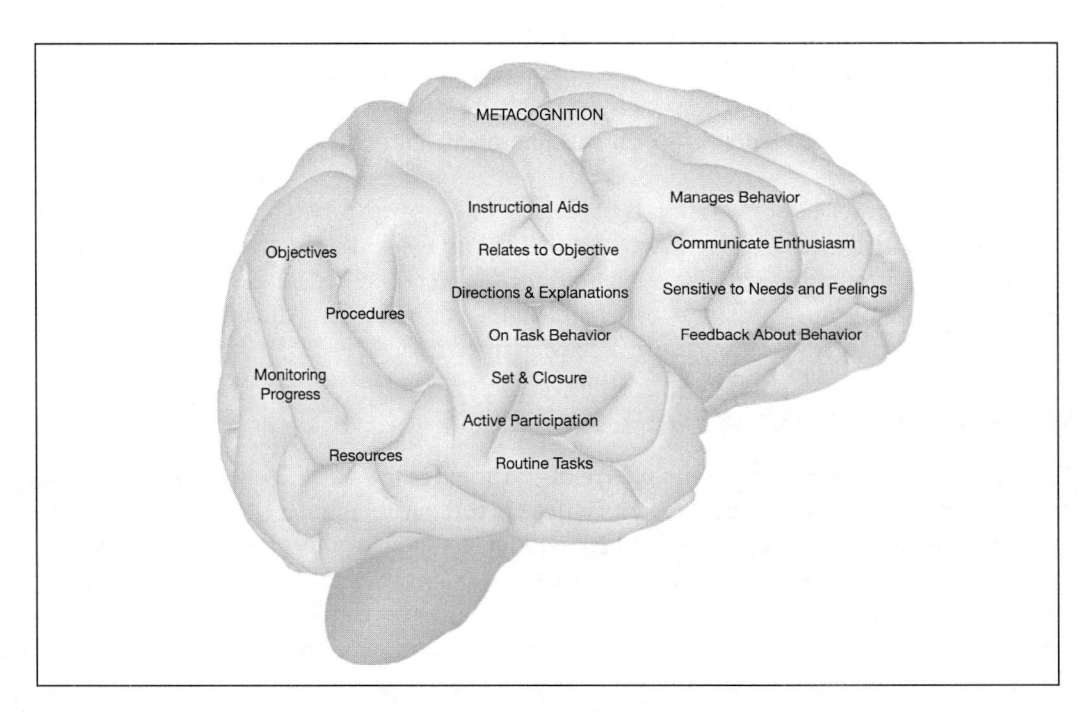

METACOGNITION

Objectives · Instructional Aids · Manages Behavior
Relates to Objective · Communicate Enthusiasm
Procedures · Directions & Explanations · Sensitive to Needs and Feelings
On Task Behavior · Feedback About Behavior
Monitoring Progress · Set & Closure
Active Participation
Resources · Routine Tasks

Both of these graphics are from *Coaching the Early Childhood Teacher* by Enz et al. Copyright © 2008 by Kendall Hunt Publishing Company. Reproduced by permission.

So how does a preservice teacher *learn* how to teach? Quite simply, this novice teacher learns a context (theories, theorists, milieu) in which the act of teaching is to take place, then, through practice and gaining of additional knowledge (scaffolding) begins the process of becoming a teacher.

The following theories add another layer of knowledge to this process. Bandura is especially interesting because he believes that all learning takes place in a social environment.

New Learning Theories and Theorists

Albert Bandura

Social Cognitive Theory

Bandura is best known for his beliefs that knowledge and learning are couched in a social context. The term *modeling* is a critical part of Bandura's theory, and it is a critical part of the lesson planning format outlined in Chapter 3. *Direct modeling* occurs when the teacher demonstrates or shows students how he would do or think through a certain problem.

Example: Maria sees Mrs. Franke write a short story.
Example: Jonathan sees Mr. Perkins, the Chemistry teacher, conduct an experiment.

Ideally, both teachers tell the students what they are doing as they do it. This process is also known as *metacognition*.

The major idea is to help students validate their own thinking as they attempt to solve problems. It is easy to see how modeling is important in the Social Cognitive Theory.

Popular news identifies other types of modeling that occur in society. For example, a young girl attempting to alter her body image by becoming bulimic or anorexic believes that the movie star *symbolizes* the correct way to look.

Another, more complex type of *synthesized* modeling occurs when a child sees a lawyer on Wall Street get wealthy and assumes the ends justify the means.

The bottom line is that learners observe the model, see the results, and emulate the model. All of this type of learning occurs in a specific context. Educational modeling occurs in the first example most of the time when a teacher demonstrates a desired behavior or skill and the student emulates it.

Robert Sternberg

Triarchic Theory of Intelligence

Robert Sternberg's Triarchic Theory of Intelligence attempts to analyze an individual's analytical, creative, and practical abilities to solve problems as a measure of intelligence.

Analytical Intelligence: Most college entrance tests measure one's ability to analyze words and math problems. These tests purport to predict one's potential for success in college.

Creative Intelligence: One's ability to adjust to situations and to find new or novel solutions to problems involves his creative ability. Education today stresses creative problem-solving.

Practical Intelligence: An old saying best defines practical intelligence. It goes something like this: "She is book smart, but doesn't have enough intelligence to get in out of the rain!" Practical intelligence, then, is the ability to solve problems in a realistic manner (albeit creative).

More information can be gained about Sternberg's Triarchic Theory of Intelligence by accessing the following web site: *http://www.lincoln.ac.nz/educ/tip/58.htm*

You should understand by now that educators think about intelligence, the types of intelligence, how to structure learning so that all types of thinkers can learn, and how to make learning age appropriate and applicable to diverse populations. All of these issues are complex and quite diverse themselves. That is why educators must learn about human development, diversity, and planning and understand how learning occurs.

Expand Knowledge of Lesson Planning to Include Teaching/Learning Strategies

In Chapter 3, a generic lesson planning guide containing nine parts set the stage for what is to follow here. The discovery of Madeline Hunter and Robert Gagne's lesson planning guides helps organize the method for delivery of instruction.

Adding the Mager-Gronland discussion about writing teaching objectives helps teachers target specific learning tasks.

Competency 4 targets the issue of instruction itself.

QUESTION
How does one actually instruct a lesson?

Answer: After planning and setting specific teaching objectives, one must deliver the instructional input or the knowledge that students are to learn. Teachers do that through a series of pedagogical methods: lecture, hands-on, see-say-do exercises, reading, modeling, and study skills among many, many other labels.

One must use varied pedagogical techniques and understand terms such as scaffolding, hands-on, and problem solving as well as design effective questioning techniques.

First, how does one instruct? Essentially, most teaching includes five styles of instruction:

1. Deductive/inductive
2. Discussion
3. Cooperation
4. Discovery learning
   a. Constructivist Theory
5. Lecture or Direct Instruction

Broadly, *induction* is coming to a conclusion about unobserved things because of what has been observed. A teacher using induction to teach a lesson from *The Scarlet Letter,* a novel, for example, attempts to show that The Reverend Dimmesdale's liaison with Hester was not acceptable in the Puritan community and could lead to nothing but a dire outcome. Inductively, the lesson being taught is that variance from the Judeo-Christian ethic will lead to a disastrous outcome.

In contrast, *deductive* lessons are more commonly used in teaching. It results when a series of arguments are proposed sufficient to determine an acceptable outcome. In competitive debate, for example, the affirmative will uphold the proposal by giving documented evidence to support it while the negative will give documented evidence to support the proposal. Either side can win determined by the efficacy of the argument. Either one can come to a logical conclusion.

By presenting thirteen chapters of the PPR, I am using deductive logic to teach this course. By giving you thirteen chapters of information containing accepted knowledge related to education, I am attempting to draw a conclusion at the end that you have the necessary tools to become a good classroom teacher.

Discussion is a term used to describe many things in the classroom, but rarely is it really discussion. Short notes appear in lesson plans over and over labeled *class discussion,* but discussion means a lot more than having the teacher ask a question then answer it. When true discussion occurs, it is hallmarked by a diversity of viewpoints given in a civil, yet lively manner. Teachers who use discussion are very aware of age-appropriateness of topics and set them up accordingly. Students in such classes feel free to agree/disagree with the teacher and know instinctively that they are safe saying what they truly believe or think about a given topic. Sometimes discussions do erupt spontaneously, and those are incredibly valued times by any teacher.

Cooperative Learning will be discussed in a later chapter, but for now, suffice it to say that this technique requires a great deal of work on the part of the teacher. If a teacher arbitrarily tells a class to group themselves and discuss a topic, the results will almost always be disastrous. Setting up groups and planning for each group member to be responsible to the group does take a considerable amount of planning. For more information on group work, see *http://www.teach-nology.com/* and type "Kagan" in the search box. Kagan is also known for his work in active learning.

Discovery Learning is a method of teaching for active learning that allows students to reach their own conclusions. The act of discovery is likened to the "Aha" or "Eureka" moment students have when they *get it*. See much more information on this teaching method at: *http://www.learning-theories.com/discovery-learning-bruner.html*

Constructivist theory is related to discovery learning in that we "construct" understanding. As learning begins, we have a mental image of what that learning represents. As new understandings occur, we simply build upon the original models to create new models.

As might be imagined, constructivists believe that ample opportunity ought to be given to children to grow through problem solving and open play, which is much like unstructured learning. Such a learning environment is very different from the lock-step of teaching to objectives and planning lessons based on very structured learning. Memorization is not valued as it forces students to make cognitive connections for which there may be no basis. The constructivist teacher faces many challenges in designing lessons that allow for students to grow at their own level of readiness.

Schema Theory

This theory is very interesting and quite logical. It simply means that the human brain has *schematics* just like the ones an architect might draw for a new house. These schema continue to build from the new experiences we have and the new knowledge we gain. In essence, schemata are like the file cabinets of information we have in our brains.

We layer this new understanding with our old attitudes and beliefs. In a sense, it is this schema that affect future learning. Either we have the basis (schema) for learning (scaffolding) new information or we do not. Both constructivist theory and discovery learning are attempts to help learners begin at the point of their existing schema and move forward.

> Example: Test your schema for logic on this short story:
> Sandra went to the movies.
> She saw the movie the Razzies named the Worst Picture.
> She did not understand the movie.
> She was deaf.

From the first line of the short story, our file cabinet assumption is that Sandra can hear; otherwise, why would anyone go to a movie? What we learn in the last line is a fact that would have been helpful at the beginning of the short story, but we are left with questions for which we have no schemata. The normal schema is based on sighted-hearing individuals who regularly see movies. At the end of the story, we are left with more questions about Sandra. Our schema will have to change (e.g., Sandra can read lips or she took an interpreter with her) so we can find a comfort zone with our understanding of why a deaf person would go to a movie. Otherwise we are left hanging with more questions than answers.

In the classroom, students who do not have the schema will often respond with "I don't know!" and sometimes, teachers will let them off the hook. The appropriate response by a teacher is, "I know you think you don't know, but if you did know what would you say?" Most often, students will respond in some way, even if minimally. Teachers must consistently work with students to increase their schema.

Therefore, when we read, study topics or courses, access different kinds of texts and styles and forms of writing, and acquire understandings of abstract concepts, we build schema. The more we read, the better the schema.

The Lecture

The lecture is by far the favored type of teaching strategy by most public school and college professors. Yet, research shows that it is the least effective method of instruction. Harry Wong, noted author of *The First Days of School,* says that many teachers go into the classroom and begin to teach as they were taught by their own college professors. He gives this model prefaced by the caveat that "There is no research to support it." He says these teachers:

- Assign chapters to read
- Assign the questions at the back of the chapter or on the worksheet
- Deliver a lecture and have students take notes
- Show a video or do an activity
- Construct a test based on a number of points. (p. 28)

In his video, Wong strikes a humorous note by saying that the lecture method is the passing of information from the professor's notes to the student's notes, effectively bypassing the brains of them both!

Surely, all young teachers remember nodding off during a lecture and vow never to teach the way they have been taught. So how does one get the information out and across if not by speech? It is done by speech—creatively.

Many different approaches to the lecture occur in instructional patterns. For example, setting up a lesson with an incredibly interesting introduction (focus, set) often involves telling a story, timing (pacing), silence, noises, voices, or setting up a problem to solve or a demonstration. Good teachers utilize imagery to draw word pictures and emphasize major points about to unfold in lecture or reading.

Teachers set up a good lecture just the way they would prepare an important speech. They give the key points with extreme clarity whether they intend to compare two events or provoke a discussion later in the class. If they are teaching sequencing in the story, they might very well tell an introductory story and point out the transitions to demonstrate sequence.

Teachers must remember to start from the concept of context. If students do not have a context for what you are about to teach, they will not (cannot) learn it. Remember the discussion about discovery learning and constructivist theory. Therefore, definitions and explanations are critically important to the lecture/learning process.

Finally, all of this speaking is done with great enthusiasm and remembering that attention span is a critical part of age-appropriateness.

Direct instruction is similar to the lecture in that it is teacher-centered and is built upon the delivery of information. It is often factual and presents overviews and summaries of a large amount of material. It is verbal, and it is linear in that it follows an organizational pattern such as a timeline based on the chronology of events.

The biggest problem with direct instruction is similar to that of the lecture. Students often label it b-o-r-r-r-i-n-g! It creates passive listeners because it is very easy to stay uninvolved. This type of delivery is very overused because its strength is that it is easy to prepare and deliver.

Wong, Harry K. (2005). The First Days of School. CA: Harry K. Wong Publications, Inc.

Teaching Strategies

Teaching strategies will be covered in Chapter 8, but keep in mind at this point that good teaching strategies help children learn. Some examples of good teaching strategies include SQ3R (or 4 R), Context Clues (reading strategies), Mapping/Webbing, Vocabulary Development, and Graphic Organizers. Any of these strategies can be researched on the World Wide Web to find out how to utilize them effectively.

Improve Personal Thinking Skills

Henry Ford had it right when he said, "Think you can, think you can't—either way you're right!" All sorts of motivational stories abound about the power of positive thinking. However, is there a process for capturing that power?

> **QUESTION**
> What is the hardest thing to do?
>
> **ANSWER:** I recall hearing this story some time ago about a man who decided as a youngster that he would accomplish difficult things in his life. He became an engineer and worked on road and bridge projects in the Andes Mountains. He hung bridges thousands of feet above wide valleys, and he dug tunnels under wide, rushing rivers. He met one life challenge after another climbing Mount Everest and sailing alone upon the open sea. Then, when he was an old man, a reporter asked him this question, "What is the hardest thing to do?" Without pausing, the old man replied, "the hardest thing to do in the world is to think a thought through to its end."

Today, educators hear a lot about teaching critical-thinking skills. Some people question whether thinking can be taught at all, yet many of us have experienced the teacher who, upon being asked a question said, "Just think about it. You'll get it!" I often thought, "I am thinking, and it's not working!"

I even recall my mother asking me from time to time, "Why did you do that?" I never had the right answer, of course, because I usually didn't know why I did that certain thing. I suppose I wasn't thinking the thought through to its end. So how do you teach young ones to think before they act? or speak? And just what is it they are supposed to be thinking anyway?

Thinking is difficult, but being able to sort through ideas and ramifications of actions can mean the difference between an ordinary life and a truly exciting, eventful life. The world treasures great thinkers, so it is no wonder that schools work consistently on developing critical-thinking skills in students.

To encourage students to higher-thinking levels, teachers learn how to structure lessons based on Benjamin Bloom's Cognitive Taxonomy (recall the KCAASE acronym). According to Bloom, the lowest levels of thinking are knowledge, comprehension, and application. However, one must have a lot of knowledge to keep building new knowledge!

The higher-order thinking skills are analysis, synthesis, and evaluation. When we gain enough knowledge about any given subject, talent, or skill, we can begin to create new knowledge.

Consider the following fable:

FABLE OF THE TWO FROGS

Once upon a time, two frogs fell into a bucket of cream. The first frog, seeing that there was no way to get any footing in the white liquid, accepted his fate and drowned.

The second frog didn't like that approach. He started thrashing around in the cream and doing whatever he could to stay afloat. After a while, all of his churning turned the cream into butter, and he was able to hop out.

Which frog are you more like? Do you have a tendency to "give up" easily at the first sign of defeat, or do you generally "hang in there" and turn your setbacks into a success?

Consider thinking in this way: we can think about things we already know, so we try to use the information we already have. We are using knowledge we have retained from prior learning. This kind of thinking helps us clarify our ideas.

✦ Retention/Use of Information (clarifying ideas)

Then, consider thinking in another way. We have the ability to think about things in terms of reasonableness, ethics and morality, social acceptability, and preferred action. This kind of thinking helps us make decisions.

✦ Critical thinking (assessing reasonableness of ideas)

Finally, think about creative thinking where we are literally *thinking out of the box*. In this kind of thinking, no wrong answers exist—only answers that must be evaluated for eventual usage. The best thing about creative thinking is that it is based on focus and safety—no judgment rendered while in process! Teachers who use this method often utilize creative problem-solving models similar to the scientific model:

✦ Determine the problem
✦ Obtain facts/parameters
✦ Match ideas with facts
✦ Evaluate the outcome
✦ Determine the solution
  ◇ Creative thinking (generating ideas)

Thinking about teaching thinking is interesting and challenging. The teacher who decides to incorporate deliberate thinking into the lesson must prepare in advance for all contingencies to assure that all students are involved at some level.

INDEPENDENT PRACTICE AND MODELING (HOMEWORK)

✦ **Scholar's Vocabulary:** Using the State-produced list of proficiencies preservice teachers should have related to Competency 4 (found in the Appendices), highlight terms you wish to place in your interactive glossary. You should have a minimum of five terms from C4.
✦ **Reflective Writing:** Using the eleven-sentence model, write a reflection over this competency. It should be uploaded into your ePortfolio.

- **Anticipatory Sets:** Rewrite the introduction to the lesson plan that you wrote in C3 demonstrating three different anticipatory sets to the same lesson. Be sure to end each anticipatory set with the same teaching objective you had in the original lesson plan (same lesson, different approach). Then, in outline form only, apply a different teaching strategy to the same lesson. You need not rewrite the entire lesson plan—just the three anticipatory sets and the outline with teaching strategies explained. Be sure to label those introductions.
- **Teaching Styles Inventory:** Take the inventory at this web site: *www.longleaf.net/teachingstyle.html* and make a copy of your scores. Keep in mind that this survey presumes you are already a teacher, so here is my suggestion: think about a teacher you have had in the past or one you have currently, and answer as you think that teacher would. Make a copy of the inventory. Then, go to: *www.members.shaw.ca/mdde615/tchstyles.htm to read about* the types of styles. Be prepared to discuss these styles in class.
- **Learning Theorists:** Research one of these theorists and write one paragraph on each of them that explains his learning theory.

  Bandura
  Gardner
  Kohlberg

Expand your knowledge of lesson planning to include **teaching strategies** for presentation of information. Create a slide for your ePortfolio that addresses your personal philosophy for active teaching strategies. In a document, create a brief chart featuring each of these types of lessons and give three teaching/learning strategies that might be used with each one.

a. Deductive/inductive
b. Discussion
c. Cooperation
d. Discovery learning
e. Lecture

CLOSURE/FOLLOW-UP

If your goal is to create interesting and fun lessons every day, I commend you. If you have unlimited resources and the freedom to teach inside and outside of the classroom, you may just pull it off; however, given the physical and financial constraints of modern education, your best bets are to:

- master what the theorists have to say about teaching and learning,
- commit to developing a wide and varied arsenal of teaching strategies, and
- take every opportunity to enhance your own teaching style by attending professional development opportunities.

ASSESSMENT

Ask yourself whether you have mastered these objectives.

- **Objective 1:** Can you identify several learning theories and theorists?
- **Objective 2:** Can you recall major theorists presented in previous chapters and scaffold new theorists to make connections between the theory, the theorist, and his contribution to how learning occurs?
- **Objective 3:** What are three teaching strategies for presentation of information? Describe a lesson you have seen with each of the three strategies.

88 Competency 4 Learning Processes

- ✦ **Objective 4:** Give five creative ways to introduce a lecture. What is important about a lecture's organizational pattern?
- ✦ **Objective 5:** How do you personally solve problems? Identify your personal thinking pattern and jot the process down in a list.
- ✦ **Objective 6:** Give an honest assessment of your own time-management skills. Keep a record of your daily activities for one week. Highlight like kinds of activities and determine where you are spending the majority of your time.

PRACTICE QUESTIONS

Now assess your learning by answering these questions. Answers are given in the Appendices.

1. "The student will be able to justify his or her opinion of the epic *Ramayana*" is an example of which level of Bloom's Taxonomy of Cognitive Domain?
    a. Knowledge
    b. Synthesis
    c. Evaluation
    d. Application

2. The application level of Bloom's Taxonomy:
    a. translates communication.
    b. applies principles.
    c. knows terms.
    d. produces new arrangements.

3. The teaching steps in Hunter's method of Mastery Learning includes all of the following *except:*
    a. input.
    b. modeling.
    c. output.
    d. checking for understanding.

4. Teachers use modeling to:
    a. organize student learning.
    b. demonstrate examples of what is to be expected.
    c. create an organizing framework for ideas.
    d. make learning a rote exercise.

5. Multiple Intelligence (MI) Theory is a tool used for classifying possible learning styles of _____.
    a. all students.
    b. gifted and talented students.
    c. average students.
    d. students in need of special education.

6. Which statement does **not** describe MI Theory?
    a. States that all people have varying levels of aptitude in certain areas and some in several areas;
    b. Tells how to educate students whose talents are geared toward one area of understanding;
    c. Describes eight areas of intelligence that occur in isolation;
    d. Was developed as a method for classifying intelligent students.

7. Multiple Intelligence Theory works best _____
   a. alone.
   b. combined with other teaching theories.
   c. when trying to find gifted and talented students.
   d. when used to predict which students will do well in your class.

8. Constructivist theory is based upon which of the following?
   a. Personal discovery
   b. Personal motivation
   c. Problem-solving
   d. All of the above.

9. An individual with native intelligence is most likely which of the following?
   a. Gifted and talented
   b. Motivated
   c. Unreserved
   d. Any student

10. If you believe that nurture is more important that nature in learning theory, you probably believe in:
    a. Maslow's Theory of Human Nature.
    b. Bandura's Theory of Social Interaction.
    c. Erikson's Stages of Cognitive Development.
    d. Mager's System of Objectives.

CAREER PLANNING

Students who enjoy creative thinking, especially when it comes to planning unique lesson plans, will probably enjoy a master's degree in curriculum and instruction. This student might also become a master reading teacher or a special education teacher.

MATERIALS NEEDED

Internet

SUGGESTIONS FOR ADDITIONAL ASSIGNMENTS

1. Research the following four theories. Create a table with four headings: theory, theorist, definition, and main points for each of the following theories:
   a. Behavioral Learning Theory
   b. Social Learning Theory
   c. Informational Processing Theory (IPT)
   d. Cognitive Learning Theory

Competency 4 Learning Processes

2. Do you believe that most tests you take are memorization of knowledge only? Do you remember much of the material later? Why do you think you forget it so quickly? (Cone of Learning)

3. Do you know students who do not know "how to behave" in the classroom (or outside either)? Why do you think they don't learn acceptable social behavior? (Bandura)

4. Metacognition is "thinking about thinking." When teachers use "talk alouds," metacognition is the teaching method used. For example, if I want my students to write a paragraph, it might be helpful if I model the process by using the overhead (or Elmo) and write a paragraph "on the spot" while you watch. As I write, I think "out loud" letting you hear the thought processes I am going through to write the paragraph.
    a. Explain how to work a math problem using the metacognitive technique.
    b. Explain how to write a short essay comparing to ideas using the metacognitive technique.

5. Further your knowledge of Piaget by researching these terms connected to his stages of cognitive development: schema, adaptation, assimilation, disequilibrium, accommodation, equilibration (note the spelling of this word). Give one personal example of your learning (any topic) and develop your thinking process as you went through the stages to develop new learning.

6. Find an explanation of Information Processing Theory on the web. Draw an analogy between IPT and the basic speech model of communication.
    a. Research information processing theory. Tell how you think the teacher knows IF the receiver (the student) is actually receiving the information he/she wants him to get.

7. What is *self-talk* or *private speech,* and how should teachers utilize it in the classroom? How does the process of *self-talk* work?

8. Find one newspaper article (maybe a letter to the editor, testimonial, or cartoon) on the subject of youth and morality. Write your personal philosophy about how today's youth are/are not the moral equivalent of a generation ago based on Kohlberg's Theory of Moral Development.

9. Using the information in the Instructional Input, give two additional examples of instructional scaffolding.

10. The following two exercises, Aladdin's Lamp and the Trying Exercise, are intended to help the student gain insight into motivational factors that influence personal learning.

ALADDIN'S LAMP

First, beside each of the categories that follow (easy, difficult, extremely difficult), write three things you would like to learn.

CATEGORIES:
    EASY
    DIFFICULT
    EXTREMELY DIFFICULT

Example:

CATEGORIES	Things to Learn	% Chance
Easy	How to bake muffins	100%
Difficult	To speak Spanish	40%
Very Difficult	Quantum Physics	10%

Next, using the example provided, list three things that you would like to learn and the percentage chance you would give yourself for doing them.

Discussion: Explain why you wrote the three things you did and why you gave yourself the percentage chance you did.

"Trying" Exercise

1. Write down four things you "tried" to do in the last year.
2. Write down whether you accomplished any of them.
3. Try to identify the motivational factors that led to the accomplishment/collapse in reaching the goal.
4. Were the goals extrinsic or intrinsic?

Motivation

"TRIED"	+ or -	FACTORS	EX or IN
1.			
2.			
3.			
4.			

Summarize

1.   What I know about extrinsic motivation:

2.   What I know about intrinsic motivation:

92 Competency 4 Learning Processes

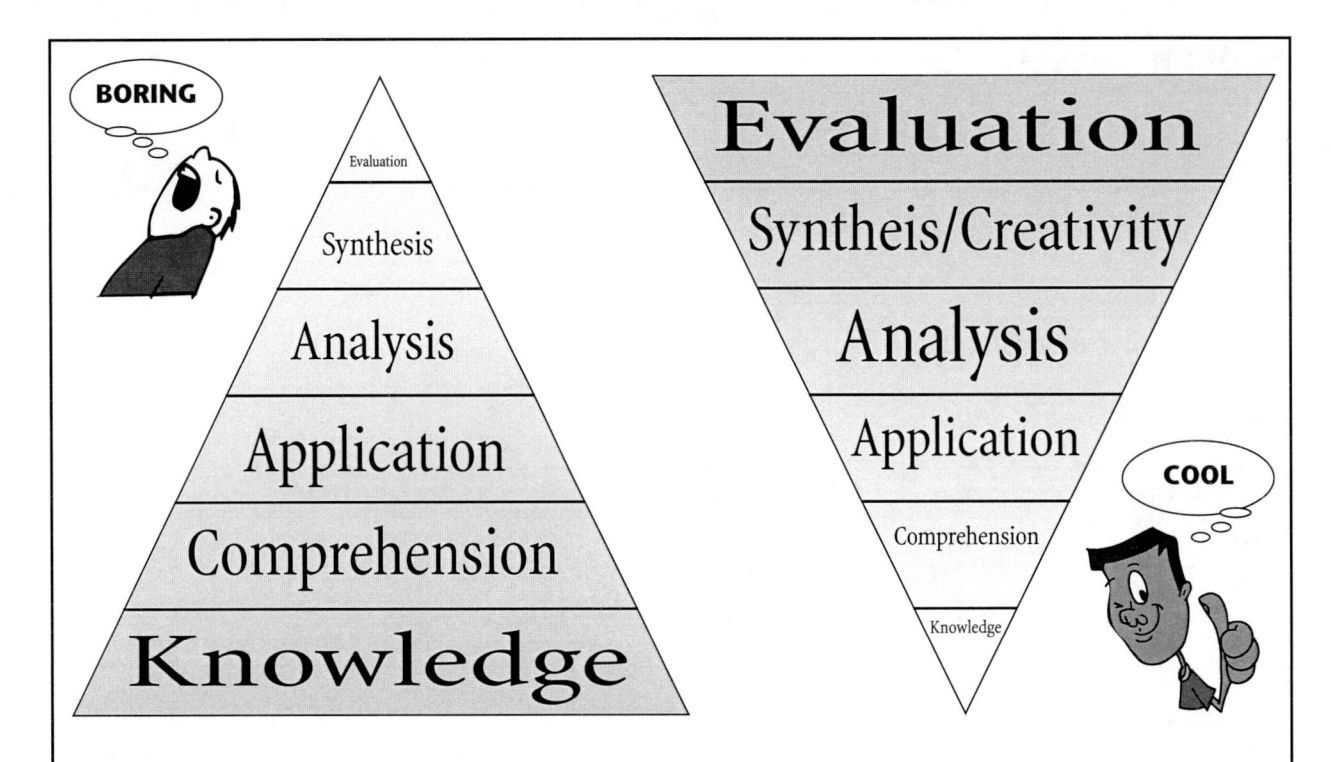

Pyramid (right-side up):
- Evaluation
- Synthesis
- Analysis
- Application
- Comprehension
- Knowledge

BORING

Inverted pyramid:
- Evaluation
- Syntheis/Creativity
- Analysis
- Application
- Comprehension
- Knowledge

COOL

Most educational programs emphasize memorization of facts, devoting most of the remaining instruction to seeing that students understand and can apply what they learn. However, research shows that students retain very little of what is learned at lower levels of thinking.

InspirEd activities teach the same content, but then require students to use what they learn to analyze, draw conclusions, problem-solve, and evaluate principles, policies, and actions. Research STRONGLY supports higher-order thinking as a means of DRAMATICALLY increasing students' retention.

InspirED can be contacted at 434-327-7919 or 434-806-9397.

Standard 2

Creating a Positive, Productive Classroom Environment

Competency 5: Classroom Environment

Competency 6: Classroom Management

Competency 5

Classroom Environment

LESSON PLAN FOR COMPETENCY 5

STATE STANDARDS: STANDARD 2, COMPETENCY 5

Competency 005: The teacher knows how to establish a classroom climate that fosters learning, equity, and excellence and uses this knowledge to create a **physical and emotional environment** that is safe and productive.

Competency 5 Classroom Environment

STATE TEACHER PROFICIENCIES

Competency 005

The teacher knows how to establish a classroom climate that fosters learning, equity, and excellence and uses this knowledge to create a physical and emotional environment that is safe and productive.

The beginning teacher:

- Uses knowledge of the unique **characteristics** and needs of students at different **developmental levels** to establish a positive, productive classroom environment (e.g., encourages cooperation and sharing among younger students; provides middle-level students with opportunities to collaborate with peers; encourages older students' respect for the community and the people in it).
- Establishes a **classroom climate** that emphasizes collaboration and supportive interactions, respect for **diversity and individual differences,** and active engagement in learning by all students.
- Analyzes ways in which teacher-student interactions and interactions among students impact **classroom climate** and student learning and development.
- Presents instruction in ways that communicate the teacher's **enthusiasm** for learning.
- Uses a variety of means to convey **high expectations** for all students.
- Knows characteristics of **physical spaces** that are safe and productive for learning, recognizes the benefits and limitations of various arrangements of furniture in the classroom, and applies strategies for organizing the **physical environment** to ensure physical accessibility and **facilitate learning** in various instructional contexts.
- Creates a **safe, nurturing, and inclusive classroom environment** that addresses students' emotional needs and respects students' rights and dignity.

TEACHING OBJECTIVES

At the end of the lesson, the student should be able to:

- Differentiate between physical, social, and emotional environments of the classroom.
- Demonstrate knowledge of how to establish routines and procedures.
- Describe basic routines and rules that enhance a classroom's environment.
- Establish democratic rules that enhance management strategies (see Competency 6).
    - ◇ Enhance student efficacy
    - ◇ Enhance student ownership/responsibility
    - ◇ Create a list of rules
- Identify elements that compose the social/emotional climate of the classroom.
- Recognize that the organization of the classroom is directly related to learning.

C5 KEY WORDS: CLASSROOM ENVIRONMENT

Terms associated with classroom environment

Physical Environment	Routines	Procedures
Emotional Environment	Social Environment	Atmosphere
Rules	Management Strategies	Student Efficacy
Classroom Climate	Engagement	On Task
Management Style	Invitational	Inviting
Seating		

> **DEVELOPING AS A TEACHER**
>
> Recall a classroom that you had a class in some time in the past and that you loved being in. Describe the classroom climate of that classroom. Can you describe in concrete terms what made it an enjoyable class?
>
> Describe the classroom climate that you wish to create in your own classroom.
>
> Theorize on how you are going to accomplish this task.
>
> What are some external factors that affect student performance? Elaborate.
>
> What are some emotional factors that affect student performance?

INTRODUCTION/FOCUS

When I was a high school teacher preparing to become a principal, many principals told me that they could walk down the hall past several teachers' rooms and tell who the good teachers were and who the bad teachers were. These same administrators also said that they could tell who had discipline under control and who did not. I wondered how that could be—I always thought they would need to spend a lot of time in a classroom to judge effectiveness in management and academics. When I became an administrator, I understood what they were saying. It is easy to see student engagement. It is easy to see a calm classroom environment. The students know, too.

TRANSITION: In short, a principal can tell a lot about who is teaching and teaching well every day by roaming the halls. He can tell which rooms are calm and well-organized, and he can tell which students are actually involved in the learning and on task. Competency 5 focuses on the classroom environment.

INSTRUCTIONAL INPUT AND GUIDED PRACTICE

What we need to know about classroom environment

The Instructional Input in this lesson plan will contain *guided practice* in the form of questions placed throughout the chapter. References to web sites will also serve as guided practice as you research topics to gain further knowledge and information and application.

> **QUESTIONS**
> Describe the feeling you get when you enter any given classroom. Do you feel warmly welcome, or do you feel like you are slightly unwelcome? This feeling can be related to the classroom climate or environment. All classroom teachers have a philosophy (stated or unstated) regarding the way they establish the physical and emotional environment in their classrooms. This belief system by the teacher is closely related to the teacher's management style. Recalling any given classroom, what can you tell about the teacher's philosophy of management? Can you tell if the teacher's management style is effective?
> Why or why not? Describe the feeling you get when you enter a classroom.

Physical, Social, and Emotional Classroom Environment

A classroom has three environments: one is **physical,** one is **social,** and the other is **emotional.** The physical environment is literally the way the room is arranged. All rooms will not be arranged the same because of the content taught in those rooms. The social environment of a classroom is related to the way the room is arranged for work. The chairs may be replaced by tables or chair/desks may be grouped for cooperative learning. The emotional environment of the classroom is the tone that the teacher establishes in the classroom. This type of environment is more difficult to describe because, again, teachers must be true to their own personalities—and personalities are very diverse.

> **QUESTION**
> It is well known that some teachers can throw erasers and "get away with it!" It is also well known that certain other teachers would be keelhauled if they ever tried to throw erasers. Why is that?

Obviously some teachers "get away with it" because students like them and accept the tossing of an eraser as an acceptable antic. Then, other teachers not so well liked, toss the eraser and students think of the throwing of any object as aggressive and unacceptable. By the way, I do not recommend throwing erasers—regardless of your personality!

> **PHILOSOPHY DEVELOPMENT**
> Reflect upon a personal philosophy of classroom environment for your ePortfolio.

Creating the perfect classroom and having it operate efficiently are topics on every preservice teacher's mind. Management of the environment relates directly to the mechanics of how you will operate your classroom so that you can teach and children can learn. Everything from the way you design your classroom to the way you respond to children is involved in classroom management. However, beyond the actual management of the physical and social environment of the room, is something a little more difficult to define: the emotional environment. Competency 5 focuses on the classroom's *atmosphere* or *environment.*

That feeling you get when you enter a school or any classroom within that school is the very first indicator that a school or a classroom is a happy place to learn. I like to call this a teacher's *invitation to the learning party,* and often, the teacher herself can be described as *invitational* in manner and tone.

> **QUESTION**
> How does a preservice teacher with no experience begin to comprehend the enormous importance of creating an invitational classroom?
>
> *Answer:* While this question can be answered many ways, you will discover that planning is the key issue in class environment just like it is in planning for a lesson. Think of it like this: you are preparing for a grand dinner party, so you want everything from the front door to the beautifully candlelit table to be perfect. You want your guests to feel welcome in your home. So it is with the classroom. Plan for the environment you want to produce in this room.

The Physical Environment

The elements of the physical environment are more complex than one might imagine. In Chapter 4, we discussed how learning occurs. Remember, learning takes place through the five senses: hearing, sight, smell, touch, and taste. Therefore, it is not such a stretch to say that the second students approach the classroom and **see** the teacher, they get a feeling about their future learning. The first words the teacher **says** and what her room **looks** like will prompt curiosity or boredom. In short, the classroom environment creates a sense of belonging. Teaching begins at the door of the classroom.

Most management experts in the field will tell you that you must establish the environment early. You do this by (1) planning, (2) organizing, and (3) reflecting on the product. Dream a little when you *design* your first classroom. Look around the room at the available resources and decide how to organize them. Look at the bulletin boards, the paint on the walls, the floors, and the space.

Once the initial organization is thought out and executed, you must plan for the actual management of your space. How will you take care of absence reports? Where will you place your desk? Are there locked files for your personal belongings? Where will you put your coat on winter days? How will you arrange student desks?

How to seat students is usually the first thing that pops into preservice teachers' minds. Try this method: assign seats at first (seating chart), but tell students that the assignment is temporary and that you will consider changing the arrangement when you have learned their names. Do not tell them that you need the time to establish control of the class to teach procedures and routines. In time, you will see whether you have difficult students or particularly talkative students in which case, you will need to maintain control of the seating through a clever rearrangement of seats. Seating arrangements also allow you to separate troublemakers without drawing undue attention to them. Following are a few suggestions for designing a seating arrangement:

1. Desks clustered facilitate group chatting, interaction.

2. Desks arranged in a circular or semi-circle design facilitate whole class discussion.

3. Traditional rows are functional for
   a. learning names
   b. observing behavior
   c. minimizing distractions

Whether you design seating arrangements in clusters, circles, or traditional rows, think ahead to test days. You will need to deter roaming eyes, so think about tri-folds (use refrigerator boxes if you do not have a budget) to separate students during independent work.

4. Atypical seating is designed for
   a. performances
   b. labs
   c. special activities

What about the teacher's desk? Some say remove it altogether and use a table or a student desk, add a high stool, and never, but never, place a teacher's desk near a door (easy for students to remove papers and leave unobserved) or where it will block the view of the chalkboard. Establish early on that your desk is private and off-limits to students. It is very wise to have at least one locked drawer for locking hard copies of the gradebook and your personal belongings such as purses or medications. You must communicate these expectations to students early in the term.

Where do you want papers turned in? If you expect homework to be turned in as students come through the door, you may want to put baskets labeled to identify the class period near the door.

What about the bulletin boards? The bulletin boards for elementary school teachers provide a stimulating environment as well as serving as a learning tool. Certainly beautiful bulletin boards take a lot of time to create. In secondary school, bulletin boards are often afterthoughts or left to a student aide. That said, bulletin boards can serve many purposes from holding work for absentees to creating a mood for the topic to be taught.

Finally, safety of children and the teacher are of concern. Books, stacks of magazines, wires, electrical cords, and any other equipment must be placed in such a manner that they do not interfere with normal walking pathways. Failure to think about this may result in injury.

The desk arrangement suggests to what degree the teacher will be structured. Consequently, the **social environment** of the classroom is established by the teacher's expectations for student involvement. If desks are clustered or grouped together, strict parameters must be set to help students monitor their own behavior. Just because desks are in close proximity does not mean students are free to talk at will and interrupt the class. The beginning teacher needs to study (Competency 4) her teaching style to determine just how much liberality she will allow in terms of behavior. Once the teacher knows how much freedom she can tolerate and still teach, she can arrange the room accordingly and design the routines and procedures at the same time.

The **emotional environment** of a classroom will scaffold on prior learning about Abraham Maslow. Maslow's Hierarchy of Needs has already been presented in an earlier competency, so think about those basic human needs of food, sleep, and shelter. After those needs are met (some schools do deliver breakfast to classrooms each morning), think about the safety needs of children in your classroom, and finally, think about acceptance. All human beings need acceptance and a sense of belonging. The emotional environment in your classroom will help establish all of those needs.

The following quote by a famous clinical psychologist, Dr. Haim Ginott, is often handed out in education courses. Born in 1922, Dr. Ginott worked with children after earning a doctorate at Columbia University in New York City. His work includes compassion and boundary setting in children as evidenced by this quote:

> I've come to the frightening conclusion that I am the decisive element in the classroom. It's my personal approach that makes a child's life miserable or joyous. I can be a tool of torture or an instrument of inspiration. I can humiliate or humor, hurt or heal. In all situations, it is my response that decides whether a crisis will be escalated or deescalated and a child humanized or dehumanized.

His ideas incorporate basic humanity of one person to another. He rationalized that if adults enjoyed fair and good treatment, children would too. His definition of good and fair treatment involved praise, attacking problems rather than people, private correction, understanding rather than dictatorial or *else* messages, and empathy.

Numerous web sites exist that provide more information about Dr. Ginott.

QUESTION
Do you believe that Ginott's quote is true and accurate?
Discuss the weaknesses and the strengths of the concepts provided in the quote.

Beyond the physical room, the emotional side of learning begins with the teacher's voice. The non-verbal elements of the teacher's voice include her personality, her gestures, paralanguage, body movement, dress, and even silence.

For the emotional environment, think of posters, banners, and signs that invite students into the classroom. Beyond the physical appearance of those things, the next most important thing is the teacher. On the first day, choose your words/speech very carefully because your goal is to create a warm, but businesslike atmosphere. In so doing, you transmit to students that you know what you are doing, that you have confidence, and that you expect appropriate behavior and effort.

> **QUESTIONS**
> How will you introduce yourself? See the Suggested Activities for Competency 5
> for an assignment on self-introduction.
> How much personal information should you reveal about yourself
> when you introduce yourself to your students?

Next, to get to know your students, plan some sort of ice breaker. See Suggested Activities for Competency 5 for an assignment on ice breakers. Begin from the first day to set your expectations for classroom rules, procedures, and routines.

Establishing Rules, Procedures, and Routines

Clarify expectations the first day—it is essential. Establish your high expectations for the class, introduce rules, and introduce one or more routines depending upon time. Specify routines for taking attendance, beginning work each day, turning in assignments, requesting help, and bathroom passes. Competency 6 goes into much more detail on establishing rules, procedures, and routines.

The Environment and Motivation Connection

Environment and motivation are very connected. Motivation is largely internal, but some students do not seem to have internal motivation. So how can a teacher help a student monitor her self-efficacy? The physical, social, and emotional environment of the classroom is one way to begin thinking about motivating your students.

The nonverbal impact of the environment includes the spatial arrangement of the room, bulletin boards, the teacher, motivation, proxemics, discipline management, and the teacher. The teacher displays her personality through her room and her body. If she has an open body she displays a willingness to know students and take them as they are. If she has a closed body, she turns students away.

A good way to draw the relationship is through this analogy:

Classroom is to Environment
As
Teaching is to Learning

Earlier in the chapter, you were asked to remember a classroom where you felt particularly welcome. Now as you remember that same classroom, visualize yourself back in that classroom. Were you more or less motivated to start and complete assignments? Why? Can you relate your motivation to some facet of the environment? Describe some ways a teacher might motivate her students through environment.

Recall that Maslow's Hierarchy of Needs looks like this:

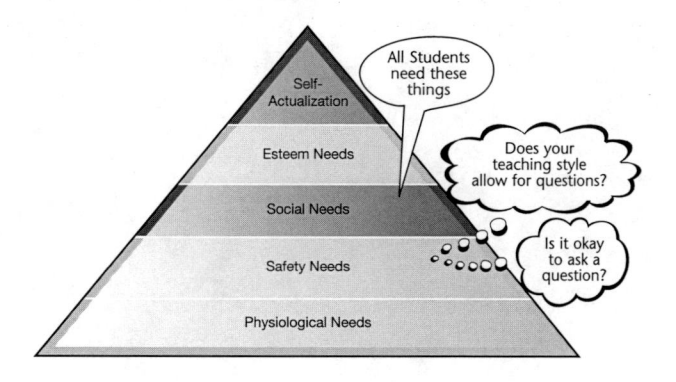

Note the questions to the right of the model. Teachers must never take for granted that their students do not have the needs expressed in this chart. Past the physiological needs, all the other levels can be impacted by the social and emotional environment of your classroom.

> Let's suppose that you have done your very best to create an open and friendly classroom environment, but you get a feeling that students do not like you or are not responding to you in the way you would like. It is time for an environmental audit.
>
> Student Question: What if . . .
>
> A student tape-recorded your class one day, and when he played it back to you to prove a point, you discovered much to your horror that a stranger was speaking?
>
> If that scenario disturbs you (it has happened, you know), periodically think about how you want to be perceived as a teacher. Visualize yourself in front of your *perfect* classroom in front of your *ideal* students. Videotape your lessons, tape record your lessons, and really listen to the tape carefully. Ask a trusted friend to help you find and correct the flaws.

What Is a Successful Teacher?

Harry Wong's *The First Days of School* states that the three characteristics of a successful teacher are:

- positive expectations for student success;
- extremely good classroom management; and
- lessons designed for mastery (Wong, 2005).

In setting high expectations, the teacher establishes a positive classroom environment that is predictable from day to day. Earlier in this chapter, it was mentioned that teachers should begin the very first day by practicing what they want to say. Friendliness and clarity are important here. The teacher establishes an invitational vs. a disinvitational persona early in the school year.

Creating the Invitational Classroom

Including and beyond the first day, the teacher should consider creating a class agenda and put it in the same place each day. This agenda might appear on the class web site, on the board, or on the bulletin board. It can even be sent home with the students a week in advance. To get class started, the teacher might consider asking questions about the previous class or asking someone to write yesterday's topic(s) on the board and asking other students to comment briefly. This easing into class will give students a feeling of security rather than being on the *hot* seat every time they step across your threshold.

The previous competency on lesson planning includes a section on modeling. Consider modeling through metacognition, using literature and history examples that students are currently studying or have studied in other classes, invite outside speakers, and above all, demonstrate respect for everyone—even those who are tardy, late with work, and those who need discipline.

After accomplishing all of these tasks and students still don't perform to your expectations, "How do you get 'em to take off?" Consider the reasons behind the students' responses.

> **QUESTION**
> What if you ask questions, but no one answers?
>
> *Answer:* Everyone knows there are two answers to every question:
>
> The wrong **answer, and**
>
> **The right answer,** which is found only in the teacher's head.

While that joke is amusing, it also has some truth in it. If students are afraid of your quick reaction, snappy come-backs, or insults, they will not talk. If students are unmotivated, they will not talk.

Consider these reasons students may be unmotivated. Perhaps they have experienced:

- a lack of success from year to year
- a lack of perception of progress
- uninspired teaching
- boredom
- a lack of perceived relevance
- a lack of knowledge about goals
- a lack of feedback

If your response to the bullets is "Grow up, I'm not your mommy!" or "They don't pay me enough to entertain them!" or "It's my way or the highway!" think about this: Educators can support students in the classroom or they can support them financially in one of the 116 Texas State prisons. (That number does not include the federal prisons or the local county jails.)

You can see that the way you talk to students has a tremendous impact upon the classroom environment. The last five entries on this bulleted list relate directly to the teacher and the teacher's role in establishing a working environment in the classroom.

INDEPENDENT PRACTICE AND MODELING (HOMEWORK)

1. **Scholar's Vocabulary:** Using the State-produced list of proficiencies preservice teachers should have related to Competency 1, highlight terms you wish to place in your interactive glossary. You should have a minimum of five terms from C5. (See the model in the Appendices.)

2. **Reflective Writing:** Using the eleven-sentence model in the Appendices, write a reflection on Competency 5. It should be uploaded into your ePortfolio.

3. Go to the American Federation of Teachers web site: *http://www.aft.org/tools4teachers/classroom-mgmt/arranging.htm* and utilize the many resources there to design your perfect classroom.

    www.aft.org/teachers/downloads/arrangeclassroomworksheet.pdf

    Read "Classroom Tips: Before the Year Begins" to start thinking about your room arrangement and the connection to discipline.

    Another helpful web site: *http://classrooms4teachers.org*

    Click on "Classroom Architect" to create your own room. Create the diagram for your room.

4. Write a speech of self-introduction for your first day in your first class. What will you say and how will you say it?
    a. Tape record your speech and bring a tape to class to play for the students, or
    b. Videotape your speech and play that tape to the class.

5. Browse through several online catalogs and decide what you will wear your first day to school. Cut and paste a picture of your ideal dress for the first day (or the first week) of school. Describe the image you want to project to your students.

CLOSURE/FOLLOW-UP

The physical and emotional environment of your classroom is both scary and tantalizing. It is fun to design your ideal classroom and to work with supplies and create wonderful bulletin boards, but when it comes to what you will say, you must think using a different part of your brain. You must think about and rehearse and play the "What If" game. In time, you will learn to think on your feet and, in time, you will have been exposed to so many student responses that you will have "heard it all" and have a good concept about how to respond. In the meantime, I reemphasize that you should think about what you will say those first days and rehearse, rehearse, rehearse. Practice smiling and practice showing and demonstrating what you expect your students to do.

Your voice sets the tone for the entire year of your first year of teaching. It is important and deserves a lot of attention.

ASSESSMENT

Ask yourself whether you have mastered these objectives.

- **Objective 1:** Differentiate between physical, social, and emotional environments of the classroom.
  - What are some external factors that affect student performance? Elaborate.
  - What are some emotional factors that affect student performance?
- **Objective 2:** Demonstrate knowledge of how to establish routines and procedures.
- **Objective 3:** Describe basic routines and rules that enhance a classroom's environment.
  - Increase academic learning time
  - Increases efficiency
  - Increased safety
  - Estimate the cost of setting up a classroom
- **Objective 4:** Establish democratic rules that enhance management strategies (see Competency 8).
  - Enhance student efficacy
  - Enhance student ownership/responsibility
  - Create a list of rules

PRACTICE QUESTIONS

Now assess your learning by answering these questions. Answers are given in the Appendices.

1. A kindergarten student comes to school with a tummy ache. He tells you he didn't eat dinner the night before or breakfast that morning. On the basis of Maslow's work, what is the best solution to this problem?
   I. Send the student to the principal's office to determine what to do with the student.
   II. Call the student's parent; request a conference to discuss the problems the child is having at home.
   III. Send the student to the cafeteria so that he can eat breakfast before class.
   IV. Send the child to the nurse's office because he may have a virus.
   V. Tell the student that he should get busy and he will soon forget about being hungry.

   a. II and III   b. II and IV   c. III and IV   d. I, III, and V

2. Jessica, a second grader, has just moved to a new school and is very shy. She is already very nervous in her new surrounding and the other children aren't welcoming her. What is the best option that you can do to help this student meet the belonging need according to Maslow's theory?
   a. Integrate group projects or games with some interaction to ensure Jill will have a chance to meet people.
   b. Introduce Jill at the front of the class and assign her to a buddy.
   c. Choose a student in the class to help Jill become more acquainted and involved.
   d. Call Jill's parents and ask them what kind of problems she's been having and offer to help.

3. Which of the following statements would best represent Maslow's Hierarchy of Needs?
   a. People will react better if they know there is promise of reward to come.
   b. People are basically evil and violent by nature.
   c. People are basically like animals, although, as rational beings, we do not act that way.
   d. People are basically trustworthy, self-protecting, and self-governing. Humans tend toward growth and love.

4. Susie has developed strong language/writing skills. However, by nature she procrastinates and must be forced to meet deadlines. There is also a possibility that Susie's grades may suffer. The teacher constantly reminds Susie that she has late work. What is the teacher having difficulty doing for Susie?
    a. Supervising one student to the exclusion of many
    b. Motivating Susie to turn in her work on time
    c. Failing to include her mother in the problem
    d. English just isn't Susie's subject

5. There are ten honor students in chemistry class; seven males and three females. The males all carry high A averages while the females are pulling high Ds and low Cs. The females begin looking for any opportunity to skip class, so they often make excuses to miss class. They also complain to the principal because they are not comfortable confronting the teacher about this issue. This issue is being caused because:
    a. females were not able to make the grades to stay in the chemistry class.
    b. males are always expected to do better in math and science related subjects.
    c. the teacher may have inadvertently created a hostile, uncomfortable environment and classroom climate.
    d. of personal problems of the females.

6. Chris, an eighth-grade student, had become a discipline problem. He disrupts class with excessive talking and distracts other students. When the teacher asked him to settle down, he said, "I can't help it because I have ADD." What should the teacher do to help alleviate the problem?
    a. Request a meeting with the special education teacher.
    b. Give the student the option to move to a different part of the room, away from distractions in order to calm down.
    c. Tell the student he had better straighten up and behave.
    d. Tell the student that if he cannot control his behavior that he can explain his behavior to his parent when a meeting is called with his parents and the principal.

7. A straight A student made her first B of the year in Calculus. She made an 88 and is upset that this will ruin her GPA and that she must be stupid. What should the teacher tell her?
    a. Encourage her by saying, "Don't worry; just do better next time."
    b. Encourage her by saying, "Next time study a little bit harder."
    c. Encourage her by saying, "To be in this class means you are capable! This class is not easy. This is just one grade out of many."
    d. Tell her that she can do extra credit to help raise her grade.

8. As a teacher walked into his classroom he noticed two boys picking on another boy. This boy was visibly upset. How can the teacher reassure the student without embarrassing him?
    a. At the first opportunity, reverse role play bullying using one of the two boys committing the bullying as the boy being picked on. Discuss with the class how it feels and ask for suggestions about what should be done.
    b. Do nothing; kids will be kids and resolve their own issues without teacher interference.
    c. Quietly ask the boy who is being bullied to stay after class; tell him what you saw, and ask him how you can help resolve the issue.
    d. Have the two boys doing the bullying stay after class and tell them that it had better stop.

9. The day of the big football game has come, and the whole school is excited about the game and anxiously awaiting the last period of the day for the pep rally. Everyone enters the fifth-period class in a heightened state of excitement, talking and laughing. It seems impossible for the teacher to get everyone's attention and get class started. What is the best option for the teacher at this point?
   a. Start sending kids to the office.
   b. Realize that there are too many distractions to teach a new lesson; this is a "Plan B" day.
   c. Sharply address the class and ask them to concentrate and begin to teach the lesson anyway.
   d. Give a pop quiz to get everyone's attention.

10. Jacob has never caused anyone a single problem; however, Mrs. Geiger suspects Jacob of walking out of the classroom with an entire set of pop quizzes she laid on the side of her desk after she had given the quiz. Jacob was one of the students who protested when she said she was giving the pop quiz as punishment because no one had completed their homework. What is the best option for Mrs. Geiger to retrieve her papers?
    a. Forget it; she will not retrieve the papers now or later.
    b. She should consider moving her desk to another area of the classroom;
    c. She should find Jacob's schedule and personally go to that class and ask Jacob whether he took the papers;
    d. She should punish the entire class tomorrow by giving another pop quiz.

CAREER PLANNING

Teachers who understand classroom environment often enjoy a pleasant relationship with students and teachers alike. These folks love teaching and normally would not think about leaving the classroom. The ability to understand one's collaborative philosophy of teaching should encourage this teacher to become a master teacher.

MATERIALS NEEDED

Internet

SUGGESTIONS FOR ADDITIONAL ASSIGNMENTS

Competency 5 deals with establishing an inviting environment in the classroom. These activities are designed to help the preservice teacher think carefully about how she can create such a climate.

1. Draw a series of classroom designs (different levels) using an interactive web site (find other interactive sites).
   + Organize a room for efficiency
     ◇ Include desks, bookshelves, pencil sharpeners, cabinets, direct traffic flow, allow for student interaction; electrical wires
   + Organize a room for aesthetic appeal
     ◇ Furniture defines space, directs attention, traffic flow
     ◇ Sit at students' level; see what they see.

108 Competency 5 Classroom Environment

2. The following terms (some are also used in other chapters) are important to establish the positive emotional classroom environment. Identify that relationship for all of these terms and give an example:
    a. cooperation, collaboration, respect
    b. supportive interactions between teacher and student
    c. peer tutoring
    d. teacher voice
        i. teacher-superiors
        ii. teacher-students
        iii. teacher-parents
        iv. consistent
    e. enthusiasm for learners/learning
    f. motivation
    g. high expectations
    h. "Speech of Encouragement"
    i. students' rights?
    j. dignity
    k. Harry Wong "Will I be treated like a human being?"

3. Prepare a speech of self-introduction for the first day remembering that your voice and tonal quality are of utmost importance. What will you say? How do you want to be addressed? What speech characteristics (from public speaking) do you want to bring to this first speech? Consider body language, dress, and bulletin boards. Write this speech out in its entirety and deliver it to the class. Tell the class what age level they are and what class they are in before you begin. Ask the class to respond as they believe that age group would respond.

4. Prepare a list of ten ice breakers; identify the age-appropriateness of each of them. Remember the ones you used to hate? Don't include those.

5. Prepare a class debate over nature vs nurture. Consider what environmental factors (classroom) and self-perception factors (self-esteem) can affect a student's learning.

    TOPIC: Resolved that nature is more important than nurture in the learning process.

6. Describe the classroom climate that you wish to create in your own classroom.

    Theorize on how you are going to accomplish this task.

    ✦ Visualize and draw a schematic of a physical classroom.

    ✦ How is a teacher involved with Maslow's Hierarchy of Needs? How does the teacher make a difference within this hierarchy?

    ✦ Find one web site/group that considers nature vs nurture. Briefly consider the nature vs nurture argument. What is your belief about what/which is more important? Why do you believe this? Write an essay with no fewer than three substantive arguments in favor of your position.

7. Draw or create a poster of a bulletin board (prototype) that exemplifies the lesson plan you wrote for an earlier chapter.

8. Interview a principal and ask about budget for supplies for his school. Ask him how much money the average teacher spends out of pocket each year to create interesting bulletin boards.

9. Start going to garage sales with the intent of finding bargains for your first classroom.

10. Create a list of things you believe will help create an invitational classroom. Visit an educational bookstore or an office supply store and price those items. Create a wish list of items you can give to your family for graduation gifts.

11. Research online for teacher supplies. Create a list of web sites that you will utilize as a future teacher.

Competency 6

Classroom Management

LESSON PLAN FOR COMPETENCY 6

STATE STANDARDS: STANDARD 2, COMPETENCY 6

Competency 006: The teacher understands strategies for creating an organized and productive learning environment and for **managing student behavior.**

STATE TEACHER PROFICIENCIES

Competency 006

The teacher understands strategies for creating an organized and productive learning environment and for managing student behavior.

The beginning teacher:

- Analyzes the effects of classroom **routines and procedures** on student learning and knows how to establish and implement age-appropriate routines and procedures to promote an organized and productive learning environment.
- Demonstrates an understanding of how young **children function in groups** and designs group activities that reflect a realistic understanding of the extent of young children's ability to **collaborate** with others.
- Organizes and **manages group activities** that promote students' ability to work together **cooperatively** and productively, assume responsible roles, and develop collaborative skills and **individual accountability.**
- Recognizes the importance of creating a **schedule** for young children that balances restful and active movement activities and that provides large blocks of time for play, projects, and learning centers.
- Schedules activities and **manages time** in ways that maximize student learning, including using effective procedures to manage **transitions;** to manage materials, supplies, and technology; and to coordinate the performance of non-instructional duties (e.g., taking attendance) with instructional activities.
- Uses **technological tools** to perform administrative tasks such as taking attendance, maintaining grade books, and facilitating communication.
- Works with volunteers and **paraprofessionals** to enhance and enrich instruction and applies procedures for **monitoring the performance** of volunteers and paraprofessionals in the classroom.
- Applies **theories and techniques** related to managing and monitoring student behavior.
- Demonstrates awareness of appropriate **behavior standards** and expectations for students at various **developmental levels.**
- Applies effective procedures for managing student behavior and for promoting appropriate behavior and **ethical work habits** (e.g., **academic integrity**) in the classroom (e.g., communicating **high and realistic behavior expectations,** involving students in developing rules and procedures, establishing clear consequences for inappropriate behavior, enforcing behavior standards consistently, encouraging students to monitor their own behavior and to use **conflict resolution skills,** responding appropriately to various types of behavior).

TEACHING OBJECTIVES

At the end of the lesson, the student should be able to:

- Demonstrate an understanding of several discipline management theories.
- Create sample classroom rules, routines, and procedures.
- Elaborate the relationship between grouping techniques and classroom management.
- Use technology to create a timeline for daily classroom activity.
- Observe and document behavior at the elementary, middle, and secondary school levels.

C6 KEY WORDS: CLASSROOM MANAGEMENT

Terms associated with classroom management

Withitness
Ignoring
Proactive
Overlapping
Rule, Routines, Procedures

Authoritative
Laissez Fair
Reactive
Smoothness

DEVELOPING AS A TEACHER

Have you observed one child for whom a given teacher's management style was ineffective? How do you know it is not effective? What might be done differently? What are the rules of the classroom you have observed? How do you know what the rules are? Are they appropriate?

INTRODUCTION/FOCUS

QUESTION
What are the two things that most frighten preservice teachers about teaching?

Answer: motivating students and classroom management

I have surveyed many junior- and senior-level students through the years asking them what frightens them the most about beginning to teach. Frequently, they will preface their answers by saying, "It hasn't been that long since I was a senior, and I saw how kids behaved. They were rude to teachers and according to students, teachers hardly ever did anything right. They made fun of teachers behind their backs and created disturbances just to get a reaction from the teacher. I'm just afraid that will happen to me."

Classroom management issues are also the number one reason many students give for choosing to teach in the elementary grades rather than at the secondary levels. Middle school students are known as "hormones on wheels" and secondary students are often identified as "bored to distraction."

TRANSITION: Wasicsko and Ross (1994) wrote a funny article some time ago entitled "How to Create Discipline Problems" in ten simple rules:

1. Expect the worst from kids.
2. Never tell students what is expected of them.
3. Punish and criticize kids often.
4. Punish the whole class when one student misbehaves.
5. Never give students privileges.
6. Punish every misbehavior.
7. Threaten and warn kids often.
8. Use the same punishment for every student.
9. Use school as punishment.
10. Maintain personal distance from students.

Obviously, the authors write tongue-in-cheek with their negative rules; they expect the reader to twist the sentences to accentuate the positive.

The truth of the matter is that kids being kids have always been rude, and they have probably always made fun of teachers behind their backs. That truth out of the way, abundant current research exists that directs beginning teachers' planning for classroom management. Research indicates that there is a positive correlation between teacher behavior and student behavior. (Do you see the correlation in the ten rules above?)

This chapter is devoted to helping preservice teachers learn how to *avoid* problems in the classroom and in the process how to keep students on task and motivated to do the work prescribed.

INSTRUCTIONAL INPUT AND GUIDED PRACTICE

What we need to know about classroom management

The Instructional Input in this lesson plan will contain *guided practice* in the form of questions placed throughout the chapter. References to web sites will also serve as guided practice as you research topics to gain further knowledge and information and application.

Theories of Classroom Discipline

No one has THE answer to managing a classroom, but many researchers have written about what works some of the time. Keep in mind that the teacher's personality must always be taken into account when designing a classroom discipline management plan; therefore, as you read about some discipline theories, think about what kind of order you would like in your classroom. You should get a feel for what might work for you.

BEGIN AT THE BEGINNING

No one likes to wait for a program to begin, and people begin to get fidgety whenever there are delays. The same thing happens when teachers get off to a late start in a classroom—kids start to get fidgety. The difference between an audience and a class is enormous, however. An audience will usually wait quietly, but a classroom will get out of control in an instant and display the same out-of-control behavior each time the class meets unless rules are made very clear from the first day. The key words in this paragraph are *wait, fidgety, late start, out of control, rules,* and *clarity*. It is simple to create rules that foresee problems these words imply.

In order to think about preventing problems in the classroom it is clear that timing is critical—clear rules and beginning on time are very important.

> **QUESTION**
> How will you maintain control of your class the first three minutes while you are calling roll, taking up homework, and listening to announcements?
>
> *Answer:* THE answer to that question does not exist. However, experienced teachers and theorists have discovered through time that many types of discipline management techniques are effective.

The First Three Minutes is the title of a book written by Steven Weinberg that details the "big bang" theory of creation over 10 billion years ago. The thesis describes how those critical minutes influenced all of creation. Playing off of that title, Dr. Bob Hawkes, a professor in the Physics, Engineering, and Geoscience Department of Mount Allison University, wrote a short piece comparing the first three minutes of class to the gigantic bang of creation. In other words, what happens the first three minutes of class influences what happens in the rest of the class period.

If teachers are well prepared at the onset of class, students will respect that organization, but if teachers take ten minutes to take the roll, students will find other things to do, and it will be like *herding cats* to get them back on track for the remainder of the class period. Similarly, if a teacher habitually allows that free ten minutes at the end of class, everything that follows is rather chaotic.

Once the initial class organization is thought out and executed, a teacher plans for daily management. How WILL you take care of all the *things* that must be done at the beginning of every class without losing control of your class? Planning will enable you to have activities for your students to do with the clear understanding that teaching related to those activities is to follow shortly. What will you do if someone does not cooperate with your initial plan? That is where a thorough understanding of discipline theory comes into play. Following are three types of discipline management, but there are many more that you may run across in your reading. Do you want to be authoritarian? Laissez-faire? Or Authoritative? In your approach to your classroom?

> **QUESTION**
> Have you heard a teacher or a principal say in reference to a new teacher "Do not smile until Christmas!" That phrase, while frightening, has some basis. Why might that be good advice—especially for new teachers?
>
> *Answer:* Principals will tell you that it is always easy to lighten up in your discipline, but it is nearly impossible to tighten up!

Discipline Management Theories

Some theories that will be covered in this chapter are Harry Wong's *The First Days of School*, Withitness, Assertive Discipline, Behavioral Modification, and Reality Therapy. In addition, a consensus of thoughts on discipline management by successful educators is offered.

I recall reading research some time ago that predicted 95 percent of all classroom problems were caused by the teacher. At first, the high number startled me. How could that be? After thinking it over and particularly after becoming acquainted with Harry Wong's work, I have a tendency to believe that, at times, the high percentage of provoking attributes of teachers might be correct.

In his best-selling book on teaching, *The First Days of School* (2004), Harry Wong is a proponent of common-sense, tried-and-true methods for developing successful classroom management.

He believes that teachers do cause teacher–student problems through disorganization and the inability to create a sense of *family* in the classroom (Competency 5). His recommendations as well as those of a myriad of other researchers are very clear: all teachers must set up desired behavior parameters in their classrooms.

Rules, Routines, and Procedures

While many educators and researchers write about rules, routines, and procedures, Harry Wong is the most outspoken proponent of routines and procedures. He says that without routines and procedures, teachers will have difficulty establishing good classroom management. He clearly distinguishes between a student's behavior and a student's failure to follow a routine. Teachers who miss this critical point (what is misbehavior?) will find themselves writing out discipline referrals by the dozens. He bases his comments on the belief that most students do not wish to misbehave nor do they wish to fall out of favor with the teacher.

> **QUESTION**
> What conclusion can a principal draw from observing that one teacher has dozens of discipline referrals to the office and another teacher has none?
>
> *Your Answer*
>
> **QUESTION**
> How does poor classroom management connect to classroom environment?
>
> *Your Answer*

A teacher establishes procedures for doing many things in the classroom; for example, a teacher calls the roll each morning and takes up lunch money. If the teacher has a seating chart, she will not need to call roll; if she has a chart that a student can manage himself to indicate he wishes to eat in the lunch room, she will not need to be involved. Instead, the teacher can open the day's lessons quickly and efficiently. There is, literally, no time for students to misbehave. The teacher must both identify the procedure she wishes to teach and then she must teach it. After the procedure is taught, she must be consistent in following the procedure herself. Soon the procedure will become a routine and students, according to Harry Wong, may not need the teacher at all! He stresses that some children take longer than others to understand the procedure and the teacher must continually reinforce the procedure over and over.

The Importance of Clear Rules and Procedures

Anyone can come up with a list of rules that youngsters should obey, but it is very important to create clearly-defined rules. Clearly-defined rules help create a predictable and comprehensible environment. Vague rules, on the other hand, may actually create behavior problems or cries of unfairness.

Clearly-defined rules minimize student confusion so academic learning time is enhanced.

When creating rules, teachers should provide students and parents with a handout that clearly explains expectations. It may even be a school requirement that parents sign a "rules and procedures" document before returning it to class.

If your teaching field needs special rules and routines for running a lab, art class, or shop activity, you should plan class rules accordingly. Remember to allow for student interaction when planning such rules. However you decide to implement consequences for the rules you write, you must be reasonable and consistent.

Even though you write the rules and send a copy home with students, that is not sufficient. You must teach rules and procedures at the beginning of the school year.

Jacob Kounin: Withitness

Some 40 years ago during the 1970s, Jacob Kounin studied discipline and management as a unit. He believed that a teacher's ability to manage instruction was critically related to discipline.

Kounin noticed a *ripple effect* among his students when he noted that correcting of one student apparently caused other students to amend their behavior. He also observed that **proactive** teachers prevented misbehaviors from occurring whereas **reactive** teachers caused a negative response from students. Proactive teachers seem to have a sixth sense about human psychology and understand when and how misbehavior is likely to occur whereas teachers who believe that student misbehavior can be corrected with a "Do not do that!" or "I've told you a thousand times . . ." are reactive.

These discoveries led Kounin to believe that there were certain teacher behaviors that could be learned and should be learned in order to prevent misbehavior. That process is known as being *proactive* rather than *reactive*. That knowledge results in more effective classroom management.

His studies led him to study prevention of misbehavior. His theories involving teacher behavior resulted in the following terms that are associated with his work:

1. Withitness
2. Overlapping
3. Momentum
4. Smoothness
5. Group focus

Borrowing from the slang of the 1960s, Kounin described a teacher with *eyes in the back of her head* as being *withit*. This teacher seems to know what is going on at all times in the classroom—note the use of the words *seems to know*. It is virtually impossible for a teacher to know everything that is going on in a classroom; however, it is possible for a teacher to impress upon students that she does.

Teachers must be able to accomplish a good many tasks at once. This behavior is known as multitasking or, as Kounin called it, *overlapping*. The idea is that the teacher is so well organized that the classroom seems to operate seamlessly as students move from one activity to another without breaks or lapses in momentum. In order for overlapping to occur, the teacher must plan for it.

Working from the concept of overlapping, the successful teacher is aware of time-on-task behavior and keeps the *momentum* of the lesson going. This teacher is quick to observe lapses in the lesson where student behavior can get out of hand and create an appropriate filler to keep things moving smoothly. This teacher is flexible. A phrase not associated with Kounin, but which is applicable, is *monitor and adjust*. This means that teachers monitor the lesson and student behavior at all times and adjust behavior accordingly—even if it means changing gears suddenly.

Similar to momentum is the term *smoothness*, and it refers to keeping students on track. In an earlier chapter, the term *birdwalking* was introduced referring to the teacher who was easily distracted and taken off-track. Sometimes, students do not deliberately try to get teachers off-track, but they do ask irrelevant questions at serious moments in the lesson. Smooth teachers can, through a variety of ways, get the lesson back on track without angering students or making them feel stupid for having asked an irrelevant question.

The final term is *group focus*, and it refers to the ability of the teacher to keep the entire class focused on the lesson. Using a variety of strategies, such as relevant and provocative discussion questions where all students are expected to participate or creating suspense in the lesson that holds their attention, the teacher can keep the group focused on the topic at hand.

DISCUSSION QUESTIONS

Give a concrete example of a *ripple effect* that you have observed. Describe the teacher characteristics of a *withit* teacher. Identify characteristics of teachers who prevent classroom misbehavior.

My example of a ripple effect: Years ago in a master's level class, I was sitting in the front row next to a young man. Everything seemed normal when all of a sudden the professor began to yell at the top of his lungs accusing the student of being lazy and copying work. No portion of the poor student's behavior went unnoticed. My heart literally stopped. I was afraid to look up from my book and notes. The class became quiet as stone while

> they waited to see what would happen next. The professor ended the tirade by demanding that the student "Get out of this classroom and don't ever darken the doors of this university again!" The man muttered some obscenity, got up, and stormed out of the door slamming it so hard I feared the glass window would shatter. Breathing hard and waiting a moment or two, the professor dismissed the class for a ten-minute break. We rose as a group, walked silently out of the classroom, and quickly dispersed. Not knowing where the professor was or the young man, we were afraid to talk to each other. We looked at each other helplessly, drank from the water fountain, and watched the clock slowly spend the ten minutes.
>
> Once back in the classroom, the man came back through the door—the anxiety of the classmates escalated fearing for the man's life until finally the professor explained he had simulated the ripple effect with the class. It took a while for our hearts to quit pounding!

This professor had assumed the persona of an aggressive teacher. It was very effective in the short term and as an example, but in the long term, it would have been sheer torture to have attended this class had the teacher's voice not changed.

Lee and Marlene Canter: Assertive Discipline

Assertive discipline is very similar to Wong's concepts of procedures and routines in that they believe you must plan systematically for discipline management. In their studies, the Cantors attacked the problem of teachers who could not control the students in their classrooms. They desired to create a system by which teachers could become the authority and in control. The result was assertiveness training where teachers have few rules, but those rules have consequences that are administered quickly and firmly. The teacher is the authority in the classroom.

> For years, my class *rules* were
>   "You have the right to learn,
>   I have the right to teach,
>   No one has the right to interfere with that process."

In a nutshell, that is the Canter theory of assertive discipline. The word *interfere* is an umbrella word that incorporates almost every misbehavior a teacher can think of. However, the three "rules" listed do not meet the Canter parameters for establishing rules. Those follow.

Words like *behavioral expectations, compliance, efficiency, behavior management, effective, assertiveness, disobey, negative consequences,* and *firmness* are associated with this theory. While these words may seem rather cold and unfriendly, the truth of the matter is that teachers must learn assertiveness to some degree before they will be effective in the classroom.

The Canters do not think of students in a negative light; they are simply convinced that student behavior must be such that a teacher can teach all students and, to make that happen, teachers must maintain control of their classes at all times. Furthermore, students must know and perceive that teachers are in charge.

When teachers first started using assertive discipline in the 1970s, they were taught the difference between aggressiveness and assertiveness. The term *non-assertive* also became relevant as a yardstick for measuring the degree to which teachers were assertive.

Aggressive: Marked by combative readiness.

This teacher's tongue is a loaded gun—a ready response for every misbehavior. This teacher might make threats and be labeled as a bully.

Assertive: Marked by bold confidence.

The assertive teacher is in charge of the classroom and sets up the classroom so that students can be themselves within the parameters of the class rules.

Authoritarian: Of or relating to blind submission.

The authoritarian teacher expects to be the leader/final authority of the classroom and sets up rules that must be obeyed.

The distinction between assertive teachers and aggressive teachers is clearly the difference between gaining compliance and making combative and hostile threats. Assertive teachers are not aggressive, but they have so defined their classroom behavior desires that they can and do act confidently when those rules are breached.

Assertive discipline also has the added benefit of helping children take responsibility for their behavior. Through consistent management with this system, the student-teacher relationship is strengthened and a bond of trust can be established.

The basic points to remember about assertive discipline are:

1. State the rules clearly (no more than five to six)
   a. Be sure that the rules are observable
   b. Provide written copies of the rules
   c. Review rules orally
   d. Rules should not violate the best interest of the student

2. State the consequences of breaking the rules

3. Be consistent

Since the introduction of Assertive Discipline in the 1970s, the trend for classroom management has become more democratic and cooperative rather than authoritarian.

DISCUSSION QUESTIONS

Discuss how children function in groups in a Canter classroom. Be age specific. Describe how the assertive teacher might set up a group activity.

Define authoritarian and authoritative approaches to classroom management. Give concrete examples.

B. F. Skinner: Behavioral Modification

The concept of reinforcement theory is based on Thorndike's *law of effect* in which he determined that people tend to repeat behaviors that have had a positive outcome for them. Conversely, people have a tendency to stop or alter behaviors that cause negative consequences. Some ten to fifteen years later, B. F. Skinner conducted experiments on animals that more or less replicated Thorndike's *law of effect*. The Skinner Box is the best-known reference to these experiments where animals (rats) would seek food at predetermined intervals if they were properly rewarded. See the following web site for more information about the Skinner Box:

http://en.wikipedia.org/wiki/Operant_conditioning_chamber

From these experiments, Skinner generalized to classroom management and became a leader in the primary discussions about reinforcement theory in the classroom. Translating Skinner's thoughts on behavior mod (as it is called in the business), children will (like the rats) seek the teacher's approval (reward) and avoid risking the teacher's disapproval (consequences) naturally.

For more information on Skinner and Reinforcement Theory refer to this web site:

> http://www.enotes.com/management-encyclopedia/reinforcement-theory

Four Principles of Reinforcement Theory

1. A teacher *positively reinforces* students through written or verbal messages, privileges granted, or external rewards such as a piece of candy or a free Friday.
2. A teacher *negatively reinforces* students by taking away something the student wants. Ultimately, the student will have to make a choice either to obey the rules or to be punished in some form.
3. The teacher must monitor a student's behavior carefully to decide whether to reinforce positively or negatively. This is called a *schedule of reinforcement*. The goal is to gain compliance from the student and to extinguish the bad behavior.
4. The teacher hopes to *extinguish* the cited behavior, so he has a couple of options: ignore the behavior and hope it will go away on its own or punish the behavior in a variety of ways according to a management plan.

Like Canter, Skinner's methods have been modernized by usage. The following formula is a nice consensus of theories that most teachers use to gain compliance and maintain order in the classroom.

William Glasser: Reality Therapy

Remember Maslow's Hierarchy of Needs? Glasser's theory is based on the idea that children *act out* because a need in the area of being loved or feeling worthwhile is not being met. He believed that people must feel needed and loved in order to be successful. Obviously, the primary place that love is given is in the home, but it can also be given through acceptance in the classroom. Therefore, it is the teacher's job to figure out how to meet these needs in all children.

The general process of reality therapy is as follows:

1. The teacher must make friends (be on good terms) with the student. This effort will cause the student to feel like he belongs and have some to trust.
2. Use personal, caring pronouns: "I care about you and your work. I do not want you to fail."
3. Establish the reality of the present. In other words, what the student is doing now, not the past behavior. Emphasize the behavior, not the feelings about the behavior.
4. Ask the student whether the present assessment is helping to make the student successful. In other words, if the student talks during instruction, does the talking interfere with understanding instructions?
5. Create an improvement plan. Keep it simple and let the student help create it.
6. The improvement plan is like a contract; get a commitment from the student.
7. Make it clear that you will not accept excuses. Encourage the student to continue trying.
8. Do not punish—just give the reasonable consequences.

Glasser uses the word *friend* in terms of this special relationship with the student, but it is wise to understand that preservice teachers are sternly admonished not to think they can be *friends* in the normal meaning of the word. You are still the teacher and still the leader of the discussion and planning about a student's behavior, and you must not forget that relationship is mentor to student. Perhaps the best thing to take away from Glasser is that he asks that you treat children humanely and proactively.

One can summarize the theories studied previously in this fashion: A teacher, in order to maintain control of students, must understand human nature, be definitive and assertive in setting rules, proactive and humane in keeping rules, and above all establish a caring and loving environment.
Some typical class rules are:

1. Follow directions.
2. Be in your seat when the bell rings.
3. Bring all materials to class.
4. Raise your hand for permission to speak.
5. Hand in all assignments on time.
6. Keep hands, feet, and objects to yourself.
7. Stay on task.

Obviously, students would be rather robotic if all seven of those rules were obeyed 100 percent of the time. So, the teacher must think of consequences. Consequences must be things students will not like, but they must never psychologically harm a student. Your consequences must be in a hierarchy. Some consequences, such as keeping students after school, are not usually possible, so you must consult the district's handbooks to be sure before you make a mistake. A list of consequences follows.

In a practical vein, the following suggestions and strategies provide a consensus of opinion on where to start.

To maintain positive behaviors, the teacher should try the following strategies in this order:

- **Proximity.** Move near the student and disrupt the student's misbehavior by standing close by until the misbehavior stops. While standing nearby, continue with the lesson. Do not do any more than look at the student as you would any other student.
- **Student's name.** Insert the student's name into the lesson. For example, you might say to Mary who is talking to Susie, "Mary, what do you think about these two rhyming words?" Of course, you will have Mary's immediate attention, and she may be embarrassed, so you will need to coach her or cue her through the question she did not hear. If she does not respond, you may ask Susie the same question.
- **Allow physical movement.** Ask the student if s/he would like to move to a different seat. You may do this privately to prevent embarrassing the student by saying something like, "Are you having a difficult time seeing the board or following the discussion where you are seated?" If the student does not get the message, you will have to be more direct: "I see that you are having difficulty . . .".
- **Signal.** A signal from the teacher may be as simple as a hand motion such as holding up the index finger as though you are starting a count-down. A finger placed to the lips for a student who does not usually cause problems is another choice of teachers. One of my favorite methods is to keep a variety of clever sticky notes handy and unobtrusively walk to the student's desk and place it where he cannot miss it.
- **Make a record.** Have your discipline records in a predictable place. When you observe a student's recurring and disruptive behavior, continue the lesson but move to the folder containing your personal notes and make a note of the behavior. You may be very silent and straight faced while doing this. Normally, the entire class will observe and become very, very quiet. You should inform the student, however, after class, that you have noted behavior in the file. Some teachers have a more public method by which marks are added to the board without ever speaking to the student.

When you do have to speak to a student about his/her behavior, do the following:

1. Discuss the behavior with the student after class and privately.
2. Begin the discussion by asking the student if he knows why you wanted to speak to him (let the student identify the problem).
3. Keep your voice calm and non-accusatory.
4. If consequences are given, do it privately.

5. Before leaving a discussion, attempt to reestablish a positive relationship with the student.
6. Separate the behavior from the child. As Baptists say, "Hate the sin, love the sinner!"
7. Remember, tomorrow is a new day. *Do-overs* allowed!

Finally, when you have had it with a student's recurring behavior, and you find you must have a personal discussion with the student, you should

1. Pick out one behavior to change;
2. Ask the student to replace that behavior with a new one;
3. Determine how you will positively reinforce the new behavior;
4. Determine how you will negatively reinforce poor performance in the future.

There are some important things to remember when deciding on the limit-setting consequences:

1. Sending a student to the principal should be the last consequence in the plan.
2. The plan must be in alignment with the ISD's behavior policy and preferably approved by the principal before it is given to the class.
3. A copy of the plan should be provided to parents.
4. The plan applies equally to all students in the classroom.
5. Provide a way for a fresh start.
6. Never delete a negative behavior as a reward for improved behavior.

When you take a classroom management course at the university level, you will be exposed to many more theories. Even though these theories appear dated, most new theories build upon these classics in some significant way.

Classroom management is closely connected to psychology in that it is truly a study of people and their responses to their environment. Obviously, the best way to prevent discipline problems is to set up a learning environment that meets the needs of students and the teacher. Remember, the classroom is established for a distinct purpose, and no student (or teacher) has the right to interfere with that process.

Grouping Techniques and Classroom Management

As described earlier in the chapter, the efficiency with which a teacher is able to get a class started applies to group management as well. Teachers must assign seating or grouping in a logical, efficient manner to keep control of the class. Stopping the rhythm of the class with techniques like these have confusing, if not disastrous, management consequences: count off seats, point to designated areas of the classroom, number students (some of whom will never remember their numbers two minutes later), self-select groups, or read down the alphabet. Students immediately begin to talk, so many of them will never hear the instructions. Therefore, more time is lost repeating or getting angry and becoming reactive with students.

When you plan a group activity, think through all the stages of the activity and plan for group movement. The successful teacher may prepare an interactive bulletin board through which students can seat themselves, use an overhead to assign seating, have students draw a seat upon entering the classroom, or assign different-colored stars to the group assignment sheet and ask students to assemble in like-colored stars to begin their assignment.

Creating a Timeline for Management

One of the most common problems associated with beginning anything new is procrastination. When you get your first teaching position, you will be elated and excited and anxious to start your first day. Preparing now for some of those first day details will enable you to get a head start.

Prepare a timeline allocating minutes for each activity you anticipate. The basic chart might look something like this:

Time	Activity	Notes: "What If"
8:00	Bell; greet students at the door; clearly state where they are to sit.	You will not be able to seat them if you are at the door. How can you make a smooth entrance to class?
8:01	Welcome	Late students? Interruptions? Announcements?
8:04	Room arrangement	

Having a chart like this to take to your first faculty meeting during inservice will be beneficial because you will be asked to hand out certain forms that require filling out or taking home to parents. What will be your procedure for handing out materials? This procedure appears later in the activities section, so you may give it more thought as an assignment.

As you can see, there is much to learn about classroom management. Its connection to the environment is unmistakable. Teachers must learn many, many tricks of the trade, so to speak, in order to keep the classroom running smoothly. The smoother the classroom, the more fun teaching can be.

INDEPENDENT PRACTICE AND MODELING (HOMEWORK)

1. **Scholar's Vocabulary:** Using the State-produced list of proficiencies preservice teachers should have related to Competency 6, highlight terms you wish to place in your interactive glossary. You should have a minimum of five terms from C6. (See the model in the Appendices.)

2. **Reflective Writing:** Using the eleven-sentence model in the Appendices, write a reflection on Competency 6.

3. **My Rules:** Construct your future classroom rules (age appropriate/grade specific) on an 8½ × 11 page. The following model would be appropriate for a middle school classroom of twelve-year-old students.

MR. SMITH'S HISTORY CLASS RULES

Responsible—for your choices.

Utilize—your time.

Listen—to others.

Envision—a peaceful environment.

Succeed—in this class.

122 Competency 6 Classroom Management

4. Teachers, of necessity, must have a rewards/consequences plan. Complete the following chart based on the rules you set in activity #3.

    If you break a rule:

    1st time _____

    2nd time _____

    3rd time _____

    4th time _____

    5th time _____

5. Describe how you will make transitions in the following situations:
    a. Materials and supplies (getting out; putting up)
    b. Words (moving from lecture to activity)
    c. Note transitions in LPs (moving from the objective to closure)
    d. Places for transitions (note the "natural" places for transitions in any LP)
    e. Use existing LP to write in transitions

6. Research reinforcers (extrinsic motivators?) for elementary school students, middle school students, or high school students. Your research may include contracts, tokens, tickets, privileges, activities, social, etc. Make a list of ten reinforcers (five positive and five negative) that you might use at the grade level you intend to teach. Write, briefly, why you believe positive and negative reinforcers should be used.

7. As you complete observations in each of the three levels, write a brief reflection about what you have seen. Did the (mis)behavior surprise you? Did the teacher's (mis)behavior surprise you? Why? What is the effect of your observations?

Misbehavior	**Interventions**
1.	
2.	
3.	
4.	
5.	
6.	
7.	
8.	
9.	
10.	

8. Create a timeline as suggested earlier in the chapter. Elaborate minute-by-minute how long you believe each thing you want to do the first couple of days in your class will take. The notes ("What If") section is for you to write unanswered questions that occur to you as you create this timeline.

CLOSURE/FOLLOW-UP

Remember a short skit on *Saturday Night Live* a few years ago about the reflective guy (Al Franken) that used self-affirmation while trying to build up his self-esteem? He had "affirmations" that he would repeat to himself. He would say things like "Gosh, I am good enough!" "I am nice enough!" "I am smart enough!" to do whatever. My advice is to self-affirm often when thinking about classroom management. Remember, you are *smarter* than your students simply because you have years more experience in school and training to draw from. You can figure out problems if you are willing to be proactive rather than reactive, if you are willing to admit you are wrong every once in a while, and if you are determined to find a win-win solution to classroom problems.

ASSESSMENT

Ask yourself whether you have mastered these objectives.

- **Objective 1:** I will create a chart comparing and contrasting three discipline management theorists.
- **Objective 2:** I will create an age-appropriate sample of classroom procedures and routines and explain how I will teach those to the class.
- **Objective 3:** Using technology, I will create a timeline for daily classroom activity.
- **Objective 4:** I will observe and document behavior at the elementary, middle, and secondary school levels and reflect upon effective methods of redirecting behavior.

PRACTICE QUESTIONS

Now assess your learning by answering these questions. Answers are given in the Appendices.

1. Melissa and John were tardy for their fourth-period class right after lunch. Mrs. Parker asked them for a tardy slip, which each presented; then Mrs. Parker asked each why they were tardy. John said that he could not find a parking place. Melissa said that she had a flat tire on the way back to school and had to call her father for help. Mrs. Parker has an authoritarian discipline plan, so what will she do?
   a. Treat both students the same and punish according to her discipline management plan.
   b. Treat both separately according to the circumstance and punish according to the discipline management plan.
   c. Accept the tardy slips from the office and do nothing.
   d. Both are good students, so she will let them slide this time.

2. What are some of the characteristics of a well-managed classroom?
   I. Students know what is expected of them.
   II. Students are kept busy on a teacher-led instructional activity.
   III. The classroom has little disruption, confusion, or wasted time.
   IV. Students know that the teacher is there to enforce rules.
       a. I, III, IV
       b. II, III
       c. I, II, III
       d. I, II, IV

124   Competency 6   Classroom Management

3. Steve is one of the well known troublemakers at school. In fact, you might say, his second home is in the office. When you get your class role for the new year, you see that you have Steve in your first period. What should you do the first day to show Steve that you are in control of your classroom?
    a. Tell the class what you expect from them and that you will hold them to these standards.
    b. Tell Steve that if he even looks at you wrong, you will send him to the office.
    c. Do not say anything hoping he matured over the summer.
    d. Decide to ignore Steve and hope he will sleep through your class.

4. Mrs. Jones, a first year teacher, consistently has problems with Jeffery. He does not follow directions primarily because he never hears directions being given in class. He is too busy misbehaving by entertaining the other students. What is most likely the reason Mrs. Jones cannot solve the problem with Jeffrey?
    a. Jeffery comes from a home that does not believe in discipline.
    b. Jeffery's peers are pressuring him to act a certain way, and he doesn't want to disappoint them.
    c. Mrs. Jones didn't begin the year by showing her students who was in charge and was inconsistent with classroom discipline from day to day.
    d. Mrs. Jones only threatens Jeffery but never follows through on what she says.

5. Students in Mr. Ooley's class know that they must be in their seats by the time the tardy bell rings and that they must begin writing in their journal the first fifteen minutes of each class. This is an example of:
    a. expected behavior in Mr. Ooley's class.
    b. a rule in the student handbook related to the code of conduct.
    c. transitional routines from one class to another.
    d. a daily routine students are expected to carry out.

6. Janie just received her third test back in Mr. Reynolds' math class. She got an F, her third failing grade for the six weeks. She griped aloud that the test was too hard and that it was Mr. Reynolds' fault that she flunked the test. After all, he didn't tell her these things would be on the test. What is Janie's real problem with the situation?
    a. Mr. Reynolds doesn't like Janie in his class, so he deliberately found fault with her work and gave her an F on the test.
    b. The test was too hard for Janie to complete correctly; she has cognitive problems.
    c. Janie needs help to understand that she must take responsibility for her actions.
    d. She is not a capable math student, and Mr. Reynolds needs to assign tutorials each day.

7. Mrs. Mills is known as a no-nonsense teacher with a list of classroom rules two pages long. She feels that the students need to know exactly what they can and can not do in her classroom; therefore, she elaborates on the rules the first day of class, turns a copy of the rules in to the principal, and sends a copy of the rules home with each student to get a parent's signature.

    Mrs. Turner is a teacher that is thought of as fair, if somewhat lenient, with her students. She feels that the classroom rules should be short and simple. She goes over the rules once and spends the rest of the day reinforcing the desired behaviors while trying to ignore the undesirable ones. She also sends a copy of the rules home to get a parent's signature.

    Which teacher's classroom policy is likely to be more effective?
    a. Mrs. Mills
    b. Mrs. Turner

8. Mr. Rodriquez is a first year fifth-grade language arts teacher assigned to a brand new classroom in Marion Webster Elementary. He is getting ready for the new school year. His classroom walls are all blank, and there is no money available for supplies. What should he do to ready the classroom for the new year?
    a. Nothing; the children will understand he is new.
    b. Use Internet "posters" to decorate the room.
    c. Let children plan decorations for the room the first day of school.
    d. Use spray paint and molding glue to create murals.

9. Mr. Riley is a physical education teacher in a small town. Many of the students that are in his classes do not like to participate because they believe that varsity athletes get all the attention. The coach is always on the lookout for athletic talent but notices that students get discouraged because they do not perform well at certain sports. How can Mr. Riley best help his physical education students and help his classroom environment at the same time?
    a. He can hold standards as high for these students as he does for his varsity athletes.
    b. He believes they should be motivated to ask for his help.
    c. He can encourage these students to develop a respect for exercise and healthy lifestyles.
    d. He can do more to persuade the athletically challenged to change their attitudes by asking varsity athletes to speak to the class.

10. Students will benefit most from which learning environment?
    a. Mrs. Smith allows her students to talk the first ten minutes of each class while she takes roll. She often flickers the lights to get the students' attention. She rarely finishes teaching a lesson during the class period.
    b. Miss Camp has a class assignment on the chalkboard when the students enter the classroom. They are required to finish this assignment by the time she has taken roll. She is also known to give the students special prizes at the end of the week when they meet their goals.
    c. Mrs. Lawson likes her students to work in groups. She promotes cooperative learning throughout the year. She has many centers in her classroom. The students are assigned by groups to a different center each week. They are required to finish certain assignments before the end of the week.
    d. Mr. Boone assigns a student to check roll each week. He has the other students write in a journal before class. He has many visual aids for each of his lessons. He has a designated helper to go around and show each student what work is missing for that grading period.

CAREER PLANNING

Teachers who are good classroom managers seem to have the complete understanding of how to be effective teachers. Teachers who enjoy the psychology of student behavior and understand the concepts of discipline will make good assistant principals. Interested teachers will pursue a graduate degree in midmanagement understanding that the role of the Assistant Principal, while somewhat varied from school to school, will entail taking care of other teacher's problems, bookroom duty, before- and after-school detention, parent conferences, and sitting in on ARD meetings from time to time.

MATERIALS NEEDED

Internet

SUGGESTIONS FOR ADDITIONAL ASSIGNMENTS

Competency 6 is connected to C5 (environment) because what is established in C6 in the way of routines and procedures helps to set an inviting climate in the classroom.

1. Create a list of negative and positive reinforcers for the grade level you are preparing to teach. Justify each reinforcer.

2. Create a **check list** of reinforcers that you may allow students to choose and come to a consensus as a class.

3. Create a **tracking form** that you can use to document rewards.

4. In one of your classroom observations, pay particular attention to the minor behavioral problems that are present in every classroom. It is important for teachers to keep students on task. Make a list of ten examples of minor off-task behaviors, and state how the teacher handles them with verbal interventions, proximity, nonverbal interventions, or ignoring the misbehavior. In the first column, describe the behavior, and in the second column describe the teacher response and whether it was effective or not.

5. Explain the difference between routines and procedures. Create a list of procedures you will set up the first two days of class, and describe how you will "teach" the procedure to your students. Identify the following elements of this classroom—subject matter, age of students, and grade level—at the top of your routines/procedures.

6. Create a daily timeline (in a table) for a fifth grade elementary-level ELA classroom beginning at 8 A.M. and ending at 3:15 P.M. Schedule these things into your classroom: attendance, lunch, instruction in ELA, mathematics, social studies, science, music, library, play time, bathroom, and physical activity. DIVIDE each activity with a transition and describe what the teacher might say to keep students on task and successfully manage the class.

7. Create a gradebook in Excel. Include a column for classroom participation. Explain in a paragraph how you will "measure" participation and how you will keep up with your measurement throughout a grading period.

8. What training in classroom management do paraprofessionals complete? Interview an ISD trainer for paras. Similarly, what training, if any, does your local ISD provide for classroom volunteers?

9. Research several ISD web sites to determine policies for behavioral management.

10. Document the rules for behavior management in several classrooms. Provide photos of classroom rules in classes that you observe. (Be sure to ask the teacher first.) Describe the differences among elementary rules, middle school rules, and high school rules.

11. Explain ways to dignify errors to promote learning. Give three examples of dignified teacher responses.

12. Explain how being prompt, consistent, and reasonable seems to be effective in managing student behavior. Why do threats seem to be ineffective in the classroom?

13. Explain how being prompt, consistent, and reasonable seems to be effective in managing student behavior. Why do threats seem to be ineffective in the classroom? (Give at least three reasons.)

14. Compare and contrast the use of behavior modification techniques and the I-message/no-lose method in terms of locus of control, freedom, individual responsibility, and philosophical belief system.

15. Use technology (possibly Excel) to create a timeline for daily classroom activity.

16. Form a cooperative learning group and have each student research and be prepared to discuss one theorist for classroom management theory.
    a. Each student should provide the group with an example of a classroom management plan based on the theorist he researched.

17. Following are a few of the typical behaviors a teacher wants. Add several behaviors of your own to complete the list.

    Follow directions
    Keep hands, feet, and objects to self
    Take turns
    Low noise level

    Play/study cooperatively
    Share
    Work independently

18. Often, teachers want to reward students who follow the rules. List five possible ways you will reward students.

19. Research the discipline policy of a local school district. Compare the district plan to the rules/consequences that you created in independent practice.

Standard 3

Implementing Effective, Responsive Instruction and Assessment

Competency 7: Communication
Competency 8: Active Engagement
Competency 9: Technology
Competency 10: Planning for Performance, Achievement and Feedback

Competency 7

Communication

LESSON PLAN FOR COMPETENCY 7

STATE STANDARDS: STANDARD 3, COMPETENCY 7

Competency 007: The teacher understands and applies principles and **strategies for communicating** effectively in varied teaching and learning contexts.

132 Competency 7 Communication

STATE TEACHER PROFICIENCIES

Competency 007

The teacher understands and applies principles and strategies for communicating effectively in varied teaching and learning contexts.

The beginning teacher:

- Demonstrates clear, **accurate communication** in the teaching and learning process and uses language that is appropriate to students' ages, interests, and backgrounds.
- Engages in **skilled questioning** and leads effective **student discussions,** including using questioning and discussion to engage all students in exploring content; extends students' knowledge; and fosters active student **inquiry, higher-order thinking, problem solving,** and productive, supportive interactions, including appropriate **wait time.**
- Communicates **directions, explanations,** and **procedures** effectively and uses strategies for adjusting communication to enhance student understanding (e.g., by providing examples, simplifying complex ideas, using appropriate communication tools).
- Practices effective communication techniques and **interpersonal skills** (including both verbal and **nonverbal skills** and **electronic communication**) for meeting specified goals in various contexts.

TEACHING OBJECTIVES

At the end of the lesson, the student should be able to:

- Compare the basics of public speaking with teacher communication,
- Compare one communication model with the 9-step lesson plan format discussed in an earlier chapter.
- Create significant class discussion,
- Demonstrate appropriate questioning techniques:
    ◇ Reinforcement Theory
    ◇ Wait Time
- Demonstrate positive responses to students' incorrect responses.
- Participate in cooperative learning as a teaching technique.

C7 KEY WORDS: COMMUNICATION

Terms associated with communication

Communication Skills
Lecture
Questioning
Higher-order Thinking
Giving Directions
Cue
Interpersonal/Group Communication
Interpersonal Skills
Establishing Rules, Routines, Procedures

Efficacy
Feedback
Discussion
Giving Examples
Closed Questions
Establishing Tone
Correcting Verbal Responses

Relevance
Wait Time
Inquiry
Problem Solving
Open Questions

INTRODUCTION/FOCUS

"Teachers are communications majors first!"

Dr. Braselton

It may surprise you to learn that teachers are communications majors first; then, they are teachers of reading, math, social studies, or physics. The point is that unless individuals can communicate what they know in a way that entices children to learn, all the head knowledge in the world won't help.

Your success, and to a degree, the happiness you will find in the classroom will depend upon your ability to communicate effectively with students, parents, administrators, and peers. How well you learn the *jargon*, the language of your chosen career, and how well you are able to apply what you learn in your classes, in fact, determines your success.

Teachers display their knowledge every time they enter a classroom. Therefore, it is important that future teachers be exposed to communication techniques that exemplify good teaching. By learning early in teacher training what constitutes good teaching delivery, student teachers can practice those skills at every opportunity.

To become a good communicator, one must seek opportunities to take public speaking courses, learn leadership skills through student government, and participate in professional development activities whenever possible. Then, one must apply what is learned consistently. Doing *what comes naturally* hardly ever works in presentational skills. Students who have teachers like this relate story after story about counting the number of 'uhs' a certain teacher uses or estimating how many times a teacher tosses his/her hair back or fiddles with change in a pocket. We study these presentation skills in public speaking but revert to our own styles of presentation, which often flies in the face of good sense.

ROLE PLAY

To prove that communication is important, think about the telephone. Consider (or turn to a neighbor and role play) likely tonal quality in the following scenarios:

+ A credit card company calls about an overdue bill.
+ You call a teacher to inquire about your child's grades.
+ The teacher calls you to request an appointment.
+ A representative for Goodwill calls asking for donations.
+ A mother calls her child by both the first and middle names!

It is not too great a stretch to imagine the tone in each of these scenarios. The teacher develops "**tones**" within the classroom. Consider the following, and imagine what the teacher's tone is likely to be:

+ A student interrupts the class to deliver an unimportant message.
+ A student is tardy—yet again!
+ A student has been absent for one day and insists on getting assignments before you can even call the roll, saying "Did I miss anything?"
+ A student openly defies you over handing in a paper.

Again, it is not difficult to imagine the **stress** in one's voice when responding to events such as these. The information contained in **Competencies 5 and 6** (establishing a good physical and emotional environment) are also applicable to this competency because the **tonal qualities** that a teacher employs in conducting the everyday tasks of teaching are extremely important in setting the emotional environment of a classroom.

TRANSITION: In addition to the **vocal attributes** described, many other types of communication take place within the classroom. Teachers need to know that communication relates directly to clear, **accurate, and developmentally appropriate language.**

School districts (thus your job) depend upon your ability to communicate with students, parents, administrators, and peers. The accurate use of educational *jargon* in all communication efforts will give you credibility and the ability to explain clearly the issues that arise in teaching.

The following discussions are meant to help you establish good communication from the very first days of inservice and classes.

INSTRUCTIONAL INPUT AND GUIDED PRACTICE

What we need to know about communication

The Instructional Input in this lesson plan will contain *guided practice* in the form of questions placed throughout the chapter. References to web sites will also serve as guided practice as you research topics to gain further knowledge and information and application.

BEGIN AT THE BEGINNING

The first days of school are extremely important in the communication process—you must establish:

+ rules, routines, and procedures;
+ an inviting environment; as well as
+ initiate instruction.

While that short list of activities seems innocuous, it is, in fact, a list filled with demands for active delivery. As discussed in previous chapters, setting up rules, routines, and procedures and establishing an inviting environment are not small tasks. Problems caused by poor decisions at this point are long-lasting. In making choices about presenting yourself as a teacher the first few days, consider your choice of words and phrasing. The language you use makes all the difference.

Some Hints

The first day of class, you may use personal pronouns such as I, you, and we. It will foster a sense of inclusion. Try phrases such as these: "This year, you and I are going to accomplish . . ."; "I want you to learn so much . . ."; "We will build a community . . .". Note that these sentences:

+ are simple in choice of words and phrasing;
+ are short and clear;
+ contain no unnecessary jargon; and
+ contain no negative speech.

As any speech teacher will tell you, you must practice and practice your speeches in order to create a smooth delivery. Because you will be very nervous the first days of school, you should follow this advice to the letter:

practice and practice in front of a mirror or a family member. Ask for advice about the "invitation" to learning in your classroom. Eventually, you will find the correct words to help you establish your positive expectations for your new class. Repeating these familiar words in front of your class will also give you confidence to move to the next stage of instruction.

Example

Practice telling students about the class rules. Does your tone have a presumption of guilt or a presumption of high expectations? Do you make clear the consequences for not following the rules? Does the delivery of your consequences seem overly negative? Did you find the right balance between being serious and yet being fair? Practice!

The Instructional Process of Communication

The first objective in this chapter is to compare the basics of speech communication with teacher communication (lecture), so we'll begin by taking a look at Aristotle's basic speech communication model.

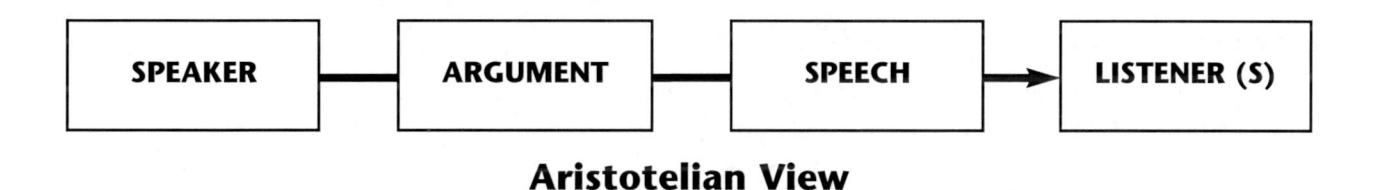

| SPEAKER | — | ARGUMENT | — | SPEECH | → | LISTENER (S) |

Aristotelian View

As you can see, this simple model begins with a speaker and ends with a listener. This model represents one-way communication.

The following graphic is simplified even further to demonstrate a basic teaching model—the two-dimensional model that follows perfectly demonstrates the concept of one-way communication often found in the lecture.

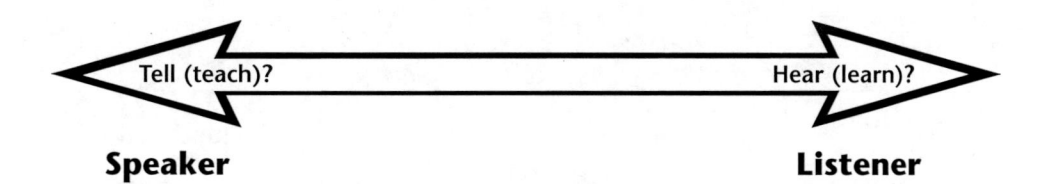

⟵ Tell (teach)?   Hear (learn)? ⟶

Speaker   **Listener**

Early Communication Model

QUESTIONS
Compare the Aristotelian Model and the more simplified "Early communication model."
What is missing?

Your Answer:

> "We have two ears and one mouth so that we can listen twice as much as we speak."
>
> *Epictetus*

Teachers who take this quote literally are lecturers. However, as you can see, this modified "early communication model" involves a teacher who tell-teaches (lectures) what there is to be learned and a student who hears-learns. Speech communications specialists learned years ago that just because someone speaks into a telephone doesn't mean someone on the other end receives the correct message if there is no feedback. Any number of distractions can occur at either end or even in the middle of the message that can destroy the original intent. Still, teachers who insist on lecturing without appropriate precautions for feedback continue to use this model of instruction.

Numerous writers have talked about the lecture and have even used it to state the obvious: the method of education delivery has not changed in over 200 years! It is even possible that many teachers who insist on using the lecture criticized it as being ineffective while they were students. Throughout college (and perhaps high school, too, in some cases) students are exposed to the lecture as the preferred teaching method; therefore, many preservice teachers may think that teaching is standing before the class talking about what you know. As a matter of fact, most teachers become very uncomfortable at prolonged silence in the classroom after asking a question. There seems to be something to the idea that "If I'm not talking, I'm not teaching!" However, research tells us that the lecture method of teaching is the least effective method of teaching! For those who cannot seem to get beyond the concept of lecturing to deliver learning, the following models may help.

Teacher Communication Models

The following graphic demonstrates what is generally thought of as the "best teaching model." This picture demonstrates the four parts of successful teaching: (1) tell, (2) show, (3) do, and (4) teach.

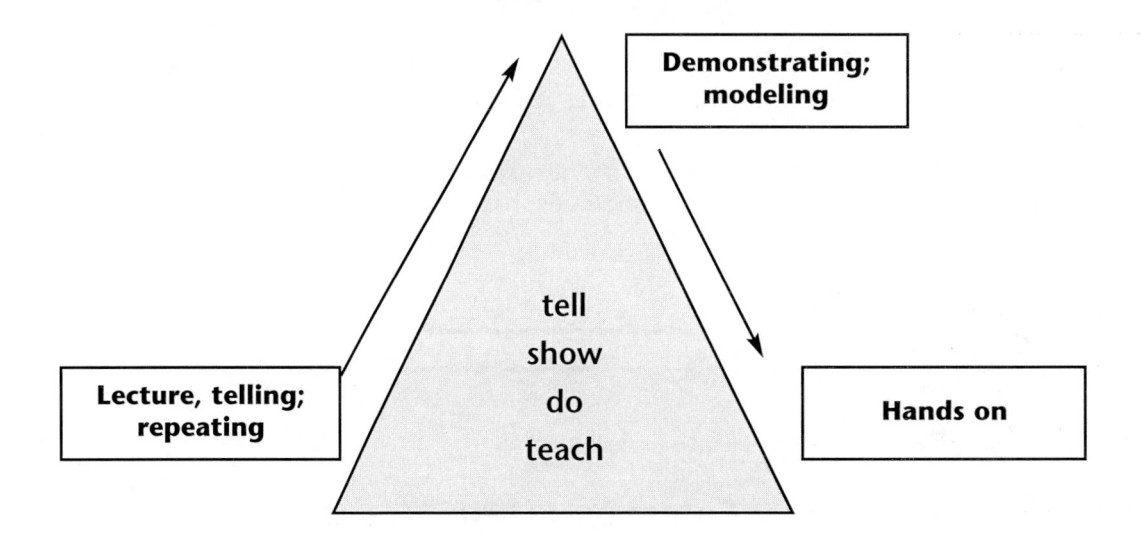

This model begins with lecturing about, or telling (auditory), what is to be learned. The lecture quickly moves to the modeling or picturing (visual) of what is to be learned. The final part is hands-on (kinesic). This part gives the learner the opportunity to try out the new information. The spiral at the last angle of the triangle suggests doing the activity so many times that one can teach it. When you can teach something, you have truly learned it. That may have been what Einstein meant by his quote:

> "You truly do not understand something unless
> you can explain it to your grandmother."
>
> *Albert Einstein*

A second model better describes the process by showing the listener as a decoder, interpreter, and encoder as he responds to the message. Educators rarely use speech models to demonstrate the process of teacher communication, but the comparison is not to be missed.

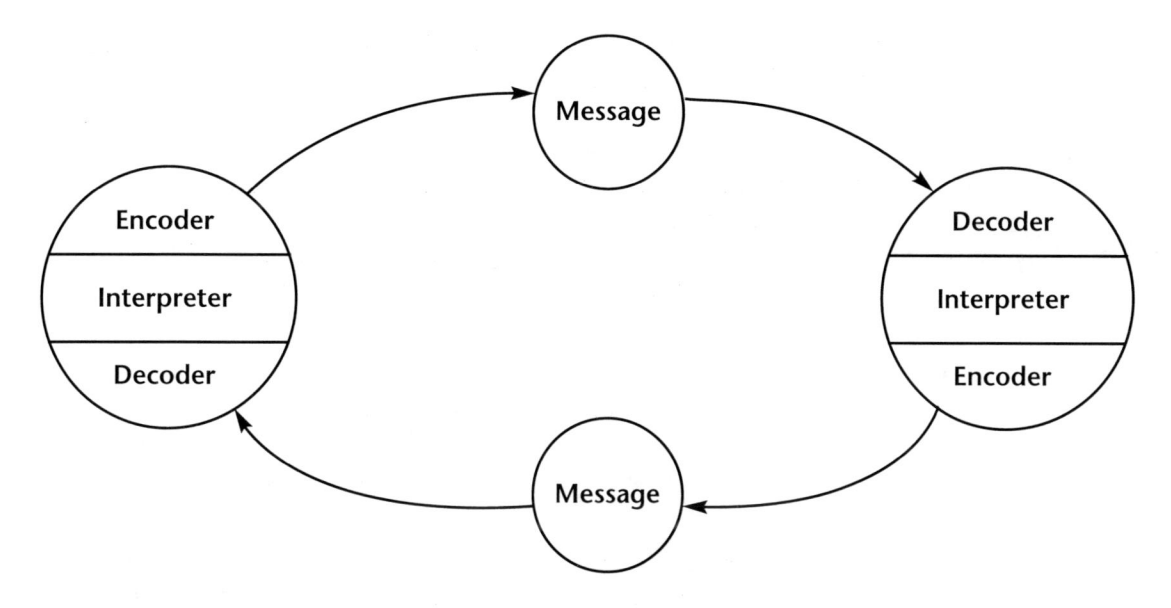

```
                    ┌─────────┐
                    │ Message │
                    └─────────┘
   ┌──────────┐                      ┌──────────┐
   │ Encoder  │                      │ Decoder  │
   ├──────────┤                      ├──────────┤
   │Interpreter│                     │Interpreter│
   ├──────────┤                      ├──────────┤
   │ Decoder  │                      │ Encoder  │
   └──────────┘                      └──────────┘
                    ┌─────────┐
                    │ Message │
                    └─────────┘
```

> **QUESTIONS**
> How do you perceive the role of listening? What is your philosophy regarding listening among students in your classroom?
>
> *Your Answer:*

When the teacher employs discussion or questioning techniques in the class (often during lecture), feedback helps the teacher to know whether students are engaged and learning. Numerous methods exist to get that feedback (see Competency 8), but the most common method of gaining feedback consists of watching student behavior.

It should be noted that the English Language Arts TEKS emphasize that speaking and listening—two of the four ELA skills—be taught at every academic level. Therefore, it is important that the *listener* be taken into account when planning lessons. (The other two skills are reading and writing.)

Discussion

When teachers write out lesson plans, they often write the word *discussion* into the lesson; yet, what actually happens during class has little resemblance to a real discussion.

Discussion is often scripted into lesson plans with one word: *discussion*. What follows in the context of a lecture may be called *discussion* but would fail abysmally as *rich discussion*. Rich discussion must be orchestrated as carefully as the lecture.

Points in the lecture where discussion can be provoked must be identified and structured in such a way to elicit comments, observations, disagreements, and arguments from most of the students in the class. While this

Competency 7 Communication

rich exchange of ideas is what teachers want and should strive for, few achieve it. When it does happen, students become excited about subjects and often want to know more. Rarely does this type of discussion take place spontaneously.

This is a good place to insert the Devil's Advocate argument. Teachers can often play the role of the devil's advocate (meaning they can take the opposite view of any student comment just to cause the student to justify his answer). Often playing the devil's advocate will cause other students to jump into the fray as well. I think it is advisable to tell students from time to time that you really like to play this role because it forces students to think about their beliefs as they are arguing for them.

Following are some tips to determine whether to call classroom response recitation or discussion in the classroom.

Identifying Role Response vs. Discussion

Recitation:

- ✦ Works well for concepts that focus on knowledge and comprehension (LOTS)
- ✦ Can help determine whether the group understands the main concepts or has the necessary background knowledge for future lessons and for higher cognitive activities (HOTS)
- ✦ In groups, does not allow for the knowledge of individual students to be checked

GOOD Discussion:

- ✦ Works well if students have the necessary prior knowledge (whether this is the result of their own experience or previous learning)
- ✦ Should vary the cognitive levels of questions geared toward higher-order thinking skills (HOTS)
- ✦ Employs Socratic questioning strategies that lead students to discover their own relationships. Socratic questioning allows students to understand complex or controversial topics better.
- ✦ Begins with open-ended questions that have no "right" answers. As a result the teacher will accept multiple interpretations of issues. This type of questioning teaches students to respect the opinions of others as well as to support their own views with cogent facts and logic.
- ✦ Keeps discussions focused on the issues
- ✦ Allows teachers to call on students from all parts of the room rather than focusing on the front and middle of the class
  - ◇ NOTE: Teachers who are right-handed frequently tend to favor the right-hand side of the room more than the left side; the converse of this tendency is often the case for left-handed teachers.
  - ◇ NOTE: Teachers often call on boys more than they call on girls. Include students of both genders.

QUESTION
Using group discussion, recall teachers who have used lecture as well as teachers who have involved you in classroom discussion. Was your learning/interest different? Did some teachers tend to call upon boys more than girls, or did they favor one side of the room over the other? What will you do?

Your Answer:

THE LECTURE AND THE SPEECH

If the lecture is so maligned as a poor teaching method, why does it continue to be the favored method of delivery? The lecture is simply the easiest way to transmit information. With so many demands on academic learning time (ALT), teachers often feel pressured to disseminate information. It boils down to quantity vs. quality. When this thinking becomes dangerous, the teacher may erroneously feel secure that information has been transmitted and that students are now responsible for it.

The good news is that many ways to lecture exist, just as there are ways to be creative with speeches. Remember, the basic components of a speech are introduction, body, and conclusion. Each of these components is similar to the basic teaching model found in the planning chapter. The introduction is similar to the focus or set and transition; the body contains the instructional input; and the conclusion is similar to the closure and assignment/independent practice phase. Even though both the speech and the lecture rely upon nonverbal input from the audience, a speaker (teacher) can never be quite sure she has taught the audience anything. The teacher must be sure she teaches for understanding. This is where the two differ. Teaching for understanding demands response from the audience.

In planning a lesson, one can use several literary devices: repetition, effective transitions, and internal summaries. One can experiment with phrases and fragments. The teacher can use concrete words, (using abstract terms to enrich), colorful language, language that appeals to the senses (remember how we learn), and devices often found in literature: similes, metaphors, analogies, alliteration, and other figures of speech.

Teachers should always use appropriate language for the audience and subject being aware of both denotative and connotative meanings. Just like one is coached in writing, teachers should use language accurately and try to use active voice.

Repeating key words, phrases, or sentences at various intervals will help students learn how to take notes. Providing students with graphic organizers, such as two-column notes, will also help students learn to take notes they can later use for studying.

Following are some of the terms that might be used to create interesting lectures/discussions. Speech profits from use of colorful language just as writing does. Most of these terms you will recognize from English classes you have had, but now they have new relevance to you, the teacher.

Vocabulary

- Style, jargon, irony
- Rhetorical device
- Contractions, cliché
- Biased language
- Colloquial expression
- Sexist pronoun
- Persons w/ disabilities
- Cultural intelligence
- Concrete, abstract
- Repetition, anaphora
- Alliteration, hackneyed
- Figure of speech, metaphor
- Mixed metaphor
- Analogy, parallelism
- Personification
- Understatement
- Allusion, hyperbole
- Onomatopoeia, simile
- Malapropism, triads
- Denotation/connotation
- Active voice, hedges
- Tag questions, antithesis

EFFECTIVE QUESTIONING TECHNIQUES

> **QUESTION**
> Is it effective to close a lesson by asking, "Are there any questions?"
>
> *Answer:* One of two things usually happens when vague questions like this are asked. One is that no one will ask anything at all—even if a question is hanging out there. Two is that someone, usually the best student in the class, will ask a question and everyone else in the class groans out loud and says, "Shut up, (insert name). It's time to go!"
>
> **QUESTIONS**
> What is an effective question? Is it one that elicits a great amount of discussion?
> Is it one that elicits the right answer? Are higher-order thinking skills always
> promoted by effective questions? Can a question be a dead end to further discussion?
> Give examples.

Certainly most students have experienced enough questions throughout their educational careers to answer these primary questions. Yet, the final definition to effective questions may not be that simple. Perhaps we must define "effective" before we can define an "effective question."

The icon of effective questioning, Socratic questioning, has been around, well, since Socrates. If Plato has it right, Socrates wandered around the streets of ancient Greece with some eight to ten young men in tow asking questions meant to elicit truth. So, *truth,* to Socrates was *effective.* In reading *The Republic,* one gets a sense of what these extensive questioning sessions were like. Socrates often focused on one or two young men at a time, so imagine what would happen to the other twenty students in today's seventh-grade classroom! Socrates was hardly limited by a bell ringing at fifty-minute intervals or lining up for a fire drill right in the middle of a math test! So, effective, in this sense, is finding the truth through an extended (sometimes torturous) line of questions and answers. That process seems a little heady for middle schoolers! Much less elementary lads.

Effective, then, in questioning today, illuminates the truth that the teacher wants to get across to students. That truth may occur in short order or it may take a little longer to accomplish, but it is essential that students be *involved* in the questioning process. Of critical importance is that the teacher must structure questions that are not dead-end questions. Instead, they must be questions that elicit opinion, fact, and evidentiary support. Such questions must be written out ahead of time. Once such questions are written and asked, teachers must practice *waiting* for the answer and coaching or **cueing** to elicit extended answers.

Wait Time

Most teachers believe they ask a lot of questions in the traditional classroom, but research shows that not only are questions infrequently asked, they are seldom designed to carry through to the inductive process mandated in the concept of inquiry as learning (e.g., getting to the *truth*). Research also shows that teachers often fail to give students enough time to answer, so students are discouraged from trying to answer once the Q&A pattern becomes established in the classroom. Did I mention that teachers often answer their own questions? The rule of thumb for **wait time** is three to five seconds. For some reason, teachers are uncomfortable with silence, but silence is not only necessary to allow for thinking, it is a method of managing classroom behavior. Ever notice how things get really, really quiet when a teacher asks a question?

It is safe to say that a few spontaneous questions promote elaborate discussions that produce those "Aha" moments of truth. It is also safe to say that teachers should work diligently to learn to ask good questions and then wait for answers.

Bloom's Taxonomy

In an earlier chapter, you were introduced to Benjamin Bloom and the Cognitive Taxonomy. Recall that the taxonomy has six levels: knowledge, comprehension, application, analysis, synthesis, and evaluation. Teachers can learn to write effective questions using that taxonomy.

By using Bloom's Taxonomy, you can focus on the levels of thinking you want your students to improve upon. This hierarchical system of thinking organization allows you to write and ask the kinds of questions you want to ask to assure yourself that students are working up to potential. Be assured that it takes a great deal of skill and practice to learn to write/ask good (effective) questions.

Divided into higher- and lower-level questions, the lower-level questions usually check for basic knowledge and comprehension or summarizing information. It is estimated that anywhere from 60–70 percent of all questions asked are lower level.

$$\left.\begin{array}{l} L \\ O \\ Ts \end{array}\right\} \text{LOTS}$$

$$\left.\begin{array}{l} H \\ O \\ Ts \end{array}\right\} \text{HOTS}$$

LOTs stands for lower-order thinking skills, and HOTs stands for higher-order thinking skills. I use this diagram "Lots of Hots" to help students remember to ask lots of higher-order thinking skills-type questions and as a reminder to keep from asking knowledge-level questions all the time. If too many class/test questions are lower-level questions, a new question arises. Do students do poorly on essay exams because they have had no rehearsal in expressing their thoughts in higher-order fashion?

Reminders

Keep from asking students too many closed questions. **Closed questions** are those to which there are a limited number of responses.

An example of a closed question is "What is the definition of a noun?"

When teachers ask too many of these kinds of questions, students who don't know the answer simply learn to wait for someone else to answer. There will always be that one student who knows the answer. Often, to the dismay of the teacher, this one student answers all the questions.

On the other hand, **open questions** may have a lot of answers, and most students can be **cued** to respond at least in a limited fashion.

An example of an open question is "Give an example of a noun." If a student responds *frighten,* the teacher might say (cue), "Is that the name of a place? A thing? Name?"

If the student says "No," then the teacher prompts again. "Will you give me the name of a friend?" This dialog goes back and forth until the student gives the correct answer.

---

adapted from first book

Teacher Responses

Teacher responses to questions can have a motivating impact or they can have a shut-down reaction. If students are encouraged to respond orally, it must be clear that all students are expected to answer. Sometimes, that means saying, "If you have already answered today, please wait until I call upon you again." To facilitate this procedure, some teachers have 3 × 5 cards with all the students' names on them; they simply work through the shuffled deck of cards. Other teachers write each student's name on a popsicle stick and draw names from a jar.

When students who normally do not answer are asked to respond, they may say something like, "I don't know."

> **TEACHER:** What is an example of a noun?
> **STUDENT:** I don't know. (This part of the process might take two or three times, but eventually, the student will answer.)
> **TEACHER:** I know you think you don't know, but if you did, what would you say?
> **STUDENT:** Well, I would say it is the name of something.
> **TEACHER:** Can you name "something?"

The conversation might need to go on another moment or two to elicit an answer from the student, and teachers must be careful not to escalate a situation like this one to a disciplinary level. (Remember how many problems teachers can cause?)

Urging a student to answer a question is similar to correcting a student's answers. The teacher must be extremely careful to respond to students in such a way that students do not become angry and shut down or become frustrated and nonresponsive. The following suggestions provide helpful hints for responding to incorrect answers.

1. Dignify the incorrect response by supplying the question to the answer that the student gave.

   For example, if a student responds that "Lincoln cut down the cherry tree" to the question "Who cut down the cherry tree?" the teacher might say, "You're thinking of another president—one who gave the Gettysburg Address. Can you think of another president . . .?"

2. Dignify the incorrect answer by rephrasing the question.

   For example, in response to the same question as above, the teacher might say, "Let's see, the President I am thinking of also had wooden teeth!"

3. Dignify the incorrect answer by putting the question in other terms.

   ✦ Which President cut down the cherry tree and was also the first President of the United States?

4. Continue to prompt the student until she is successful.

QUESTION
Give an example of a question to which a student gives the wrong answer.
Then provide additional questions with subtle clues/cues that can prompt a correct answer.

Actually, the responses to items 1, 2, 3, and 4 are correctly handled. When asked to think of your own example, did you have a difficult time thinking of a question and writing examples? It takes practice to employ the patience needed to motivate reluctant students to answer. While you are coaching a student to the correct answer, here are a couple of things to remember:

+ Avoid moving on to another student even if another student is dancing in his seat to answer;
+ Avoid making the student guess.

Once the correct answer is given, the teacher should repeat the answer, then clarify and extend on the answer if warranted.

The teacher must also determine whether the student truly does not know the answer and cannot move forward. If that is the case, the teacher provides help by giving the student some control over the situation. Ask the student to explain "where" he is in the lesson or ask the student to verbalize what he does understand about the problem in question. That verbalization can jump start a reluctant responder's thinking and help him move forward.

Finally, do not stay too long with one student. Extended questioning reaches a point of diminishing returns and risks losing the attention of the entire class.

Motivation

One of the most consistent questions future teachers ask is "How will I be able to motivate my students?" The answer to that is simply, "You can't!" However, that cursory statement is hardly the quitting point—it is the starting point. Preservice teachers need to know about two types of motivation: extrinsic and intrinsic. I would hazard a guess that most of you have intrinsic motivation. That is, you have looked at your employment options and interests and decided that teaching is a potential career. That *something* that pushes you into action is called intrinsic motivation: you want it, so you *work* to get it.

Still, it is certain that you can be further motivated by some external factors. Would you be more willing to take a class online if you knew the work was easier than the classroom? (or vice versa?) Would you be more willing to take a class where the teacher gave "blanket A's" for minimal work? Would you be willing to work hard in this class knowing you were assured of getting your dream job? All of these things have some extrinsic rewards. Within the public school classroom, however, the extrinsic rewards may be as simple as candy, pencils, stickers, or a Friday movie/popcorn day.

Your job researching motivation is to compare the temptation of "bribery" to get students to do what you want them to do versus developing a pride in doing work for work's sake. Remember researching Maslow's Hierarchy in the chapter on environment? Think about those levels of basic needs, and relate his theory of needs to a child's likelihood of motivation. Think, too, about what happens to the child when he gets to high school and he/she has had ten years of "gimmes" for learning. You are the high school teacher! What kind of students have you inherited? What's more, how will you motivate them?

The State of Texas recognizes that teachers must understand that the principles of **motivation** affect group and individual behavior. Ultimately, motivation affects learning so teachers must have enough understanding to promote student learning.

Teachers develop philosophies of motivation. For example, do you believe that everyone can learn? Why would one choose not to learn? Do you believe that teachers value students' opinions and ideas? If students don't participate in discussion and class inquiry, how do you know whether they are valued or not? Do you believe that teachers can give feedback that motivates students? Do you believe that teachers often teach to get jointly constructed meaning between the teacher and the student?

> **DEVELOPING AS A TEACHER**
> What is your philosophy of motivation? Further research the concepts of extrinsic and intrinsic motivation, then write your beliefs about it.
> (Include this "Motivation to Teach" in your ePortfolio.)
>
> *Your Answer:*

To someone without teaching experience, the tendency might be to answer *yes* to all of those questions, but after some experience, the answers might be a little more difficult. The beginning teacher might begin to work on creating motivation by writing original lessons that are relevant; that is, relevant lessons are situated in the students' own experiences. Teachers can also create motivation by helping students develop a sense of pride in their work. Finally, young teachers need to know about Effective Schools Research.

EFFECTIVE SCHOOLS RESEARCH

Effective Schools Research took place in the 1980s, but it is still relevant today. The final research report had six correlates including Instructional Leadership, Clear and Focused Mission, Safe and Orderly Environment, Climate of High Expectations, Frequent Monitoring of Student Progress, Positive Home-School Relations, and Opportunity to Learn and Student Time on Task. The fourth correlate, Climate of High Expectations, is relevant to this discussion. Teacher expectation is important to student achievement.

> "If you think you can or you think you can't, either way you're right!"
>
> *Henry Ford*

This quote embodies the heart of the teacher expectations research. It is the teacher's job to help students understand that they can do the work and to create a sense of *self-efficacy* within each of them. While pushing students forward, however, it is important that teaching must match students' abilities. Too complex material and few students succeed; too easy and few students succeed in meeting their potential. Numerous web sites exist featuring the correlates. Many scholarly articles on ESR can be found on ERIC.

COOPERATIVE LEARNING

Personal Communication within Classrooms

When asked whether they like group work or not, classes of students will often vote 50-50 yes-no; sometimes, there is a much stronger negative reaction to group work. Reasons given for hating group work are legend: "I have to do all the work, and people who do nothing get the same grade!" Reasons for loving group work are just as well known: "I enjoy having others to work with!"

From the group to the teacher, good group communication is essential to your success as a teacher. However, good communication is easier to *give lip service* to than it is to accomplish. Group communication is very tricky because groups will take on special characteristics according to the dynamics of the members. Suppose you wind up in a group made up of some of these characters:

Mr. Perfect: He is ALWAYS right!!! He is great at the art of ONE-UPSMANSHIP. He is also known as Super Cool, Big I, Junior God, Bragger.

Miss Do-It-All: She will be the leader! She will do it all (sigh) because no one else can do it up to her standards.

Miss Complainer: It is always too hot, too cold, too much work; or "No one ever helps ME." This person is known for her pickiness, negative attitude, and grumbling.

Mr. Put Down: He goes through life building himself up at the expense of others. He is aka Mr. Cut Down . . . he never fails to make examples of others . . . loudly.

Miss Jealousy: All sizes, shapes, ages, she can tell you so sweetly how happy she is for you . . . but JUST wait until she gets behind your back. She can become bitter and depressed.

Mr. Cynic: He thinks he has a great wit, but he is actually the two-edged sword of sarcasm. He does not trust himself much less others. His cracks are often followed by "I was just kidding. Boy, some people can't take a joke." (Least of all him!!)

Miss Moody: Her attitude fluctuates daily, like a kite blowing in the wind. One day she is happy, the next minute she is crying. She pouts, misinterprets your words or actions, and is unduly sensitive.

Mr. Phony: He comes on like gangbusters: "How Great Thou Art!" He gives the impression that he thinks, "I am snowing this babe!"

Miss Sick: She enjoys hurting others. She laughs at the misfortune of others and seems to deliberately enjoy destroying meaningful relationships. Her whole attitude often seems warped. She might also literally enjoy complaining about her health.

Mr. Negative: It won't work! THEY won't let us. Why try? Every time we think of.....!

Chicken Little: The sky is falling! EVERYBODY will think we are stupid; EVERYONE else does it! ALL of my friends think so.

Mr. Do-Nothing: He will do nothing. First, Miss Do-It-All has already declared herself, and because she always makes A's, the teacher obviously loves her. He will simply use the group time to daydream or catch up on other, more important classes.

You have probably been in one or more of these groups.

STUDENT QUESTION
How does a teacher create and maintain successful group work knowing full well that the potential for most of these characters exists in her classroom?

Your Answer:

The answer to this question is that the teacher must design group work meticulously and play the "What If" game frequently. In other words, "what can go wrong, and if it does, how will I manage the issue?"

This competency requires that teachers realize that they are communicators first, then teachers of content. By recognizing that input (or the lesson) represents the model of a good informative speech, teachers can deliver meaningful lessons day after day.

Some specific types of communication that a teacher will need to practice are the following:

Inquiry, questioning	Higher-order thinking	Giving examples
Problem solving	Giving directions	Interpersonal skills
Wait time	Interpersonal skills	Giving feedback
Correcting verbal responses	Establishing rules, routines, procedures	

INDEPENDENT PRACTICE AND MODELING (HOMEWORK)

1. **Scholar's Vocabulary:** Using the State-produced list of proficiencies preservice teachers should have related to Competency 7, highlight terms you wish to place in your interactive glossary. You should have a minimum of five terms from C7. (See the model in the Appendices.)

2. **Reflective Writing:** Using the eleven-sentence model in the Appendices, write a reflection on Competency 7.

3. Write a three-minute speech (about 2.5 pages) introducing yourself to your students on the first day. Be sure to indicate the grade level of the students and subject matter you are teaching.

4. Create a PPT to go along with your speech of self-introduction. Use personal artifacts in this PPT. NOTE: Assignments 3 and 4 may be used under the "credentials" part of the ePortfolio (all about me), and/or they may be used as evidence for Competency 7.

5. Give an example of a question, an incorrect response, and a rephrased question that will help the student get on track.

6. Ask a principal for a copy of the teacher evaluation instrument that s/he uses to evaluate teachers' teaching ability (called the PDAS). Review this form carefully (this is most likely how you will be evaluated). Compare this form to the basic speech model, which includes feedback. (You may use the "T" Chart model found in Suggestions for Additional Assignments.)

CLOSURE/FOLLOW-UP

One of the objectives for this chapter is to get you to draw parallels between the act of teaching and speech communications models. Rethink the communications models from the simplest, one-dimensional model to the most complex model you may have seen in a speech textbook (you can also research many models online). Note the emphasis on the listener in every modern model—the audience. One of the best rules for preparing a speech is to know your audience. Prepare for them, and speak directly to them. Yet, this rule is often overlooked because students in speech classes are speaking to their peers—every time! When it comes to your classroom, however, you cannot overlook identifying the different groups of students in your classroom. Almost every competency/proficiency that the State requires of its teachers connects to *developmentally appropriate instruction*. In fact, this one rule of *knowing your audience* may undergird your success as a teacher.

ASSESSMENT

Ask yourself whether you have mastered these objectives.

- **Objective 1:** I can compare the basics of public speaking with teacher communication.
- **Objective 2:** I can compare one communication model with the 9-step lesson plan format discussed in an earlier chapter.
- **Objective 3:** I know how to create significant class discussion.
- **Objective 4:** I can demonstrate appropriate questioning techniques.
- **Objective 5:** I can demonstrate positive responses to students' incorrect responses.
- **Objective 6:** I can design for maximum participation in cooperative learning groups as a teaching technique.

PRACTICE QUESTIONS

1. Miss Alacon believes that her fourth-grade classroom is fine with very little decoration or color. She is a strict authoritarian disciplinarian and thinks that children should learn how to function in all kinds of environments and that to provide bells and whistles just confuses them and gives them a sense of expectation. Furthermore, as an emigrant, she believes that children learn dependence that, in turn, encourages laziness and creates expectations within the child that can never be met. Her children do very well on exit exams, and she has no parental problems. Miss Alacon probably:
   a. praises the children through words, eye contact, and smiles.
   b. feels that praise "spoils the child."
   c. disciplines consistently creating an atmosphere of fear, thus learning.
   d. never hesitates to mark "F" for poor work.

2. Mrs. Remmer is an excellent speaker who uses excited bodily movement and eye contact. She shows superior vocal ability in her English classes. She tells the most interesting stories from her homeland and speaks with a pleasing tone. However, English literature is not Mrs. Remmer's first field of study, so she has to use the textbook each and every day.

   On the other hand, Mrs. Longfellow is an English teacher who specialized in English literature. She is not incredibly enthusiastic, and she teaches sitting at a lectern. Her nonverbal communication is less effusive. However, she is able to explain difficult concepts independently without the help of a textbook. Which teacher is more effective and why?
   a. Mrs. Remmer: Form should be valued over content.
   b. Mrs. Remmer: Interest and enthusiasm help students learn better than teacher knowledge of a subject.
   c. Mrs. Longfellow: Has more in-depth knowledge of literature.
   d. Mrs. Longfellow: Calmness is more effective in traditional subjects.

3. During the last three weeks, Mr. Jimenez has taught about the Gulf of Mexico and cities near or on the gulf including the city of Corpus Christi, Texas, Mr. Jimenez' home town. He assigned four groups to research the history of this area and then prepare an oral report based on the information. In one group, there are two students that are very shy and who avoid speaking in front of the class every time they are asked to do so. This time, however, the oral report is an important part of the grade for the six weeks. What should Mr. Jimenez do to make the grading fair for all students? Mr. Jimenez should:
   a. not ask these shy students to talk in front of the class.
   b. allow the shy students to turn in a written report on their findings.
   c. should deduct points for each student not giving an oral report.
   d. construct an alternative assignment for these students requiring speaking competency.

148 Competency 7 Communication

4. There are twenty students in Mrs. Jacoby's seventh grade Texas History class located in Goliad, Texas, some 100 miles from San Antonio, the location of the Alamo. She is teaching lessons about the Alamo that will last three weeks. She wants the students to have a more hands-on approach, so that they will remember the Alamo throughout their lives. What is the best teaching strategy she can use to emphasize this learning experience?
    a. She can lecture about the missions of the area and show slides that she has taken on prior visits she has made.
    b. Group students and ask parents to take them to the various missions. Require students to take pictures and create PPT presentations on their visits.
    c. Create handouts utilizing materials she has gotten from the missions and from the Chamber of Commerce. Ask a local historian to speak to the students.
    d. Plan a field day to a local mission in Goliad located on the Battleground of one of the Texas wars and have the curator talk about similarities between the Alamo and his mission.

5. It is very important that teachers listen to students. We can learn a great deal about their experiences, their abilities, their families, and their ambitions if we choose to listen and be observant. What would be the most productive form of feedback to assure the students that you see them as real people?
    a. Caring concern, but careful not to get too personal.
    b. Corrective feedback on behavioral issues (you're the model).
    c. Positive feedback on every paper or report students do.
    d. Negative feedback when essential.

6. What form of communication is used between the teacher and the student?
    a. Cross-generational communication
    b. Need self-disclosure
    c. Relationship development
    d. None of the above

7. Ms. Theodore grouped her senior English students into groups of four to discuss the themes occurring in *Beowulf*. The teacher expected the individuals in each group to participate equally and actively. A few groups were not successful in their cooperative learning groups. A reason the groups did not succeed may be:
    a. each group member contributed different opinions to the topic.
    b. the instructions to the groups did not provide for equal participation.
    c. one person in each group took charge, refusing to allow other group members to assist.
    d. the assigned group members had personality conflicts.

8. Mr. Zavala is an experienced elementary teacher. He believes young students should not be required to remain seated all day long. Mr. Zavala incorporates hands-on activities, experiments, and demonstrations to help keep the attention of his students. Which type of method is Mr. Zavala using to educate his students?
    a. Active student participation
    b. Passive student participation
    c. Cooperative learning groups
    d. Feedback techniques

9. Mr. Butterworth, a fifth-grade Social Studies teacher, wishes to incorporate cooperative learning groups into his Social Studies class. He learned in college that cooperative learning groups would promote communication of concepts of the materials to be learned. Because he is a new teacher and has never set up cooperative learning groups, which would be the best method of grouping his students and why?
    a. Group different ability levels together so the strong students can help those less able.
    b. Group them in alphabetical order to assure fairness.
    c. Group them into like-ability groups so the strong students can push each other to higher levels of achievement.
    d. Group the students randomly to assure that he is not showing favoritism or labeling his students.

10. As a new teacher, you are afraid that the classroom will get out of control if you allow casual conversation in the classroom, so you decide to limit communication in the classroom through rules. Philosophically, too, you believe that a quiet classroom is a productive and learning classroom. Should you consider changing your philosophy?
    a. No, students learn best when they are quiet.
    b. Yes, I could have guest speakers knowing students would be respectful and not take advantage.
    c. No, the principal emphasized that he did not need more students in the office, and heads would roll if they were sent.
    d. Yes, the nature of language includes being able to express oneself and validate learning.

CAREER PLANNING

Teachers who enjoy communications and demonstrate effective skills in working with students, parents, other teachers, and administrators can become involved with the system's communications services committees (sometimes called the Superintendent's Communication Committee) or even become a director of communications for a school district. If choosing to stay in the role of a teacher, these teachers often get to do special activities among faculty: they plan get-togethers and programs; they often get asked to make presentations to administration on behalf of faculty.

MATERIALS NEEDED

Internet

SUGGESTIONS FOR ADDITIONAL ASSIGNMENTS

"Teachers are communicators first; then, subject-specific trainers."

Dr. Braselton

1. "T" CHART

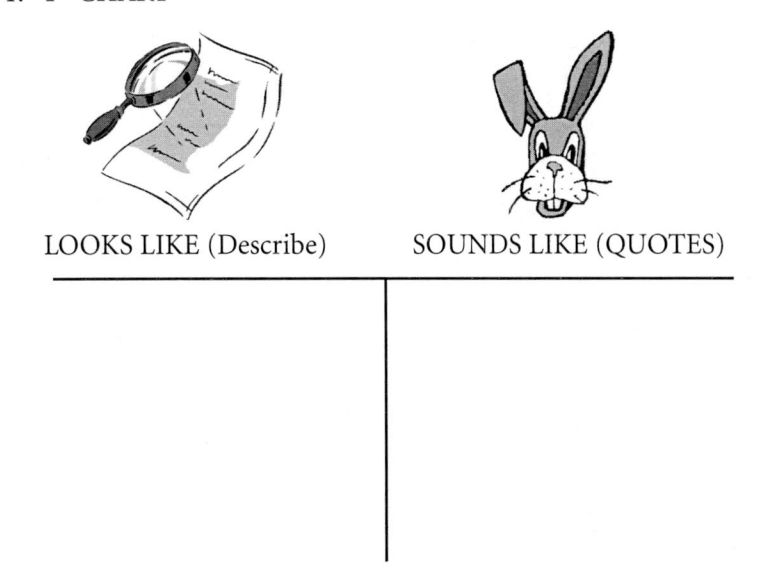

LOOKS LIKE (Describe)   SOUNDS LIKE (QUOTES)

The "T" Chart is a great graphic organizer that can be adapted for use with many assignments. In this assignment, recreate the chart and compare the 9-step teaching model with a common speech model.

2. Teaching in Parables: The reason for including this unusual literary device is to emphasize the need for careful planning when working on lecture material. The parable is just one literary device that is very effective in lectures.

   ✦ Jesus Christ was a master teacher and storyteller. He used literary devices to help listeners:
   ✦ remember his lessons,
   ✦ ponder them, and
   ✦ determine their responses.

   Think for a moment . . . isn't this the outcome you seek when you teach? You want students to remember the lesson, think about it (reflect), and figure out where they stand in relation to the information presented.

   Obviously, parables originated with the Greeks: Para: means *alongside* and Bl: means *throw* or *cast* (origin of "ball"). Literally, the parable is the earthly thrown alongside the heavenly. More clearly, the definition of a parable is an earthly story that has a heavenly meaning. However, the learning goes beyond the literal truth revealed. It works to help students flesh out their own beliefs and philosophies.

   Some characteristics of a parable include drawing unforgettable pictures (helping students visualize) and teaching undeniable lessons. Other characteristics are:

   ✦ makes a single point
   ✦ is plausible
   ✦ emphasis isn't on story, but ending
   ✦ figurative or allegorical elements
   ✦ one main point/few secondary points

- memorable metaphor/simile from everyday life
- enlighten and call for a response
- starts in Matthew 13:
    - mower/reaper (farming)
    - weeds
    - mustard seed
    - yeast

Your assignment is to research several of the parables in the bible to discover how brief and to the point each is. Then, create an example of your own secular parable for use in a lesson. HINT: Remember, the outcome is the truth you want to impart.

3. Remember several other literary devices from English class? These devices are also used in the bible.

    Hyperbole—an exaggeration intended to be taken figuratively rather than literally. Example: "And if your eye causes you to sin, pluck it out..."
    Metaphor—a comparison without using *like* or as. Example: "I am the vine; you are the branches..."
    Simile—a comparison using *like* or as. Example: "the kingdom of heaven is like treasure hidden in a field..."
    Proverb—a short, meaningful saying. Example: "Love your neighbor as yourself."
    Poetry—verse composition. Example: "Glory to God in the highest, and on earth peace to men on whom his favor rests."

    Your assignment is to use each of those literary devices as an introduction to a lesson on nouns. Be creative.

4. Practice writing good questions. Using Benjamin Bloom's Cognitive Taxonomy, choose one topic; then write six questions over the same topic but going from LOTS to HOTS.

    Second, after you write the six questions, practice asking each question aloud, and count five seconds of wait time. Get a feel for wait time, then write a brief reflection about the discipline it takes to wait that long for a response.

5. Suppose the questions you wrote for Assignment #4 were a test. Write the directions for Assignment #4 making it clear to students that they must use a correct essay format for their answers.

6. Research the nonverbal online usage known as *Netiquette*. Describe in written form how you would know improper nonverbal responses. Describe in written form how you will know whether a student understands your "lecture."

7. Describe active listening, and give at least two ways you can facilitate active listening in a classroom.

8. Identify several web sites that discuss motivation; identify themes that run through these web sites. Write a short philosophy of motivation.

9. Develop your personal theory about motivation; that is, what do you think motivates students and under what circumstances?

10. Connect Maslow's Hierarchy of Needs to motivation in a written essay.

Competency 7 Communication

11. What does the theory "constructivism" (based upon Piagetian concepts) mean? Connect constructivism to motivation in essay form.

12. What motivates you? Analyze your personal motivational attributes, and write a short essay describing the same.

13. Compose a list of ten ways to introduce a lecture. Now from an earlier lesson plan that you wrote, use three of those ways to introduce the SAME lesson.

Competency 8

Active Engagement

LESSON PLAN FOR COMPETENCY 8

STATE STANDARDS: STANDARD 3, COMPETENCY 8

Competency 008: The teacher provides appropriate instruction that **actively engages** students in the learning process.

STATE TEACHER PROFICIENCIES

Competency 008

The teacher provides appropriate instruction that actively engages students in the learning process.

The beginning teacher:

- Employs various **instructional techniques** (e.g., **discussion, inquiry, problem solving**) and varies teacher and student roles in the instructional process, and provides instruction that promotes intellectual involvement and **active student engagement** and learning.
- Applies various **strategies** to promote student engagement and learning (e.g., by structuring lessons effectively, using **flexible instructional groupings, pacing lessons** flexibly in response to student needs, including **wait time**).
- Presents content to students in ways that are **relevant** and meaningful and that link with students' prior knowledge and experience.
- Applies criteria for **evaluating** the appropriateness of instructional activities, **materials, resources, and technologies** for students with varied characteristics and needs.
- Engages in continuous **monitoring of instructional effectiveness.**
- Applies knowledge of different types of **motivation** (i.e., internal, external) and factors affecting student motivation.
- Employs effective **motivational strategies** and encourages students' self-motivation.

TEACHING OBJECTIVES

At the end of the lesson, the student should be able to:

- Define active engagement.
- Create a plan which motivates learners.
- Identify types of instruction.
- Design lesson plans that feature active engagement.
- Apply problem-solving strategies to lesson objectives.
- Understand the connection between teacher expectation and student performance (Effective Schools Research).
- Applying knowledge of learner's preferred styles to lessons.
- Practicing positive feedback by:
  - Valuing students' opinions, ideas, comments
    - Developing a sense of pride in students
  - Situate learning in students' own experiences
  - Providing opportunity for jointly constructed meaning

C8 KEY WORDS: ACTIVE LEARNING

The following terms are often associated with active learning. Create your own glossary for these terms by accessing at least one good web site for each term and defining each term from the web site.

Terms associated with active learning

Cooperative/Collaborative Learning	Problem Solving	Instruction
Hands-on Learning	Discovery Learning	Constructivist Learning
Teaching Styles	Learning Styles	Motivation
Didactic	Deductive	Inductive
Thematic	Brainstorming	Meaningful Reception Learning
Dale's Cone of Learning		

INTRODUCTION/FOCUS

> "Coming together is a beginning.
> Keeping together is progress.
> Working together is success."
>
> *Henry Ford*

A teacher opened a lesson on context with this demonstration. She divided the students into four groups and secretly gave each group one of the following artifacts:

Group 1: a colored picture of an apple
Group 2: a block outline of an apple
Group 3: a plastic apple
Group 4: a real apple

Each group worked together to describe the artifact they had been given, and after a brief time, each group stood, revealed the artifact and described it to the rest of the class.

The teacher asked the class as a whole, "Which group described its artifact the best?" The answer was overwhelmingly Group 4. The teacher then asked "Why was the description of the real apple the best?" The students answered "Because the apple is real. All we had was paper and plastic!"

TRANSITION: This "apple" demonstration shows that there is no substitute for the real thing. Once children have a *context* for learning, they have more meaningful learning. Teachers should try to replicate this concept in lesson planning. This competency focuses on active engagement.

INSTRUCTIONAL INPUT AND GUIDED PRACTICE

What we need to know about active engagement

The Instructional Input in this lesson plan will contain *guided practice* in the form of questions placed throughout the chapter. References to web sites will also serve as guided practice as you research topics to gain further knowledge and information and application.

BEGIN AT THE BEGINNING

State Proficiency #1 States That the Teacher:

✦ Employs various **instructional techniques** (e.g., **discussion, inquiry, problem solving**) and varies teacher and student roles in the instructional process, and provides instruction that promotes intellectual involvement and **active student engagement** and learning.

Instructional Techniques

Some terms related to instruction include **didactic** (which is teacher centered); **deductive** (which moves from general to specific); **inductive** (which moves from specific to general); **thematic instruction,** and **collaborative or cooperative learning.** From previous chapters, one might believe that lecture is the only way to teach. Lecture is a strategy, as previously discussed, and it is the prime example of **didactic teaching.** In fact, didactic means the art or science of teaching. The didactic lecture may be subdivided into deductive- or inductive-type lessons that may be designed around themes and utilize collaboration or cooperative learning.

Work that students must accomplish might move **deductively** from general to specific. For example, in a study of "wars," the class moves to the study of individual wars such as the War of 1812. Another example might be to study "parables" as a subject, then move to individual parables as examples. If the lesson is **inductive,** it moves from specific to general. For example, "Sweet 'n Low" and "Equal" are types of artificial sweeteners. Another example is the thirteen competencies. Each competency is a specific example of proficiencies the State of Texas wants you to know in the more general standards.

Thematic instruction may work within the classroom or across the entire school. For example, if the site-based team at an elementary school decides to study dinosaurs for a semester, the science classes study dinosaurs, the math classes count dinosaurs, and the English classes read stories about dinosaurs.

The teacher can also plan lessons that require students to work together collaboratively or cooperatively. The process of setting up collaboration or cooperative learning groups has been discussed from the standpoint of planning. In this chapter, cooperation and collaboration refers specifically to active learning.

In an earlier chapter on developing good discussion, methods of inquiry and problem solving were discussed. In this chapter, these terms arise again—this time almost as a mandate to teachers to integrate each of these methods of instruction because they "promote intellectual involvement and active student engagement."

Often called by different names, **problem solving** is a mainstay strategy of most science classrooms. However, all content areas can utilize one of the basic formulae for solving problems. A basic problem-solving formula for any class might be composed of these seven steps:

1. Define and identify the problem
2. Analyze the problem
3. Identify possible solutions
4. Select the best solutions

5. Evaluate solutions
6. Develop an action plan
7. Implement the solution

Applied in an English or History classroom, however, the "problem solving" might be called "brainstorming" or "**inquiry.**" When students brainstorm an issue, they do these things that convey the same principles as basic problem solving:

- Define a problem
- Collect thoughts
- Try for quantity, not quality
- Review thoughts
- Evaluate thoughts
- Edit and focus

Still another method for problem solving is given by Billstein, Libeskind, and Lott when they revised Polya's 1945 formula for solving problems in their Four-Step Process.

1. Understanding the problem
2. Devising a plan
3. Carrying out the plan
4. Looking back

Teachers can help with the successful completion of the problem-solving process by providing clear instructions, clearly structured problems, graphic organizers, and explaining the problem-solving model as it relates to the problem at hand.

Well-Structured vs. Ill-Structured Problems

Much emphasis is placed on writing good problems to be solved or good inquiry starters, so the following definitions of both terms should be helpful. Note that the ill-structured problem does not necessarily mean one that is poorly written.

A **well-structured problem** is one that leads to a correct answer that is found through the application of a certain process.

Example: Solve an algebraic equation for x.

> **NOTE**
> Teachers may utilize a type of grouping for well-structured problems called STAD (Student Teams-Achievement Divisions). STAD works well with direct instruction leading toward a correct answer (e.g., math problem). Students are grouped in such a manner that they can assist each other in learning the concepts leading to the correct answer. Students test individually.

On the other hand, an **ill-structured problem** does not lead to one certain answer. At the end of the research of an ill-structured problem, researchers may not come to consensus; rather, they may construct new hypotheses for further research. This type of problem can lead to rich discussion and opposing views on outcomes.

Example: Determine the three main reasons for World War II.

Five sample questions for getting at the answer:

1. What did you see? Notice? Observe?
2. How are these things alike? How are they different?
3. Why?
4. What would happen if . . .?
5. How do you know?

As you can see, these questions require higher-order thinking. Used repeatedly in class, these questions teach students that they need to read with these purposes in mind. Teachers might even print these questions on a 3 × 5 card, give one to each student, and remind them as they begin to read, "These are the questions I will ask at the end of reading."

> **QUESTION**
>
> Do you have a favorite method for solving problems? Select one of the three models discussed, and explain why the order of the steps is critical to successful completion of the assignment.

SEATWORK

Teachers give seatwork on a daily basis, so a discussion of the purposes and problems is in order.
The purpose(s) of seatwork can vary. Teachers may wish students to:

+ practice skills and apply concepts;
+ provide students with opportunities to ask questions; or
+ check for student understanding.

Several problems are associated with seatwork, however.

+ When teachers make irrelevant assignments (busy work) or assignments that are not educationally sound, students quickly identify the work as busy work and lose motivation.
+ When teachers give assignments that are not within the Zone of Proximal Development (ZPD), students can be bored or challenged beyond their means of achievement.
+ When teachers do not give clear directions and seem unapproachable by students, students will "zone out" and deem the assignment undoable or not important.
+ When teachers give seatwork and return to their desks to do other tasks, students can misbehave because they are not monitored.

Someone once said that "Students respect what teachers inspect!" Apply that caveat to finding solutions to making seatwork successful.

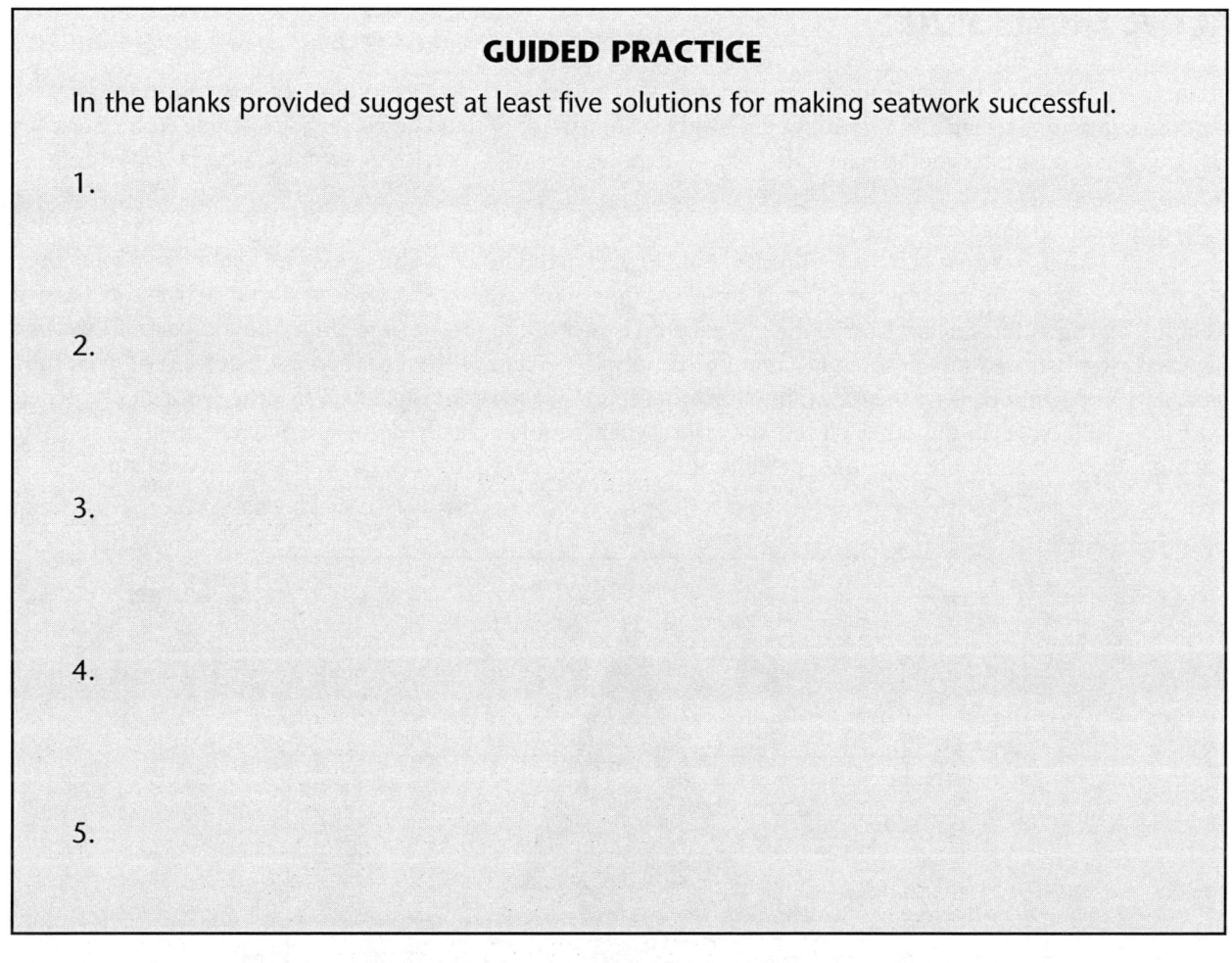

> **GUIDED PRACTICE**
>
> In the blanks provided suggest at least five solutions for making seatwork successful.
>
> 1.
>
> 2.
>
> 3.
>
> 4.
>
> 5.

Related to brainstorming or problem solving is constructivism or inquiry. Inquiry often begins with a question, problem, or hypothesis that must be researched. Establishing good **inquiry** parameters that are **relevant** to students will lead to learning.

When I was going through teacher training, the ONE word of advice every education professor gave was *relevance*. "Just make it relevant!" they would say, "and you will be successful." Although teacher training is now based on years of research and practice, that one word is still applicable to teaching today. Relevance means, simply, that whatever the subject, task, strategy of choice, the content and context must be something that the student can relate to from his own experience. When that relationship isn't made, students may as well be learning an ancient language.

> **Example:** I taught American literature in high school for several years. One year while introducing *The Crucible* written by Arthur Miller, I thought it would be interesting to mention that Miller had once been married to Marilyn Monroe—an American icon—a piece of Americana—a piece of American cultural literacy! Met by absolute blank stares, I realized immediately that Marilyn Monroe was simply not relevant to these students!
>
> **Example:** On the other hand, talking about a text message I had gotten from someone brought absolute response! "You text message?" Relevant.

ACTIVE ENGAGEMENT

Because teachers display their knowledge every time they teach a class, it is important that future teachers be exposed to teaching techniques that exemplify good teaching usage of that knowledge. By learning early in teacher training what constitutes good teaching delivery, student teachers can practice these skills at every opportunity.

Active (learning) engagement means students should be involved in their learning rather than passive observers. That means teachers should not expect students to be passive listeners while they expound/read/explain for long periods of time. Various researchers have written about active and passive teaching/learning, but Edgar Dale's Cone of Learning is one of the most interesting. The top part of this *cone* says that after two weeks, people tend to remember only 10 percent of what they read, 20 percent of what they hear, and 30 percent of what they see. This chart that follows labels this as *passive* learning—if it can be called learning at all. Note on the other end of the cone, when people actually *do* or are actively involved in their learning, they can remember up to 90 percent of it. That, according to Dale, constitutes active learning.

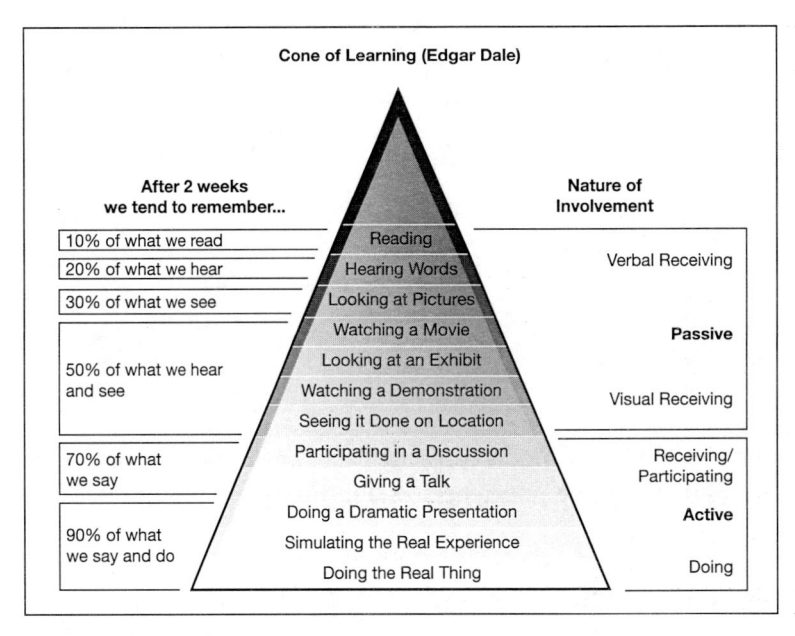

Cone of Learning (Edgar Dale)

After 2 weeks we tend to remember...		Nature of Involvement
10% of what we read	Reading	Verbal Receiving
20% of what we hear	Hearing Words	
30% of what we see	Looking at Pictures	**Passive**
50% of what we hear and see	Watching a Movie	
	Looking at an Exhibit	Visual Receiving
	Watching a Demonstration	
	Seeing it Done on Location	
70% of what we say	Participating in a Discussion	Receiving/ Participating
	Giving a Talk	**Active**
90% of what we say and do	Doing a Dramatic Presentation	
	Simulating the Real Experience	Doing
	Doing the Real Thing	

Adapted from Dale, *Audio-Visual Methods in Teaching*, 1E, © 1969 Wadsworth, a part of Cengage Learning, Inc. Reproduced by permission. www.cengage.com/permissions

Dale's Cone of Learning certainly reinforces the idea that teachers should strive to make lessons active or hands-on in order to help students learn more effectively. To create active lessons, teachers should have a repertoire of teaching strategies. Therefore, let's take a look at some of the following strategies and determine whether they require active or passive involvement.

QUESTION

Develop an example of a well-structured problem and an example of an ill-structured problem.

State Proficiency #2 States That the Teacher:

+ Applies various **strategies** to promote student engagement and learning (e.g., by structuring lessons effectively, using **flexible instructional groupings, pacing lessons** flexibly in response to student needs, including **wait time**).

GROWING AS A PROFESSIONAL

Describe a personal experience with cooperative learning. What is your philosophy of cooperative learning? What are the key components of cooperative learning? How can a cooperative structure enhance learning? Contrast competitive learning with cooperative learning. (Use a graphic organizer.)

Your Answer:

Flexible Instructional Groupings

Possible groupings of students for learning are many and varied. For example, you can utilize dyads (two students), triads (three students), or groupings of multiples of students. You can place less-capable students with stronger students for more peer coaching; you can utilize static groups or change groups as the need arises. All of these types of groups have advantages and disadvantages. The key to successful groupings is, once again, based on teacher planning and management of these events:

+ What is the problem to be solved?
+ What grouping is best suited to the solution?
    ◇ How will leaders/role players be identified?
+ How will you divide the group efficiently?
+ How seamlessly do the groups move into work?
+ How will you time the activity?
+ How will you monitor group progress?
+ How will you conclude the activity with the same ease of motion as groups were formed?
+ How will reports be given?
+ What is the class responsibility for learning the output from other groups? (See Jigsaw Strategy below.)

SAMPLES OF GROUP WORK STRATEGIES

Jigsaw

The Jigsaw Strategy is at first glance rather intimidating; however, it is well worth the effort because it provides for whole-class learning. Each student is assigned a portion of the main concept to learn and to teach to his/her peers; each student then learns about the entire concept as each peer assigned a specific topic teaches his/her section.

The strength of this strategy is that each person has an assignment and is responsible to his/her group peers as well as class peers.

Jigsaw II

Jigsaw II is similar to Jigsaw I; however, in this adaptation of the strategy, each student is provided an overview of the entire concept before being assigned a portion as in Jigsaw 1.

Again, the strength of this strategy is that each person has an assignment and is responsible to his/her peer group as well as class peers.

Group Investigation (or Group Inquiry)

The teacher places students into small group to investigate a clearly-defined topic. The students are then responsible for determining how to divide the tasks. As a check, teachers can ask for a short report outlining who has each task.

Teachers should set up clearly-defined evaluations: peer assessment, self-assessment, and teacher evaluation. As part of the assessment, the "recorder" of the group will keep a daily record of group accomplishment.

Example of Group Investigation Reporting

Self/Group Evaluation:

    Student A: Responsibilities

        Today I...:

Today we...:

Student B: Responsibilities

        Today I...:

Today we...:

Individual Peer Evaluation

Student A:

    Comments about his/her contributions

Student B:

    Comments about his/her contributions

Self-Evaluation

    Comments about your own contributions

State Proficiency #3 States That the Teacher:

✦ Presents content to students in ways that are **relevant** and meaningful and that link with students' prior knowledge and experience.

If materials you teach are not meaningful/relevant to students, no learning will take place. Every topic has a relevance, but that does not mean the students automatically relate to it.

State Proficiency #4 States That the Teacher:

✦ Applies criteria for **evaluating** the appropriateness of instructional activities, **materials, resources, and technologies** for students with varied characteristics and needs.

One of the major problems confronting new teachers is how to corral their enthusiasm and desire for a "fun classroom" into productive teaching practices (which can still be fun). Many preservice teachers criticize teachers they have had in the past for "not being fun" or "planning activities that were not fun." The intent to create "fun" activities must never overshadow the need for planning fun activities that have a teaching objective. Following are two evaluative questions that will help a teacher design fun lessons that are also effective.

✦ "Does the lesson match the TEKS/teacher objective?"
✦ "Did I follow through AFTER the activity to be sure students understand what they were to have learned?"

Competency 9 which follows deals specifically with resources and technology, and a portion of that chapter is devoted to the evaluation of resources.

State Proficiency #5 States That the Teacher:

✦ Engages in continuous **monitoring of instructional effectiveness.**

The importance of this proficiency should not be underestimated. There is increasing national conversation (as well as State) about connecting the results of your students' TAKS tests to your instructional effectiveness. The rationale is clear: if you are doing an effective job of teaching your students, they will do an effective job of taking and succeeding on any test the State deems appropriate.

To help you stay abreast of your own professional development toward becoming an effective teacher, each year, your school district will require you to complete forms describing the steps you have taken to increase your effectiveness and to evaluate the things you have done and how effective you believe them to be. These reports will become part of your personnel file and be used in part to determine your growth as a teacher.

If you are deemed ineffective by your evaluators, you may be required to go through additional training (either in-house or at a college) and testing. These extreme measures are intended to improve your teaching not to discourage you from being in the classroom.

State Proficiencies #6 and #7 State That the Teacher:

✦ Applies knowledge of different types of **motivation** (i.e., internal, external) and factors affecting student motivation.
✦ Employs effective **motivational strategies** and encourages students' self-motivation.

In an earlier chapter, motivation was discussed in terms of *extrinsic* and *intrinsic*. In this chapter, motivation once again becomes relevant because of the term *active engagement*. What is known about drawing students into the lesson is that the more interactive it is, the more motivating it is to students. Some of the connections made in active learning lessons are through:

✦ Peer teaching
✦ Discovery
✦ Relevance
✦ Graphic organizers
✦ Confidence
✦ Provocative questions
✦ Simulations

Modeling
Investigation
Getting ideas from others
Defending my point of view
Someone believes I can
Discrepancies
Music—movement

Step-by-step instructions
Dilemmas
Interpretation

Active engagement
Problems to solve
Inexplicable event

164   Competency 8   Active Engagement

- Process thinking by writing
- Repetition
- And CHOICES is the number 1 motivator.

Student-led discussions
Coherence (hear it in Math, Sci, Eng)

Argumentation
Inquiry

Guided Practice 1: Active or Passive?

Think, Pair, Share	Word Sorts	Directed Reading
SQ3R (or 4R)	K-W-L Charts	Q-Notes
Webbing	Maps	Problem-Solving
Mapping	Anticipation Guides	Acronyms
Venn Diagrams	Think Alouds	Outline

1. Pick a partner.
2. Choose one strategy from the list above.
3. Google the name of the strategy and read additional information about the strategy.
4. Report to the class whether and under what circumstances the strategy is active or passive.
5. Fill in the graphic organizer that follows.
6. Which circumstance do you prefer?
7. Compare your preferences with the class.

GRAPHIC ORGANIZER

Use with Guided Practice #1: Active or Passive?

Strategy?	Active?	Passive?

INDEPENDENT PRACTICE AND MODELING (HOMEWORK)

1. **Scholar's Vocabulary:** Using the State-produced list of proficiencies preservice teachers should have related to Competency 8, highlight terms you wish to place in your interactive glossary. You should have a minimum of five terms from C8. (See the model in the Appendices.)
2. **Reflective Writing:** Using the eleven-sentence model in the Appendices, write a reflection on Competency 8.
3. **Lesson Plan for Active Engagement with A-PTL:** Use this model to construct a lesson based on active engagement A- PTL.: Active Planning, Active Teaching, and Active Learning.

   Grade Level:

   Subject/Topic:

Active Planning	Active Teaching	Active Learning
In this column describe, using bullets, the active steps you will take in the planning process for this lesson.	In this column describe, using bullets, the active teaching process you will provide for the students in your class.	In this column describe, using bullets, the active learning processes students will use to learn the material you will teach.

   You have been exposed to a traditional lesson planning model in Chapter 3. Do not forget the parts of that model as you are planning for this active lesson. Be sure to develop this lesson on a specific topic and plan as though you will teach it tomorrow.

4. Find a current newspaper article from the *New York Times*.
   - Apply one of the strategies you learned about in Learning Activity 1 (you do not have to use the same one you used in Learning Activity 1) as you read the article.
   - Write one paragraph (at least five complete sentences) telling how this strategy helped you understand the article.
   - Discuss your findings with a Think, Pair, Share partner.
   - Expand the Think, Pair, Share to four students.
   - Revise your paragraph, thinking as needed.

5. CREATE A LESSON

The History of American Education

This is a peer-teaching assignment: Utilizing these parts of a traditional lesson plan for this assignment—teacher objectives, focus, input, guided practice (make clear the active part), closure, and assessment—create an ACTIVE lesson requiring student ENGAGEMENT on one of the following periods of educational American History:

1. (1607–1775) The Colonial Period
2. (1775–1820) The Early National Period
3. (1820–1865) The Common School Movement
4. (1890–1930) The Development of the American High School
5. (1940–present) Modern Schools and Nationalism

RULES

- *Active* means "hands on"; (use any strategy(ies) you wish).
- *Engagement* means the student must have a "product."
- Make the directions clear.
- Assessment: create a six-question assessment utilizing all six levels of Bloom's Taxonomy (KCAASE).
    ◇ Include sample answers for each question.
- Please document all references (including web sites) you use.

6. Create a timeline using Excel.

    Timelines cross many curriculum areas such as science, social studies, literature, mathematics, and technology. One can also use a timeline to outline the story of someone's life or historical events.

    Use a Microsoft Office Excel spreadsheet to create a timeline:

    1. Begin by making a rough draft of your timeline. (You may use the one you created in an earlier chapter.)
    2. Open an Excel spreadsheet.
    3. Type a title across the top of the spreadsheet, and format the text (Arial, 12 pt. preferred).
    4. Skip several rows and type in the days (Day 1/Day 2) and times (beginning bell/ending bell). (You will have two different spreadsheets; one for Day 1 and one for Day 2.)
    5. Type a short description of your predicted activity above or below the date or time cell.
    6. Format the description by clicking on the **format menu;** click **cells.** In the **format cells box,** click the **Alignment** tab, **and adjust the line orientation** according to the angle you wish. Click **OK.**
    7. Save your timeline periodically while you are working.
    8. Additional formatting can be added such as pictures, borders, fill color, or clip art.

Assignment: Create a timeline of your predicted activities for the first two days of school. Be sure to include enough detail; for example, if you are teaching a routine or a procedure, name the procedure and estimate the amount of time it will take to teach it to the class.

CLOSURE/FOLLOW-UP

Creating active lessons that require student engagement is a time-consuming task until you get the hang of it. The good news is that each successive year, you will create more and more active lessons and tweak the ones you did in previous years. Begin each lesson preparation with this thought in mind:

> "If I cannot lecture, how can I get this idea across to my students? Then, how can I assess it to be sure they learned what I wanted them to learn?"

Literally thousands of teaching, learning, reading, and study skills strategies exist on the Internet. By Googling any one of these terms, you can access a huge number of materials. Be aware that most will not be congruent with your teaching style, so use your imagination to create the lesson you want.

ASSESSMENT

Ask yourself whether you have mastered these objectives.

- ✦ **Objective 1:** Have I planned a lesson that motivates learners?
- ✦ **Objective 2:** How do I define active engagement?
- ✦ **Objective 3:** What are the types of instruction and their descriptions? identify and describe the types of instruction.
- ✦ **Objective 4:** Have I designed lesson plans that feature active engagement.
- ✦ **Objective 5:** What problem-solving strategies have I incorporated into active lessons?
- ✦ **Objective 6:** What is the connection between teacher expectation and student performance (Effective Schools Research).
- ✦ **Objective 7:** How have I demonstrated applied knowledge of a learners' preferred styles to lessons.
- ✦ **Objective 8:** What are some sample scenarios demonstrating positive feedback in the following ways:
  - ◇ Valuing students' opinions, ideas, comments
  - ◇ Developing a sense of pride in students
  - ◇ Situate learning in students' own experiences
  - ◇ Providing opportunity for jointly constructed meaning

PRACTICE QUESTIONS

1. Mr. Strain, a middle school teacher, tries all kinds of new techniques to enhance his students' learning. He is very creative, so he loves having his students write skits, simulations, and role plays. Sometimes he lectures a little bit, but he is careful to use good techniques for lecturing. He evaluates his students through authentic assessment using portfolios and art projects, and he uses cooperative learning wherever possible to meet his objectives. Mr. Strain seems to read current research and apply it, so he knows that in spite of all the good things that are written about cooperative learning:
   a. cooperative learning provides a very good social environment—and even if students get off task, they are learning how to get along.
   b. cooperative learning lessons are much more difficult to develop and take much more of his time.
   c. cooperative learning provides students with other ideas.
   d. cooperative learning promotes team effort.

2. Mrs. Lethargy notices with some relaxed interest that Mr. Strain's students are different from hers. He has excited kids in his classroom. However, she does not read much research because she has too many things to do at home, and, besides, she likes things quiet in her classroom. Still not convinced that she wants any part of the cooperative methods Mr. Strain uses to create all that excitement, she discovered in talking to Mr. Strain one day in the hallway, that she might try cooperative learning because it:
   a. is one way to increase students' dependability.
   b. is one way to make sure the project is done.
   c. provides some rest time for the teacher.
   d. breaks the monotony of the day-to-day activity.

3. Mr. Strain invites Mrs. Lethargy into his classroom for observation. He explains to her that cooperative learning may in fact:
   a. be a simple way to get all children involved.
   b. be designed to keep kids quietly on task.
   c. be more difficult to plan than other activities.
   d. make shy students extroverted.

168   Competency 8   Active Engagement

4. Ms. Wimbley teaches her English students to attack text a certain way: (1) skim the material; (2) construct questions about material; (3) read, using questions as guidelines; (4) think about what you have read; (5) answer questions; (6) organize information so you can remember it. What is this an example of?
   a. Outlining
   b. SQ4R study skills strategies
   c. Two-column notetaking
   d. Context clues

5. Mrs. Reynolds the eighth grade reading teacher is teaching her class how to map out stories. They are learning about the specific technique where they organize information of characteristics about the story. The information is webbed together and is called:
   a. graphic organizer.
   b. fishbone map.
   c. webbing and mapping.
   d. Both a and c.

6. Ms. Green stands in front of the class spoon feeding the students with a prepared lecture. She tells them the information in their Science textbook and often refers to the page number the information can be found on. The students are not required to respond, as all questions are rhetorical. The students are required to sit, listen, and take in all of the information the teacher is giving them. What type of presentation method is this?
   a. Inductive presentation by lecture
   b. Deductive presentation method
   c. Cooperative presentation method
   d. The Green method

7. Mr. Applegate is very exciting and interesting to listen to. His students love to come to his class and learn. Yesterday, he taught longitude and latitude and made the lesson relevant by telling students that, with his method, they could explain to someone how to find out exactly where they were in the wilderness without a map. He used a beach ball and a tennis ball to teach this lesson and guided students by asking lots of questions. Mr. Applegate asked specific questions in order to bring the students to the correct conclusion. What type of lecture is this?
   a. Traditional lecture
   b. Guided discovery learning lecture
   c. Jigsaw lecture
   d. Elaborative questioning lecture

8. Mrs. Mears presents a problem to the class, and the students have to explore alternative points of view and find acceptable solutions to the problem. What type of lecture style is this?
   a. Comparative lecture
   b. Formal oral essay
   c. provocative lecture
   d. Problem-centered lecture

9. Mrs. Reynolds knows that students need a great vocabulary to be good readers, so every spare moment she plays vocabulary games with her class. She keeps games such as vocabulary bingo, vocabulary concentration, and vocabulary hunt on the computer ready to go at a moment's notice. What is Mrs. Reynolds trying to do with all of the vocabulary games?
   a. Develop students' vocabulary
   b. Have fun while learning usage
   c. Pass the time to keep students occupied
   d. Currying favor with her students

10. Mr. Scharbauer always asks his students these five questions about lessons read or studied: (1) What did you see? Notice? Observe? (2) How are these things alike? How are they different? (3) Why? (4) What would happen if . . . ? and (5) How do you know? These questions are designed to get the class to think about what they are reading or studying beyond the knowledge level. This an example of what type of strategy?
    a. Advanced organizers
    b. Critical-thinking skills
    c. Notetaking
    d. Evaluations

CAREER PLANNING

Students who enjoy working with teaching strategies **and** like implementing new and exciting plans into lesson planning will enjoy graduate work in curriculum and instruction. They may become curriculum coaches, master teachers, or peer coaches for their campuses or districts.

MATERIALS NEEDED

colored picture of an apple; outline of an apple; a plastic apple; and a real apple; Internet

SUGGESTIONS FOR ADDITIONAL ASSIGNMENTS

Competency 8 stresses the importance of active engagement. Following are some activities that will enhance your understanding of this competency.

1. Define at least four instructional techniques (teaching styles: didactic). Set up a learning center based on each of the techniques.

2. How do you define engagement? Create a matrix (rubric) for the different levels of student engagement that you plan to assess.

3. Relevance "Who are your Students?" Each year, Beloit College publishes the Beloit College Mindset, which describes likely experiences each incoming class might know about. Access the following web site and do a little research.

    http://www.beloit.edu/mindset/2012.php

4. Create a matrix (rubric) that establishes your criteria for evaluating a written assignment.

5. Describe how you will use the informal evaluation process of monitoring. Write three different things you might say to get a student back on task.

6. Describe motivation strategies that you might use for an academic assignment.

7. Describe how you will teach for transfer of knowledge.

8. **Lesson Planning with a Constructivist Environment:** Utilizing the following format, complete a lesson plan with a partner:

Teachers' Names:

Grade Level:

Subject Area:

Lesson Title:

Standard:

Teacher Objective:

Teacher Preparation: Student knowledge needed prior to the lesson (vocabulary, math skills, etc.):

Instructional Strategy Model

What type of active learning model will you use? Cooperative/collaborative learning groups, problem-based task, project-based task, or other? Identify your strategy and then decide how you will arrange materials and the room.

Constructivist Instructional Principle

Which of the following constructivist principles will you use?

- O Identify learner's prior knowledge and experiences before setting up instruction—that is the student's context for scaffolding new learning;
- O Create the learning opportunity by utilizing active strategies;
- O Identify which of the senses will be paramount for the students to construct meaning;
- O Develop a process for learning new concepts presented in the learning objectives. How will students think about the concepts? test them? and create new knowledge (Dewey's reflective activity);
- O What opportunities for communication and social interaction will you prepare for students?; and
- O How much time and opportunity will you provide for new learning while remembering that it is internally controlled and mediated by the learner and it takes time.

> **PROCEDURE**
>
> Create your lesson plan by relating all desired learning back to your teaching objectives. Be sure to write clear instructions.
>
> **ASSESSMENT**
>
> How will you assess the learning? Informal (checking for understanding) and Formal?

1. As a chat group, decide on a topic and write a question for each level of **Bloom's Taxonomy.** Continue the activity with the same group and the same topic, and write a question for each level of the Affective Domain and the Psychomotor Domain as well.

2. Create a list of investigative teaching strategies.

3. Provide an overview of Bruner's approach to discovery learning, stressing the following points: active versus passive roles for the student; motivation; responsibility; creativity; initiative; insight; and techniques.

4. Outline Ausubel's Meaningful Reception Learning. Be sure to discuss the following terms: reception learning; rote learning; discovery learning; meaningful learning; advance organizers; and learner's set.

5. The following web site presents different teaching styles. Refer to the links for more information: http://web.indstate.edu/ctl/styles/tstyle/html

You may take an additional learning style inventory at this web site:

http://www.2.ncsu/edu/unity/lockers/users/f/felder/public/ILSdir/ilsweb.html

One way research speaks to the issue of teaching/learning styles is that teachers prefer to teach the way they learn. After taking these two inventories, document the styles and analyze them in this way:

✦ Is your learning style compatible with your teaching style?
✦ Do you agree/disagree with the statement "teachers prefer to teach the way they learn"? Explain.

Competency 9

Technology

LESSON PLAN FOR COMPETENCY 9

STATE STANDARDS: STANDARD 3, COMPETENCY 9

Competency 009: The teacher incorporates the **effective use of technology** to plan, organize, deliver, and evaluate instruction for all students.

STATE TEACHER PROFICIENCIES

Competency 009

The teacher incorporates the effective use of technology to plan, organize, deliver, and evaluate instruction for all students.

The beginning teacher:

- Demonstrates knowledge of basic terms and concepts of current technology (e.g., **hardware, software applications** and functions, **input/output devices,** networks).
- Understands issues related to the appropriate use of technology in society and follows guidelines for the **legal and ethical** use of technology and digital information (e.g., privacy guidelines, **copyright laws, acceptable use** policies).
- Applies procedures for acquiring, analyzing, and **evaluating electronic information** (e.g., locating information on networks, accessing and manipulating information from secondary storage and remote devices, using online help and other documentation, evaluating electronic information for accuracy and validity).
- Knows how to use task-appropriate tools and procedures to **synthesize knowledge,** create and modify solutions, and evaluate results to support the work of individuals and groups in problem-solving situations and **project-based learning activities** (e.g., planning, creating, and editing word processing documents, spreadsheet documents, and databases; using graphic tools; participating in electronic communities as learner, initiator, and contributor; sharing information through online communication).
- Knows how to use productivity tools to communicate information in various formats (e.g., **slide show, multimedia presentation, newsletter**) and applies procedures for publishing information in various ways (e.g., printed copy, monitor display, Internet document, video).
- Knows how to incorporate the effective use of **current technology; use technology applications in problem-solving** and decision-making situations; implement activities that emphasize **collaboration and teamwork;** and use developmentally appropriate instructional practices, activities, and materials to integrate the Technology Applications TEKS into the curriculum.
- Knows how to **evaluate students' technologically produced products** and projects using established **criteria** related to design, content delivery, audience, and relevance to assignment.
- Identifies and addresses **equity issues** related to the use of technology.

STATE TECHNOLOGY STANDARDS

The State of Texas has established a special set of Standards for Texas teachers.

Technology Applications Standards I–V

1. All teachers use technology-related terms, concepts, data input strategies, and ethical practices to make informed decisions about current technologies and their applications.
2. All teachers identify task requirements, apply search strategies, and use current technology to efficiently acquire, analyze, and evaluate a variety of electronic information.
3. All teachers use task-appropriate tools to synthesize knowledge, create and modify solutions, and evaluate results in a way that supports the work of individuals and groups in problem-solving situations.
4. All teachers communicate information in different formats and for diverse audiences.
5. All teachers know how to plan, organize, deliver, and evaluate instruction for all students that incorporates the effective use of current technology for teaching and integrating the Technology Applications Texas Essential Knowledge and Skills (TEKS) into the curriculum.

At this time, the State has four strands devoted to **technology applications:** (1) foundations, (2) information acquisition, (3) solving problems, and (4) communication. In foundations, students learn the basics of computer technology and its uses; in information acquisition, research is taught; in the third strand, solving problems, research, and problem-solving strategies are introduced; finally, the communication aspect is devoted to teaching students appropriate methods of communication as well as communication possibilities inherent in the virtual world. Resource: http://www.sbec.state.tx.us/SBECOnline/standtest/standards/

The Texas Essential Knowledge and Skills for children at all grade levels can be found at:

http://ritter.tea.state.tx.us/rules/tac/chapter126/index.html.

TEACHING OBJECTIVES

At the end of the lesson, the student should be able to:

✦ Prepare a PowerPoint presentation using rules for professional PPT construction.
✦ Prepare a digital representation of a desired classroom utilizing interactive web sites.
✦ Review and comment on the "Core Rules of Netiquette."
✦ Describe the current/future issues regarding handheld devices.
✦ Describe how to utilize a one-computer classroom.
✦ List print, visual, technology, manipulative, and human resources as you can relative to what you will teach.
✦ Construct a professional ePortfolio.

C9 KEY WORDS: TECHNOLOGY

Terms associated with technology

Web Quests	ePortfolio	Handhelds
Manipulatives	Computer Assisted Instruction (CAI)	Backup Files
Visual Resources	Human Resources	Print Resources
Privacy	Copyright	Acceptable Use
Public Domain	Fair Use	Intellectual Property

Additional technology terms can be found on this web site:

http://www.matisse.net/fi les/glossary.html

On this web site, there is a dictionary of technology terms.

INTRODUCTION/FOCUS

About six years ago, I addressed a packed audience made up of school superintendents from around the State and presented the technology initiatives West Texas A&M University undertook with the assistance of an Amarillo National Resource Center for Plutonium (ANRCP) math/science grant. At the end of the presentation, I asked for questions, and a superintendent from South Texas stood up near the back of the room and clearly articulated a problem endemic in many school districts: "The problem with teacher education today is that you're teaching students all about technology at the university, then, I hire them to teach in my school district, and they want all this equipment. We simply cannot afford it!"

176 Competency 9 Technology

Then fast forward to August 2009 when I attended a TXE conference in Austin, Texas, produced by the Texas Education Agency. Attended by 200 public school teachers and college professors, the opening session featured two award-winning public school teachers who spoke to utilizing blogging in their classrooms as a teaching tool. I should mention that throughout the room the participants were twittering and utilizing cell phones for a myriad of functions. Open before them were their laptop computers where several of them had begun to blog about the conference! This scene mirrored the description of today's student who is simultaneously doing several things at one time—yet supposedly paying attention to a speaker.

WHAT IS ONE TO DO?

TRANSITION: Competency 9 of the Standards refers to the technological aspect of teaching, so students must acknowledge the role of technology in planning, organizing, delivering, and evaluating instruction. The State Technology Standards also address the need for teachers to integrate technology in their classrooms. With those goals in mind, teacher preparation would be remiss to ignore the role of technology in classrooms. Independent School Districts are responsible to No Child Left Behind (NCLB), Title II, Part D not only for increased scores in academics but also for reaching technology goals.

INSTRUCTIONAL INPUT AND GUIDED PRACTICE

What we need to know about planning and presenting lessons using technology

The Instructional Input in this lesson plan will contain *guided practice* in the form of questions placed throughout the chapter. References to web sites will also serve as guided practice as you research topics to gain further knowledge and information and application.

This competency mandates that teachers use a variety of educational resources to enrich individual and group learning. While, at first glance, this competency seems very simple—"Just get a guest speaker, and you're good to go!"—the word *enhanced* carries with it an admonition to the classroom teacher. **Resources are to be used as tools to assist in the learning process, not as a *replacement* for quality instruction.** Neither are movies to be used as a replacement for quality instruction.

BEGIN AT THE BEGINNING

State Proficiency #1 States That the Teacher:

✦ Demonstrates knowledge of basic terms and concepts of current technology (e.g., **hardware, software applications** and functions, **input/output devices,** networks).

Rather than provide a very long glossary of terms, the following links will take you to various web sites that specialize in defining technology terms.
  http://4teachers.org/ is a web site designed for teachers who teach with technology. Its primary purpose is to help teachers integrate technology into their courses. On the same web site is a link to the glossary that provides technology terms used in the publications of the 4teachers Organization. *http://4teachers.org/techalong/glossary/*. The site also has a translator link to Spanish.
  The following web site includes technology "buzz words" for students: *http://www.tekmom.com/buzzwords/*
  This web site from MIT provides a space for you to type in the technology term you wish to define: *http://web.mit.edu/teachtech/glossary.html*. On this web site you will find the term *educational technology,* which refers to technology used in educational settings.

The following Standards taken from the State Board for Educator Certification, (SBEC) outline the technology knowledge all beginning teachers should know. These standards will be tested in future certification examinations.

TECHNOLOGY APPLICATIONS STANDARDS

For All Beginning Teachers

Standard I

All teachers use technology-related terms, concepts, data input strategies, and ethical practices to make informed decisions about current technologies and their applications.

Standard II

All teachers identify task requirements, apply search strategies, and use current technology to efficiently acquire, analyze, and evaluate a variety of electronic information.

Standard III

All teachers use task-appropriate tools to synthesize knowledge, create and modify solutions, and evaluate results in a way that supports the work of individuals and groups in problem-solving situations.

Standard IV

All teachers communicate information in different formats and for diverse audiences.

Standard V

All teachers know how to plan, organize, deliver, and evaluate instruction for all students that incorporates the effective use of current technology for teaching and integrating the Technology Applications Texas Essential Knowledge and Skills (TEKS) into the curriculum.

Furnishing Your Classroom

Before beginning to furnish your classroom, the most important thing to remember about any resource is to make it relevant! A few years ago, the State defined this competency in this way: "The teacher uses a variety of educational resources (including people and technology) to **enhance** both individual and group learning." If technology does not **enhance** learning, you do not need it.

At the end of each chapter in these lesson plans, you will see a materials box. It is wise to list the things you will need to teach each lesson before you begin the lesson. Let this materials box serve as a reminder for each lesson you prepare. It is not fun to work hard on a lesson only to discover at the moment of truth that you do not have enough copies or supplies for everyone.

The first thing a new teacher sees is the classroom with its desks and chairs. If you are lucky enough to get a well-endowed room that hasn't been scavenged by other teachers before your arrival, you may have many useful items. Schools ordinarily have a budget for supplies, and new teachers may get preferential treatment to get necessary equipment. Inquire about supplies during the interview process.

Past the overall "big" equipment a teacher is likely to take for granted (overhead, television monitor, black or white boards), the teacher should consider in the planning phase of every lesson which "materials" will be necessary to complete that lesson. Every new teacher will soon discover that materials and resources do not miraculously appear nor do they pay for themselves! Sometimes, the school will provide a budget for each

Copyright © by the Texas Education Agency. All rights reserved. Found at *http://www.sbec.state.tx.us/SBECOnline/standtest/standards/techapps_allbegtch.pdf*

teacher; but more often than not, the teacher provides his/her own materials out of his/her own pocket. The Internal Revenue Service recognizes this expense and provides teachers with an automatic yearly $250 deduction from income taxes!

Another option for obtaining resources for supplies or equipment includes writing a grant. In public schools, however, teachers are pretty much on their own in finding grant resources outside the school, but if you do find one that you would like to write, be sure to gain approval from district officials before you start this laborious process. Remember, grants take months to write and secure, so plan at least a year in advance. Another resource is the community, but teachers should be very careful to get permission before asking anyone in the community to fund an event or purchase equipment. Again, always ask.

> **PROFESSIONAL DEVELOPMENT**
>
> The following site links to good educational resources and equipment. It may include grant and funding resources as well: *http://www.pitsco.com*

Teachers most likely will find other resources to supply their classrooms. Past the wonderful finds at the Dollar Tree, teachers should always be on the lookout for free or sale items. Garage sales (especially those of retired teachers) or second-hand stores are surprisingly fruitful. One garage sale I went to provided seasonal bulletin board items that the retired teacher proudly gave me because she wanted a "teacher" to have them. I used them in my classroom until I left, at which time my lucky replacement inherited them. Sometimes, students can ask for donations more easily than you can, but again, make sure you do not "assign" students to provide your supplies.

Find the local Chamber of Commerce to discover listings of organizations that might respond to educational needs. Find ways you can work service learning into community organizations in return for a donation to your program. Most organizations are looking for "worthwhile" projects to fund. Learn which times of the year organizations make their monetary commitments for the year.

Become an innovator. Just because you "did it that way last year" does not mean you should do it the same way this year. As a matter of fact, there is an old adage around that says, "There are those teachers who have taught twenty years one time; and there are those teachers who have taught one year twenty times." That means some teachers teach the same way, the same lessons for twenty years in a row, while others find new and creative ways to teach lessons by utilizing new resources every year. Get in the habit of looking at things in unusual ways: The popsicle sticks you used to build a log cabin this year might be used to make umbrellas the next year; a cotton ball is no longer a household item used to remove makeup—it is the tail of a rabbit or a cloud in the sky; pencils become scrolls; plastic sleeves from newspapers provide raw material for crocheting; and paper towel rolls make excellent rain sticks!

The term *resources* means much more today than the old brass bell and hickory stick of yesteryear. Teachers who have mastered this competency have learned the difference between the art of teaching and science of teaching and have decided to integrate the two. Your competency with resources is directly related to how students learn and ultimately how much they learn. These ideas are provided to help young teachers understand that planning resources for the year will certainly result in better accumulation of resources for the long term, and the collection of resources doesn't have to break the bank.

Introduction to Technology

Become computer literate and stay that way! If this is indeed the age of technology, you are part of it . . . be a competent part. It may be that your campus has state of the art computer labs or that you may not even have access to computers. Find a way to adapt to the level of technology on your campus. Know what is there. When my Student Council students introduced AutoCad as a potential resource for our council scrapbook, we worked collaboratively with the technology teacher to set a new standard in the State. The result: a State Award-Winning

Student Council scrapbook, and being the first school in the state to use technology in this way.

Your technology skills will enable you to find resources for yourself online. Millions of web sites exist that tell teachers how to teach every subject under the sun. Take advantage of that valuable resource.

> **NOTE**
>
> The competency standard also requires you to evaluate what you find on the Internet:
>
> 1. All teachers identify task requirements, apply search strategies, and use current technology to efficiently **acquire, analyze, and evaluate** a variety of electronic information.
>
> Thus, you must know that everything you find must be filtered through your own knowledge and competency with the content before you present it as quality teaching.

Competency 9 is closely related to Competency 4: how learning occurs. In another chapter, you learned that students learn in different ways, but most frequently, students must hear, see, and do before they learn. After doing an exercise, students must practice (or do over and over) before they become proficient. What better way to "do" than to work with a computer?

State Proficiencies #2 and #3 State That the Teacher:

✦ Applies procedures for acquiring, analyzing, and **evaluating electronic information** (e.g., locating information on networks, accessing and manipulating information from secondary storage and remote devices, using online help and other documentation, evaluating electronic information for accuracy and validity).

✦ Knows how to use task-appropriate tools and procedures to **synthesize knowledge,** create and modify solutions, and evaluate results to support the work of individuals and groups in problem-solving situations and **project-based learning activities** (e.g., planning, creating, and editing word processing documents, spreadsheet documents, and databases; using graphic tools; participating in electronic communities as learner, initiator, and contributor; sharing information through online communication).

Teachers might think about following a four-part plan when acquiring, analyzing, and evaluating electronic information as well as constructing a technology plan for their classrooms. First they must **plan,** then **organize, deliver,** and finally **evaluate** the effectiveness of technology.

Planning: A new teacher surveys the school resources (including the Region Service Center) to discover what resources are available. When you interview for a teaching position, ask the principal about available technology resources. After you are hired, approach the media specialist (formerly the librarian) to see what technology is available and do it early in the semester. Finally look at the support resources available with your textbook. If they are missing, call the publisher and ask for new copies (or go through your assistant principal in charge of textbooks).

Always be open to exploring new instructional materials. Creative teachers can use the same materials for a variety of teaching strategies. Modeling this creativity may help students become more creative and independent.

Organizing: Once you know what equipment is available, visualize how you will organize it. Will you have locked closets to store it in, or is the building security safe enough to leave things out over the weekend? Be sure to check with your principal for building policies. Find out how much in advance you must order from the Region Service Center or the building media center so that you may mark your calendar appropriately. Ask whether you can use equipment of your own in place of school equipment if it is more up to date. Be sure to ask if the school might buy you some software to compensate for the use of your own equipment. Check out light bulbs in overhead projectors and check the wall or screen for PPT.

Delivering: When the time arrives to utilize the equipment, you must know how to utilize it effectively. Be prepared by having materials ready to go within minutes of starting a lesson. No one wants to watch someone fiddle with technology—especially kids who will find other things to do while you are not focused on them.

Evaluating: Factor in the one-computer classroom, whether or not you will have one computer or a bank of computers. The wisest way to think about this limitation is to think about the ways the teacher can use the computer and then think about ways the student can use the computer. The hope is that a teacher would not have to share a computer for obvious reasons, but if she does, precautionary measures for privacy of information would have to be taken.

Always evaluate any software you use by connecting it to the objectives you wish to achieve. Blind use of a computer—even drill exercises—may be largely ineffective and treated somewhat like a mindless game by students if objectives and further assessment is ignored.

Beyond that a student(s) can use the computer for special assignments including drill and practice or for assignment creation including publication applications. In some classrooms, students may be able to use the computer to strengthen basic skills through preloaded programs, or they may be able to enrich their learning through innovative problem-solving assignments.

If you are limited to one computer, you must design a plan that will allow for eventual use of the center by every student. Take into account whether students have access to computers at home and whether you will be allowed to communicate with students through their home computers. Plan for access and security if you only have one computer.

Obviously, having a bank of computers requires the same security concerns, but several computers will allow more access by all students.

Other State Proficiencies State That the Teacher:

✦ Knows how to use productivity tools to communicate information in various formats (e.g., **slide show, multimedia presentation, newsletter**) and applies procedures for publishing information in various ways (e.g., printed copy, monitor display, Internet document, video).
✦ Knows how to incorporate the effective use of **current technology; use technology applications in problem-solving** and decision-making situations; implement activities that emphasize **collaboration and teamwork;** and use developmentally appropriate instructional practices, activities, and materials to integrate the Technology Applications TEKS into the curriculum.

Competency 11 speaks to communication with parents. Knowledge of various formats of technology, including slide shows, multimedia presentations, and newsletters, are three ways to facilitate your communication with students as well as parents. Developing the HOT ePortfolio establishes expertise in slide shows and multimedia presentations. Learning to create class newsletters is a fun skill for which multiple web sites exist.

Education World provides hundreds of free templates. By clicking on the web site that follows, then clicking on "miscellaneous," you will find a large assortment of newsletters.

http://www.educationworld.com/tools_templates/index.shtml

There are a few caveats that you must keep in mind for creating newsletters:

1. If you start a newsletter, decide early when and how the newsletter will be distributed (check with your principal).
2. Keep the same formatting for the newsletter from one edition to the next; if you are unhappy with your first choice, change it next year.
3. Try to include each and every child's name in the newsletter; excluding some children's names can be very discouraging to students.

The chapter on active learning included a discussion on cooperative and collaborative learning. Obviously, however you decide to develop thematic units that utilize the computer, you will have to take into account the number of computers and the controls the school district places on them.

The following discussion involves other kinds of resources in addition to computer technology. With each type of resource is included a web site or two that provides additional information.

> **QUESTION**
> What are the types of resources you might look for that will help you set up problem-solving assignments for students?
>
> *Answer:* Print, visual, technology, and human resources are the first ones to think about.

Consider the following resources:

PRINT RESOURCES: books, journals, magazines, flyers, brochures, atlases, newspapers

http://www.recordedbooks.com provides recorded books.

http://www.windowsphotostory.com enables students to create electronic books.

http://storycenter.org will assist with narratives.

http://blabberize.com provides creative fun by making a photo "speak."

VISUAL RESOURCES: DVDs, videos, posters, bulletin boards, maps

These four web sites are essentials for teaching today: *http://www.pbs.org/teachersource*. The main purpose of the Public Broadcasting Service (PBS) is to provide information on using video as a tool for learning in the classroom.

http://www.si.edu is the Smithsonian Institution web site from which photos can be downloaded.

The Library of Congress can be accessed at this site: *http://www.loc.gov*.

Likewise, the interactive National Geographic site can be accessed at: *http://www.nationalgeographic.com*

COMPUTER RESOURCES: software, Internet, computer-assisted instruction, web pages

http://www.sitesforteachers.com will take you on tours to virtual museums and much more.

http://www.dictionary.com is an essential part of any classroom today. If you are teaching ESL, you may need this web site: *http://www.learnthenet/english/html/103wiki.htm*

Note: Many interactive web sites are devoted to all aspects of learning English.

OTHER TECHNOLOGY RESOURCES: While outdated, some schools still maintain the equipment to support audio-visual resources, such as filmstrips and slides

http://www.scholastic.com provides classroom activities, games, curriculum programs and materials, software, and film and video information. It also provides access to reproducibles, articles, and lesson plans.

MANIPULATIVES/LABS: pentaminos, dominos, cards, counting bears, money, markers, beakers, 3 × 5 cards. The following web site takes you to the National Library of Virtual Manipulatives:

http://nlvm.usu.edu/en/nav/vLibrary.html

while *http://nlvm.usu.edu/en/NAV/category_g_4_t_3.html* takes you to virtual geometry manipulatives for older students. Type "virtual manipulatives" into your search engine for more sites.

182 Competency 9 Technology

> Although this website could be listed under several headings, *http://www.ecarter.k12.mo.us/dept/elementary/fourthgrade/ccrites/etipslesson1.html* will assist you if you are lucky enough to have a SMARTboard.
> *http://www.edhelper.com/crossword.htm* will help students create a crossword puzzle.
> *http://www.wordle.com* provides other links for making crossword puzzles.

HUMAN RESOURCES refer to experts from the community, such as specialists, guest speakers, parents, other students

SPECIALIZED RESOURCES: Special education requires many specialized resources as does music, theatre, art, and physical education. Teachers in these areas must make good connections in the community. One resource that provides a good starting place is the Region Service Center for your specific area.

REGION SERVICE CENTERS

http://www.esc16.net is the web site for the Region 16 (Amarillo area) Service Center.
   Substitute your own regional service center in the web site to see what resources are available free to you as a teacher. A guide to each region service center in Texas is provided below the following map.

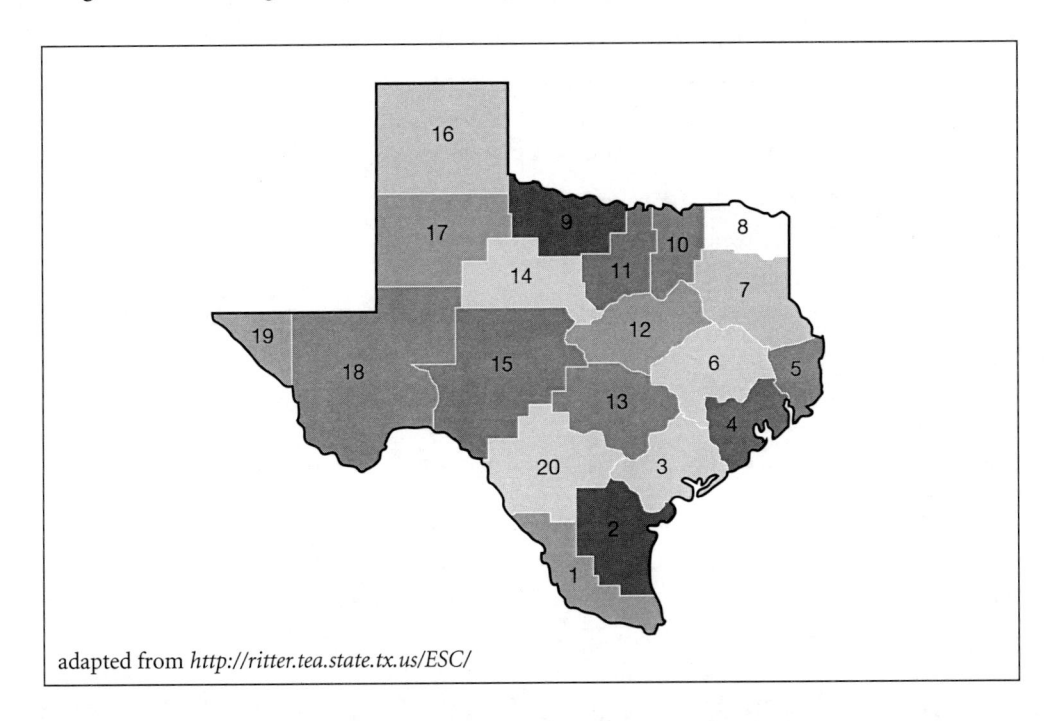

adapted from *http://ritter.tea.state.tx.us/ESC/*

Region Headquarters 1 Edinburg 11 Fort Worth 2 Corpus Christi 12 Waco 3 Victoria 13 Austin 4 Houston 14 Abilene 5 Beaumont 15 San Angelo 6 Huntsville 16 Amarillo 7 Kilgore 17 Lubbock 8 Mount Pleasant 18 Midland 9 Wichita Falls 19 El Paso 10 Richardson 20 San Antonio Texas

The Final State Proficiency States That the Teacher:

✦ Knows how to **evaluate students' technologically produced products** and projects using established **criteria** related to design, content delivery, audience, and relevance to assignment.

HOW ARE RESOURCES USED?

Teachers should use resources as tools to extend or widen the learning process rather than as a replacement for quality instruction. In other words, good lessons or required objectives should be made better rather than having technology or other resources being offered to students as the lesson itself. Teachers who do not make sure their resources have a "point" are creating a "fluff" day where little learning takes place. Also, teachers should judge if their addition is really appropriate to the student age and so forth. The teacher is accountable for many benchmarks sometimes including a resource. Sometimes a resource, though outstanding in and of itself, may be a waste of learning time for students because it does not correlate with the subject matter. In some cases, a purchased resource may not turn out to be as advertised, yet having spent the money, a teacher feels compelled to use it even though it is not an addition to the lesson.

WEBQUESTS: The first webquests were developed in 1995 by Bernie Dodge, a professor of educational technology at San Diego State University. At its best, a webquest is a focused, inquiry-based lesson that uses Internet resources to discover answers.

Numerous webquests can be found online. The web site that bills itself as the "most complete and current source of information about the WebQuest Model" is *http://www.webquest.org/*.

On this web site, click on the "find webquests" link in the grey left-hand column. You will find a place to type in any subject on which you want to find a lesson. Review at least one lesson at this web site. Then, click on the link directly underneath the first "Create Webquests" and discover how to create your own webquest for use in your classroom. The introduction on this page further describes what a webquest is and what it is not. Of importance is that the webquest utilizes higher-order thinking.

STUDENT QUESTION
How does a teacher use a movie in a classroom that a student will actually listen to and respond to?

Answer: You ask this question sincerely remembering quite well the students who put their heads down and slept through *The Great Gatsby*, no doubt! The answer to this question is not simple, but it is rather repetitious to answers given before. Teachers must **plan carefully** for class movies, filmstrips, or slides just like they would plan for any other day. Provide a graphic organizer, preview the video with students, ask provocative questions that students will have to answer after watching, stop the video at intervals for discussion, and set up a signal for students to know that something important is coming. Of course, all of these ideas assume the teacher has viewed the video before showing it to the class!

Netiquette

In years past, teachers taught children how to be polite when answering a telephone or having a good telephone conversation. Today, that instruction seems so old fashioned in light of the immediacy and frequency of technology use. This venue of technology as an information-gathering device has opened up such a new realm of legal and ethical questions that netiquette must find a place in the curriculum.

It is always important to use appropriate etiquette whether in the classroom, a social gathering, or on the Internet. The appropriate use of etiquette in technology is called **netiquette.** Review the core rules as cited on the following web site as a reminder about acceptable rules of conduct online:

http://www.albion.com/netiquette/corerules.html

Be sure to review web sites such as Net Nanny, Safe Eyes, and CYBERsitter, which were created for the sole purpose of protecting students who are utilizing the computer under your supervision. Check and understand to see what safety precautions are in place at your school. You should be able to explain these precautions to any parent who asks.

Handhelds

Handhelds for a classroom cost approximately $1000 and require a great deal of work by the teacher. The following web site by Education World describes four districts that are using handhelds in the classroom: *http://www.educationworld.com/a_tech/tech083.shtml*

This web site from Teacher Tap provides additional information about the use of these devices: *http://eduscapes.com/tap/topic78.htm*

The bottom line on handhelds is that they can be amazingly useful for immediate feedback, testing, and active learning. As always, however, the teacher must plan for their use and have the ability to think of creative ways to integrate these devices into the classroom. I have seen teachers with these devices stash them in closets never to see the light of day! Then, I have seen/participated in events where the instant results are exciting.

Privacy and referencing web sites: Students and teachers alike must be very aware of privacy, copyright, and acceptable use laws. Understand the term *public domain* and its relevant dates, copyright (including copyrighted music) rules, and acceptable use by teachers. Normally "fair use" includes giving teachers the right to copy just enough material to make a point, prove a point, research, critique, and report. Otherwise, be very careful that you do not infringe upon someone else's intellectual property.

Intellectual property includes products that individuals have created out of their own intellect and that have commercial value. This property includes copyrighted property.

QUESTIONS
Is forwarding e-mails you receive considered a breach of privacy?
Are sites such as Facebook, MySpace, and YouTube private?

Answer: Most e-mails can be considered private UNLESS you send it from a school computer—in which case its contents belong to the school. Before you forward any e-mail, you should ask permission. Web sites such as those listed may not be private—college graduates have not been hired because of "private" postings on such web sites. Try *http://www.schooltube.com* for a safe and free media-share site.

NOTE
Be sure your e-mail address is a dignified, professional address. Somehow I can't see a principal being too impressed with an address like "Bigsexy@hotmail.com"!

Understand the difference between creating and referencing. You are "creating" an original ePortfolio that "references" outside sources not original to you.

For a complete understanding of fair-use copyright laws, access this web site: *http://www.copyright.gov/fls/fl 102.html*

State Proficiency #7 States That the Teacher:

✦ Identifies and addresses **equity issues** related to the use of technology.

Certainly it seems that every child has a cell phone today! Many district and classroom discipline issues involve cell phones, and many districts have policies ranging from "losing access to your cell phone" to "redeeming your cell phone for a price." It may surprise you to learn that the future of cell phones may include delivering information via the cell phone! Obviously, that practice would very definitely cause some equity problems.

Mentioned in an earlier chapter, Governor Perry of Texas has stated that within four years (schools actually predict ten years) Texas public schools will transition to digital textbooks. Issues of *equity* will be of concern because not all children will have access to a computer at home that will support the technology of an online textbook.

Some predict that the iPad is the future of public education. That means the State will provide iPads to all students. The cost is unfathomable in these economic times. Even the cost of electronic textbooks has not been calculated, but individual districts expect the costs to be out of reach for several years.

All of these issues pertain to equity. It is clear that not all children, in fact, not all school districts can afford computers for every child. Known as the *digital divide,* school districts will continue to be faced with equity issues. Still, the State believes its students must be exposed to cutting edge technology to be competitive in the workplace.

INDEPENDENT PRACTICE AND MODELING (HOMEWORK)

1. **Scholar's Vocabulary:** Using the State-produced list of proficiencies preservice teachers should have related to Competency 9, highlight terms you wish to place in your interactive glossary. You should have a minimum of five terms from C9. (See the model in the Appendices.)

2. **Reflective Writing:** Using the eleven-sentence model in the Appendices, write a reflection on Competency 9.

3. Utilize one of the following web sites, and design your ideal classroom:

    http://classroom.4teachers.org/

    http://www.aft.org/teachers/downloads/arrangeclassroomworksheet.pdf or you may find a web site of your own choosing to accomplish the same assignment.

4. The ways that technology is integrated into education are endless. Most students today must take a course called Educational Technology or Instructional Technology at the university level. Some departments of education are even constructing CDs with technology assignments on them that students must complete before graduation (including Twittering, Blogging, and WebQuests). This course is designed with a project-based learning tool called the ePortfolio, which demands that students utilize several technological skills to complete. Create a list of all the technology tools you have used in the process of creating your ePortfolio. Be sure to provide a "full text" link in the ePortfolio.

CLOSURE/FOLLOW-UP

The teacher is sometimes caught in the squeeze between the twin technology issues of finance and ability. Teachers may not have much technology and still do a great job of teaching; others may have a lot of technology provided but be reluctant to learn to use it. The most important thing to remember about technology is that you should not use technology for technology's sake; you should use it to *enhance* learning.

ASSESSMENT

Ask yourself whether you have mastered these objectives.

- **Objective 1:** Prepare a digital representation of a desired classroom utilizing interactive web sites.
- **Objective 2:** Review and comment on the "Core Rules of Netiquette."
- **Objective 3:** Describe the current/future issues regarding "handhelds."
- **Objective 4:** Describe how to utilize a one-computer classroom.
- **Objective 5:** List print, visual, technology, manipulative, and human resources relative to what you will teach.
- **Objective 6:** Prepare a PowerPoint presentation using rules for professional PPT construction.
- **Objective 7:** Construct a professional ePortfolio.

PRACTICE QUESTIONS

Now assess your learning by answering these questions. Answers are given in the Appendices.

1. An example of a manipulative is:

    I.   modeling clay
    II. jigsaw puzzles
    III. base ten blocks
    IV. dominoes

    a. I
    b. II and III
    c. I, III, and IV
    d. All of the above.

2. Before a teacher brings in a guest speaker, he or she should:

    I.   talk with other teachers.
    II. send notes home asking for permission.
    III. be able to relate the subject to class activities.
    IV. be aware of school law that might pertain.

    a   I and II
    b. I, III, IV
    c. III, IV
    d. II, IV

3. What is the most appropriate time to include a human resource in a unit of learning during which the students will be exposed to material for which they have no background?
    a. At the beginning of a unit to introduce material.
    b. At the end of the unit as a means of closure.
    c. Any time during the unit is fine; you must accommodate the speaker's schedule.
    d. You should avoid human resources for lessons where students have no background knowledge.

4. The main purpose for using resources in the classroom is to:
    a. enhance student learning.
    b. expose students to a variety of lessons.
    c. give the teacher added support in the classroom.
    d. provide an interesting lesson that will aid in classroom management.

5. Magazines, postcards, flyers, day calendars, web sites, telephone books, and restaurant menus are categorized as which of the following resources?
   a. Technology resources
   b. Print resources
   c. Computer resources
   d. Specialized resources

6. Competency 9 emphasizes that it is the teacher's job to enhance student learning by using a variety of resources. Which of the following examples expresses the best effort in enhancing the variety of resources used to promote optimal learning?
   a. A math teacher uses marbles and M&M candies to help students better understand the concept of grouping similar objects.
   b. A science teacher reads *The Magic School Bus on the Ocean Floor* to her class and brings in different objects from the ocean to elaborate on her lesson about things that belong in the ocean.
   c. A physical education teacher has Arnold Schwarzeeggger come and talk to her class about the importance of staying healthy.
   d. All of the above.

7. Jason is a twelfth-grade honor student at Seymour High School, a small 2-A school in West Texas. He has decided to research The Effects of Aspartame on the Memory of Lab Mice. However, the school media center does not have a lot of information on this topic. Which would be the most beneficial choice for Jason to gain initial information for his research?
   a. He could interview with a lab psychologist in the field.
   b. Use an Internet search engine.
   c. Review some science journal articles.
   d. A & C only

8. Mr. Jacobs, the high school band director, has decided that his students need to become better acquainted with the computer world as it relates to music. You are the instructional technology resource person for the campus. How can you help him?
   a. I cannot. There is no connection between music and computers.
   b. Let him type his concert program on my word processing program.
   c. Prepare a PPT on electronics and music for his class.
   d. Show him how to access music computer sites with outside links.

9. Over the past forty years, Mrs. Thompson has developed an outstanding reputation as a math teacher. Her students make top scores on statewide exams, and she has been honored with many awards for her outstanding results. However, Mr. Wallace, a new teacher, informs her and the rest of the math faculty in a meeting about some interesting tools that just came out on the market that could help all of them. Mrs. Thompson felt intimidated by the young man, so she responded that math is ageless, and the school does not need any new tools. Where is the flaw in Mrs. Thompson's logic?
   a. Mrs. Thompson should be willing to try new things that might help her students.
   b. Mr. Wallace has no right to inform Mrs. Thompson of new tools because he is a new teacher.
   c. Mrs. Thompson is tired and should retire.
   d. Statewide scores do not always determine how effective a teacher is.

188 Competency 9 Technology

10. When you arrive at your new classroom for the first time, you notice the world maps that you are supposed to teach with are old. Germany is still divided, and the Soviet Union is as big as ever. You tell your principal that you need new maps, and he tells you that they do not have the money budgeted to replace them. He also said that Mr. Storm the teacher you replaced managed just fine with them and never complained. What can you do?
    a. Raise the money, and buy new ones yourself.
    b. Tell the superintendent and the school board that you have outdated maps.
    c. Use the maps anyway. You have to use what you have sometimes.
    d. Use overheads you copy out of a book.

MATERIALS NEEDED

textbook; Internet

SUGGESTIONS FOR ADDITIONAL ASSIGNMENTS

1. Create a resource list using these three columns:

   People   Technology   Print

   Your resource list should be a dreamer's list of things you have seen or heard about and hope to have in your own classroom someday.

   Construct a three-column table listing supplies you anticipate needing when you become a teacher in the first column. In the second column, list how you will utilize these supplies. In the third column, assign a realistic cost of each of these items.

   Create a landscaped five-column table with the following headings: print resources, visual resources, computer resources, human resources, and other resources. Under each column list at least fifteen entries for each heading.

2. Provide a list of the "antiquated" items that teachers "used to use."

3. Think of manipulatives that you might use for each of the following subjects: Math, Reading, Science, History, Writing

   Be sure to tell how you would utilize the manipulative and under what circumstances you would use it.

4. What are some of the limitations to using human resources in your classroom? What legal considerations should you consider? (Hint: religious or moral.)

5. Explain the connection between Constructivist Theory and using manipulatives.

6. Privacy, copyright law, and acceptable use issues are very important when using documentation from the Internet. Demonstrate the proper way to document a citation from the Internet. Be sure to cite your resource!

7. Utilizing the following web site *www.webquest.org,* **create a short webquest** on the subject *educational technology.* Be sure to include this link in the ePortfolio.

8. Create a list of web sites relevant to the subject you hope to teach.

9. What technological resources still "scare" you? How can you become familiar with them during your fieldwork?

10. Some additional exercises that you may undertake include:
    a. creating an ExCEL gradebook
    b. creating templates (news letters)
    c. creating backup files
    d. using realistic/clip art graphics
    e. creating spreadsheets-timelines
    f. creating a greeting card
    g. creating a PPT with multimedia
    h. inserting closed captioning in a video
    i. inserting music into a PPT
    j. demonstrating the principles of Podcasting

11. Demonstrate expertise at locating information each of the following items, which are pertinent to the profession of teaching in Texas:
    a. TEKS Curriculum
    b. TRS
    c. TAKS
    d. SBEC
    e. TEA
    f. TheCB
    g. ETS (certification examinations)
    h. STAR requirements
    i. NCLB

12. Begin a technology resource library by collecting relevant publications. For example, an excellent basic PowerPoint reference is a small book entitled, *Save Our Slides* by Earnest. Compare your ePortfolio slide creation with the model given in this book.

13. Describe the digital divide and equity in technology.

14. Create a list of time-management tools (e.g., calendar, appointment software).

15. Set up an educational newsgroup; consider blogging. Access the following web site for help with creating a blog, generating a test, constructing a rubric, generating a timeline, among other things: *http://kathyschrock.net/cooking/*. This web site also provides instruction on creating wikis.

16. Develop a plan of personal technology growth including becoming a Master Technology teacher. Access the following web sites for current information on technology purchases, reviews, and the latest gadgets. There is also instruction on blogs, podcasting, and technology.

    http://www.cnet.com and *www.esc11.net*. If your personal learning plan includes learning how to create wikis, access these web sites: *http://www.pbwiki.com/academic.wiki*, *http://www.wetpaint.com*, and *http://www.wikispace.com*.

Competency 10

Planning for Performance, Achievement and Feedback

LESSON PLAN FOR COMPETENCY 10

STATE STANDARDS: STANDARD 3, COMPETENCY 10

Competency 010: The teacher monitors student **performance** and **achievement,** provides students with timely, high-quality **feedback;** and responds flexibly to promote learning for all students.

STATE TEACHER PROFICIENCIES

Competency 010

The teacher monitors student performance and achievement; provides students with timely, high-quality feedback; and responds flexibly to promote learning for all students.

The beginning teacher:

- Demonstrates knowledge of the characteristics, uses, advantages, and limitations of various **assessment methods** and **strategies**, including technological methods and methods that reflect real-world applications.
- Creates assessments that are congruent with **instructional goals** and **objectives** and communicates assessment **criteria and standards** to students based on **high expectations** for learning.
- Uses **appropriate language** and **formats** to provide students with timely, effective feedback that is accurate, constructive, substantive, and specific.
- Knows how to promote students' ability to use **feedback** and **self-assessment** to guide and enhance their own learning.
- Responds flexibly to various situations (e.g., lack of student engagement in an activity, the occurrence of an unanticipated learning opportunity) and adjusts instructional approaches based on **ongoing assessment** of student performance.

TEACHING OBJECTIVES

At the end of the lesson, the student should be able to:

- Define basic testing and measurement terms.
- Explain the purposes for student assessment.
- Explain the difference between measurement and evaluation.
- Give examples of checking for understanding as informal assessment.
- Construct both formative and summative tests.
- Assess test results to determine achievement.
- Design appropriate feedback to assist students in their future learning.

C10 KEY WORDS: ASSESSEMENT

Terms associated with assessment

Intelligence	Basic Skills	Aptitude
Entity Theory	Single-Subject Achievement	Competence
Incremental Theory	Achievement	Mastery
Norm-Referenced (Carroll/Hunter)	Criterion-Referenced	High-Stakes Tests

Other terms are included within the text for testing and measurement.

# INTRODUCTION/FOCUS

Americans are consumed with numbers. For the sake of startling statistics, let's say that these numbers that appeared on the Internet anonymously are accurate:

A. A billion seconds ago it was 1959.
  1. A billion minutes ago Jesus was alive.
  2. A billion hours ago our ancestors were living in the Stone Age.
  3. A billion days ago no one walked on the earth on two feet.
  4. A billion dollars ago was only 8 hours and 20 minutes at the rate government is spending it.

B. Congress allotted $250 BILLION to rebuild New Orleans.
  1. Each of the 484,674 residents of New Orleans (every man, woman, child) gets $516,528.
  2. Or, each of the 188,251 homes in New Orleans gets $1,329,787.
  3. Or, each family of four gets $2,066,012.

How we evaluate the results of the test is usually based on **norm-referenced** (compared with others) or **criterion-referenced** (compared with defined criteria and also includes **Mastery Learning**) comparisons. More information about these types of evaluation is included in the glossary.

TRANSITION: People work with numbers constantly to determine the amount of body fat each of us has, the number of deaths attributed to H1N1, and how much money the health bill will cost the American people in taxes. Debate abounds over the (in)efficiency of the space program and calculates the number of miles cars get on a tank of gas. All of these issues refer to assessment in some form or another, so it is no surprise that schools must assess learning and assess it frequently and accurately because each child's future hangs in the balance. Called **high-stakes testing,** the State, as a result of No Child Left Behind, has imposed significant testing criteria upon every child in the State (TAKS, soon to be STAR).

INSTRUCTIONAL INPUT AND GUIDED PRACTICE

What we need to know about assessment

The Instructional Input in this lesson plan will contain *guided practice* in the form of questions placed throughout the chapter. References to web sites will also serve as guided practice as you research topics to gain further knowledge and information and application.

State Proficiency #1 States That the Teacher:

✦ Demonstrates knowledge of the characteristics, uses, advantages, and limitations of various assessment methods and strategies, including technological methods and methods that reflect real-world applications.

By now most of you have had approximately fifty to sixty teachers and/or professors. Each of these individuals, as well as State agencies who make laws, have "assessed" your abilities time and time again. You have been required to take mandated test after mandated test and from those scores, information is gained about you that has been used to "place" you in an ability-level class and to assign your grade for the course or term. Standardized scores may not even have had much meaning for you. Most of us are just interested in "did we pass" and if so, "by how much?" The truth of the matter is that, as a teacher, you will need to know much more about assessment than who passes and who does not. You will need to use the results of the assessments you give to your students, but perhaps most importantly, you will need to know enough about assessment to determine if you are really testing what you think you are testing and if students are learning what you want them to learn. Furthermore, if you are not testing properly or students are not learning properly, you must know what to do. One study found that elementary teachers spend as much as one-third to one-half of each day assessing students! Yet, many teachers do not understand the assessment process well and may even view testing as inconsistent with helping students.

Assessment activities involve three types of activities: (1) **collecting information** about how much knowledge and skill students have learned (measurement) and (2) **making judgments** about the adequacy or acceptability of each student's level of learning (evaluation). **Measurement** is the (3) **assignment of numbers** to certain attributes of objects, events, or people according to a rule-governed system (e.g., How many words can Suzie type per minute?). **Evaluation** involves the use of a rule-governed system to form judgments about the value or worth reflected in a set of measures. Evaluation calls for attaching meaning to test scores in terms of general instructional objectives (e.g., What does it mean to say that a student answered eighty out of one hundred earth science questions correctly?).

Assessment refers to the process of gathering and analyzing information in order to make instructional, administrative, and/or guidance decisions about or for individuals. Remember, however, that assessment information should be used as a means for making instructional decisions NOT as an end in itself. Remember, too, that assessment is never precise because it deals with human properties rather than physical properties. When we assess aptitude, attitude, and achievement, we know that the results of such testing can vary from one time to another; thus, the results are not precise.

> **STUDENT FORMATIVE QUESTION**
> What is the distinction and the relationship between measurement and evaluation?
> Provide a classroom example of each of these concepts.

State Proficiency #2 States That the Teacher:

✦ Creates assessments that are congruent with instructional goals and objectives and communicates assessment criteria and standards to students based on high expectations for learning.

With that important introduction to assessment out of the way, let's turn to assessment's three major parts: performance, achievement, and feedback. This competency also focuses on the teacher's role of monitoring each step of a student's learning.

Of tantamount importance to any assessment is the connection between the teaching objectives and the test itself. Failure to test what you teach is a fruitless endeavor.

PERFORMANCE

Performance refers to the design of an assignment that will ultimately require some form of assessment. In other words, the assignment will be *tested* through a weekly examination, a unit examination, a mid-term examination, or perhaps, a semester examination. When a teacher plans a lesson, he or she should automatically plan for assessment. Following are some testing principles.

GENERAL TESTING PRINCIPLES

I. Planning the Test

A. Plan the lesson: plan the construction/administration of the test.

1. Do not wait until the day before to create a test; build the test over time; avoid creating all items in one sitting.

2. Announce the test date early.
3. Test only material (objectives) presented in class.
4. Test the material proportionally to the amount of time spent on it.
5. Do not use words or word items out of a textbook.
6. Arrange the test in order of difficulty.
    a. The first few items should be easiest to answer.
    b. The last few should have the highest difficulty level.
    c. Test language should be at the appropriate developmental level.
7. Test should have no more than 30–40 percent subjective items.
8. No single item should be worth more than 10 percent of the total points.
9. Objective test items should require a clear method of response.
10. Subject test items should feature clear language.
11. Avoid speed as the critical factor in creating a test; the primary emphasis is on self-empowerment.

II. Administering the Test

A. Make test directions clear and concise.
B. Read directions aloud for each section in the exam.
C. Directions standardize the test behavior of the students.
    1. The test should be typed and reproduced.
    2. One copy per student (enhances validity and reliability).
D. Do not put questions on the board or read orally.
    1. Reading test questions orally may affect test reliability and validity because oral reading may compromise the test environment.
E. Proof every test. Correct mistakes; preferably before duplicating/distributing the test. If an error is found after the fact, go over the mistake with students before they take the test. Write corrections on the board as well.

III. Giving Test Feedback

A. Construct a method of feedback for all students.
B. Return tests promptly.
C. Go over tests in class with students. (See the section on **feedback** that follows.)

ACHIEVEMENT

The second part of the competency is **achievement.** How much knowledge/skill did the students achieve? Knowing how to evaluate assessments once given is important for the results in order to determine the next step: reteach, reinforce, or move forward to scaffold new information. The preservice teacher should know about formative and summative evaluation. Other names for formative and summative evaluations are informal and formal evaluations.

FORMATIVE AND SUMMATIVE EVALUATIONS

Two types of measurement that teachers should know about include **formative and summative evaluation.** Formative evaluation monitors students' progress and can be used to plan supplementary or remedial instruction. Formative evaluations are a type of Informal evaluation, and they can take place at any time during a lesson. This type of evaluation can also be called checking for understanding (CFU), an identifiable part of lesson planning. While conducting a lesson, the teacher can ask for a show of hands for those who understand, ask students to show a red card or green card indicating understanding, or she can simply read the nonverbal feedback at a check point. Following are some forms of informal evaluation that a teacher might use sporadically or on a daily basis:

1. One-Minute Writing
2. 2Qs
3. 3-2-1 Express

This evaluation is also called informal assessment.

Summative evaluation will provide a clear, meaningful, and useful accounting of how well a student has met the teacher's objectives.

Summative evaluations are those tests that are given at the end of a unit of learning. These are usually tests that are announced in advance and the ones that students dread the most because the grades on such tests usually account for most of the term's final grade. This evaluation is also known as formal evaluation.

STUDENT SUMMATIVE QUESTION

Outline the major distinctions between formative and summative evaluation strategies. Explain when and why a teacher might use such concepts in order to provide effective instruction.

State Proficiencies #3 and #4 State That the Teacher:

✦ Uses appropriate language and formats to provide students with timely, effective **feedback** that is accurate, constructive, substantive, and specific.
✦ Knows how to promote students' ability to use **feedback** and self-assessment to guide and enhance their own learning.

FEEDBACK

The third part of the competency is **feedback.** The work of a British project called Student Enhanced Learning through Effective Feedback (SENLEF) was published in 2004. The entire report can be accessed at *www.ltsn.ac.uk/genericcentre/senlef.* This group identified seven principles of good feedback:

1. Facilitates the development of **self-assessment** (reflection) in learning.
2. Encourages teacher and peer dialogue around learning.
3. Helps clarify what constitutes good performance (**goals, criteria, expected standards**).
4. Provides **opportunities to close the gap** between current and desired performance.
5. Delivers **high-quality information** to students about their learning.
6. Encourages **positive motivational beliefs** and self-esteem.
7. Provides **information to teachers** that can be used to help shape the teaching.[1]

Types of Tests

Written tests are composed of a set of written questions or statements asking the student for a written response (sometimes called **essay**). These tests reveal how well students can recall, organize, and clearly communicate previously learned information on such higher-level abilities as analysis, synthesis, and evaluation. **Selected-response** tests are brief statements where the student selects one of the provided options as the correct answer: these include multiple choice, true-false, matching, and interpretive items. **Short-answer** tests ask for short answers. Sometimes called **identify** or **fill in the blanks,** students may limit their study of a subject because they know they will only be required to have limited knowledge. **Performance** tests measure how well people perform a skill or set of skills under more or less realistic conditions (**authentic assessment**). An example of performance testing would be the mini-teach or the portfolio.

Additional Information about testing:

1. Connect the test to the teaching objectives:

    a. Teacher-made tests are often the best tests because they match the teaching objectives to the test items. The problem with teacher-made tests is that they may require lower-order thinking (e.g., knowledge level or memory-based questions). Problems with language may also pose a problem. If a teacher creates his own tests, he should be sure to "take the test" himself in advance of duplicating it for distribution to a class.

    b. Publisher-ready tests are often easier to administer because they are formatted neatly and offered in electronic fashion, so with the click of a button, tests can be created, printed, and administered. The obvious drawback to such tests is that they are not always matched with the teaching objectives, so students see items that they know nothing about. Once confronted with issues with tests, teachers must back down, give credit, or face irate parents.

    c. Alternative assessment (authentic, portfolio, performance) as described previously measures how well people perform a skill or set of skills under more or less realistic conditions. An example of an assignment that meets the criteria for authentic assessment is the ePortfolio.

STUDENT SUMMATIVE QUESTION
Discuss the use of performance tests as a means of assessing student learning.
In your answer, describe the general goal of performance testing, describe the four general types of performance tests, discuss at least five characteristics of performance tests, and comment on some current concerns about performance testing.

---

   d. Self and Peer Assessments can be added to your testing repertoire as a means of asking students to evaluate their own performance on a task as well as the performance of their peers. For example, if you have assigned a group project, this type of assessment might provide some insight into who contributes to the final product and who does not.

   e. Standardized testing involves very specific terminology, some of which you have probably been exposed to when you got the results of your standardized tests. Often counselors, teachers, or even parents will abbreviate the results by saying something like, "My little Charlie scored in the top 97 percentile of all third graders!" That oversimplification, however, involves much more complex terminology:

   Standard deviation (SD)—a measure of variability that tells how far all the scores in a distribution deviate from the mean. The higher the SD the more the scores vary; the lower the SD the less the scores vary from the mean.

Normal Curve—a theoretical distribution where scores cluster around the center. Moving away from the center in both directions, fewer and fewer scores occur. The normal curve is symmetrical and the mean, median, and mode are all placed at the center.

Reliability—an indicator that under the same circumstances, the measurement will occur over and over.

Validity—a test that measures what it is supposed to measure.

Frequency Distribution—a tabulation of scores from high to low, or low to high, showing the number of individuals who obtain each score. Frequency distributions are used to determine tables of percentile ranks.

Percentile—the point in a data distribution at or below which a given percentile of scores fall. For example, the 67th percentile means 67 percent of the scores in the distribution are AT or BELOW that number.

Generalizability—generalizes only to like populations (i.e., urban students to urban, rural students to rural).

Additional Terms Associated with Standardized Testing

APTITUDE TEST: Test intended to give educators some idea of the level of knowledge and skills students could acquire with effective instruction.

COMPETENCY: A test that determines if potential graduates possess basic skills.

Example: You will take competency tests (TExES) at the end of your university program.

CRITERION-REFERENCED: Test that indicates the degree of mastery of objectives.

Example: Each course assignment focuses on mastery of a certain standard/competency.

DIAGNOSTIC TEST: A single-subject achievement test intended to identify the source of a problem in a basic subject and perhaps study skills.

GROUP TEST OF SCHOLASTIC APTITUDE: Test administered by a school district as part of its testing program that attempts to measure ability to cope with the intellectual demands of classroom tasks.

Example: Otis-Lennon Mental Ability Tests

INDIVIDUAL INTELLIGENCE TEST: Used if a student is considered for a special program of some kind.

Example: Stanford-Binet or Wechsler Intelligence Scale

NORM GROUP: A sample of individuals carefully chosen so as to reflect the larger population of students for whom the test is intended.

NORM-REFERENCED: Test that compares one student with another.

PERFORMANCE-BASED: An assessment system that attempts to gauge how well students can use basic knowledge and skill to perform complex tasks or sole problems under more or less realistic conditions.

Example: The ePortfolio.

RELIABILITY: The similarity between two rankings of test scores obtained from the same individual.

SINGLE-SUBJECT ACHIEVEMENT TEST: A test designed to assess learning or achievement in a particular basic school subject, such as reading or math.

Examples: The AP examinations; CLEP tests.

SPECIAL PURPOSE ACHIEVEMENT TEST: The National Teacher Examination must be taken before being granted a teaching certificate in some states.

STANDARDIZED TEST: Items presented and scored in standard fashion; result reported with reference to standards.

Examples: TAKS; STAR

VALIDITY: How accurately a test measures what users want to measure.

Common testing and measurement terms

The following terms are associated with assessment. All teachers will be expected to know these terms and be able to explain scores to parents from time to time.

Measures of Central Tendency: These measures should be performed each time a test is given. Teachers may choose to post these results on the board or not.

Mean—arithmetic average
Median—the middle number of an odd number of data points, or the mean or middle two numbers of an even amount of data points.
Mode—the most-often repeated number (bimodal if two; trimodel if three).
Range—the difference between the lowest and highest data points.

ITEM ANALYSIS

After the mean, median, mode, and range are determined, teachers should do an item analysis of each question. How many students missed each question? Is it clear why students missed the question? Does the missed question match a specific teaching objective?

STUDENT SUMMATIVE QUESTION

Discuss the following aspects of conducting an item analysis on an exam: procedure, rationale, and objective.

What is your philosophy about curving grades, omitting a certain question if more than 50 percent of students miss it, and giving a second test?

The Final State Proficiency States That the Teacher:

✦ Responds flexibly to various situations (e.g., lack of student engagement in an activity, the occurrence of an unanticipated learning opportunity) and adjusts instructional approaches based on ongoing assessment of student performance.

During the 1980s Madeline Hunter's Mastery Learning became the standard for ongoing assessment. If the student "mastered" the teaching objective, he was able to go on to the next objective or to be "enriched" with a more challenging form of the same objective. If the student "failed" to master the objective, he was relegated to "reteach" of the same objective and "retesting" until he could show mastery.

Ongoing assessment is very much like the mastery concept. The teacher provides feedback to the student about performance and continues with a watchful eye on the student's progress. At periodic intervals, the teacher completes progress reports and assesses the progress of the student for the administration and parents. This process, which is ongoing itself, permits early intervention of a child who is not progressing at the rate he should be progressing.

Early intervention programs are in almost every school, particularly in the areas of math and reading. Students who are identified as "at risk" are often the recipients of this early intervention. Specialists are brought in to assist the child in overcoming weak areas of learning.

INDEPENDENT PRACTICE AND MODELING (HOMEWORK)

1. **Scholar's Vocabulary:** Using the State-produced list of proficiencies preservice teachers should have related to Competency 10, highlight terms you wish to place in your interactive glossary. You should have a minimum of five terms from C10.

2. **Reflective Writing:** Using the eleven-sentence model in the Appendices, write a reflection on Competency 10.

3. Create a formative test (ten questions) and a summative test (essay, multiple choice, short answer, matching) based on portions (you choose) of this lesson (and provide answers).

4. Write a brief philosophy of testing.

CLOSURE/FOLLOW-UP

To say that tests and testing form a small part of what teachers do would be to underestimate the role assessment plays in a teacher's daily life considerably! With the Texas Essential Knowledge and Skills (soon to be STAR) tests determining promotion and graduation, teachers are very concerned with teaching to the test versus *teaching*.

Soon you will be involved in this very important debate. Keep in mind what preceded competency exams when you enter into the discussion and inform yourself. Make no mistake, testing is a part of your daily life as a teacher and faculty team.

ASSESSMENT

Ask yourself whether you have mastered these objectives.

- **Objective 1:** Define basic terms used in testing and measurement.
- **Objective 2:** Explain the purposes for student assessment.
- **Objective 3:** Explain the difference between measurement and evaluation.
- **Objective 4:** Give examples of checking for understanding as informal assessment.
- **Objective 5:** Construct both formative and summative tests.
- **Objective 6:** Assess test results to determine achievement.
- **Objective 7:** Design appropriate feedback to assist students in their future learning.

Competency 10   Planning for Performance, Achievement and Feedback

PRACTICE QUESTIONS

1. What is the purpose of administering certain standardized tests to students?
    a. To measure a student's Intelligence Quotient and subsequent placement in a gifted and talented program.
    b. To obtain accurate, representative samples of some aspects of a student's learning.
    c. Determine SES placement to assure success.
    d. None of the above.

2. Which of the following is not a standardized test?
    a. Achievement test
    b. Diagnostic test
    c. Content validity test
    d. Aptitude test

3. Which of the following best demonstrates the concept of measurement?
    a. Keisha likes to do math worksheets.
    b. Gregg runs fast on the playground.
    c. Donzelle loves to read books about sports.
    d. Anna scored in the 96th percentile on a math aptitude test.

4. Which of the following best represents an evaluation?
    a. Ian answered eight out of ten quiz questions correctly.
    b. Catrina earned an A in algebra.
    c. Antonio has an IQ score of 132.
    d. Jennifer scored higher on the test than Helen did.

5. If Ms. Choi, a third-grade teacher, decides to engage in formative evaluation, she should:
    a. give a test at the end of a grading period to find out how well students have mastered objectives.
    b. give a test at the beginning of a grading period to determine how much background knowledge students possess.
    c. give a test to determine student strengths and weaknesses.
    d. give tests periodically to find out how well students are progressing so that remedial instruction can be implemented, if necessary.

6. Mr. Li is a seventh-grade English teacher. If he wants to design his semester-long testing schedule in order to best facilitate his students' learning, research suggests that giving ____ tests may be the most effective.
    a. a moderate number of
    b. a large number of
    c. a small number of
    d. no

7. Which of the following is *not* an advantage of using selected-response tests?
    a. They allow you to cover quickly a large amount of material.
    b. They have reliable scoring procedures.
    c. They provide quick and easy feedback to students and teacher.
    d. They encourage meaningful learning.

8. Well-designed essay questions require:
    a. the recall of facts rather than elements of complex learning.
    b. the students to respond verbally rather than in writing.
    c. higher-level cognitive abilities, such as basic terminology and definitions.
    d. that students recall, organize, and clearly communicate what they have learned.

202 Competency 10   Planning for Performance, Achievement and Feedback

9. How well someone can do something under realistic conditions would be best measured by a(n) _____ test.
    a. diagnostic
    b. performance
    c. intelligence
    d. written

10. Which of the following is a characteristic of performance tests?
    a. They emphasize summative evaluation.
    b. They may vary in how "true to life" they are.
    c. They eschew computer-based simulations as instructional tools.
    d. They emphasize open-ended, well-structured problems.

11. Which of the following is a norm-referenced approach to grading?
    a. Before the beginning of a report period, figure out the minimum test scores necessary for various letter grades.
    b. Compare the score of each student to scores of other students.
    c. Provide clear and specific objectives and test on those objectives.
    d. Score each test in terms of a scale of points and add up totals.

12. Which of the following objectives would be best evaluated by a criterion-referenced test rather than a norm-referenced test?
    a. How much students know about biology, compared with students in other schools.
    b. Which reading test produces the highest reading comprehension scores.
    c. How well students have mastered English grammar.
    d. How well your students do in their first year of college.

13. If you decided to use a mastery approach, you would do all of the following *except:*
    a. use instructional objectives.
    b. compare test scores of different students when assigning grades.
    c. allow students to work at their own pace.
    d. provide opportunities for retests.

14. All of the following describe disadvantages of the mastery learning approach *except:*
    a. establishing a standard for mastery is no more difficult than establishing a standard using regular instruction.
    b. students may not study for the first test administration, knowing they can take the test another time.
    c. mastery learning requires more teacher preparation than other forms of instruction.
    d. students work through the material at different paces; thus, a teacher has to keep the faster ones occupied while the slower ones catch up.

15. The best kind of test:
    a. emphasizes only part of the relevant material, so students who have studied that part will perform well on the test.
    b. touches on every point made by the teacher, so it is clear what the student does and does not know.
    c. is a representative sample of all behavior deemed important by the teacher.
    d. is completely subjective, so a teacher can take students' personal circumstances into account when determining grades.

16. If you wanted to evaluate how well students perform a dance routine, it would be desirable to use:
    a. a list of psychomotor objectives.
    b. a rating scale.
    c. a table of specifications.
    d. summative evaluation.

17. An item analysis can be used to determine:
    a. the reliability of a test.
    b. the validity of a test.
    c. which items should be revised, discarded, or retained.
    d. which items contribute to the teacher expectancy effect.

CAREER PLANNING

Plenty of opportunities exist in public education for making meaningful contributions if you enjoy working with testing and assessment. You have probably noticed that every competency within the PPR uses the term *assessment*. Every administrator works with numbers in determining how many students drop out, succeed, go to college, qualify under Title 1, etc. Teachers who master the art of grading and maintaining records can grow into a number of positions in public education.

MATERIALS NEEDED

Internet

SUGGESTIONS FOR ADDITIONAL ASSIGNMENTS

1. Research "teaching to the test" vs teaching from the TEKS. Write a position paper on your beliefs.

2. Construct both a formative and a summative test over the types of tests given in this chapter.

3. Create hardcopy documents representing these three types of feedback to a teacher:
   a. Test feedback (you choose what kind of test)
   b. Scheduling a test for gifted and talented
   c. Explaining to a parent why his child is in standard English classes

4. Explain the advantages and limitations of using the following types of tests: essay, multiple choice, and short answer.

5. Reread the teaching objectives for this chapter. Connect each objective to test questions that you create.

6. Research at least one academic article regarding the language of tests. Write a summary critiquing the article.

7. Research one academic article regarding a student's ability to use feedback (article). Write a summary focusing on one point in the article that surprised you.

8. Define your concept of an unanticipated learning opportunity. Then, define the following terms:
   a. Reteach
   b. Madeline Hunter's Mastery Learning

---

[1] Juway, C., D. Macfarlane-Dick; B. Matthew, D. Nicol, D. Ross, and B. Smith. 2004. *Enhancing student learning through effective formative feedback*. York, England: The Higher Education Academy. Contact information: ISBN 1-904190-58-8; email: gcenquiries@ltsn.ac.uk; www.ltsn.ac.uk/genericcentre

204 Competency 10 Planning for Performance, Achievement and Feedback

9. Research "Checking for Understanding" online and create a list of items that you could use to check for understanding (Note: three are given in the lesson).

10. Write a position paper on high-stakes testing. Do you believe high-stakes testing benefits children?

Assessment: CHECKING FOR UNDERSTANDING

Match the following terms with their definitions or descriptions.

_____ 1. Portfolio
_____ 2. Authentic assessment
_____ 3. Performance assessment
_____ 4. Performance-based assessment
_____ 5. Contract activity package

A. Student demonstration of a skill
B. Fits well with multiple intelligences theory
C. Presentation of body of work
D. Performance assessment measure
E. Performs skill in real-life setting

Match the following terms with their associational definitions.

_____ 1. Informal assessment
_____ 2. Observational data
_____ 3. Multiple-Choice questions
_____ 4. Student interviews
_____ 5. Essay tests

A. Must be nonthreatening, ungraded
B. Scoring Rubric
C. Checksheets, inventories
D. Reliability, validity highly suspect
E. Associated with *always, never*

Match the following terms with their associational definitions.

_____ 1. Validity
_____ 2. Formative data
_____ 3. Criterion-referenced
_____ 4. Reliability
_____ 5. Norm-referenced
_____ 6. Test bias
_____ 7. Curriculum-based assessment

A. Consistency of results over time
B. Fairness of test
C. Measures current student achievement
D. Measures what it says it does
E. Standardized test based on curve
F. Measures mastery of specific skills
G. Generally criterion-based

11. Type a one- to two-page paper stating whether you believe that accountability and high-stakes testing will improve the quality of education or harm it. Do not take a "middle of the road" approach. Take one side of the argument and provide rationale in support of your position. Use correct grammar, spelling, and sentence structure in this paper.

Standard 4

Fulfilling Professional Roles and Responsibilities

Competency 11: Family Involvement
Competency 12: Professional Knowledge and Skills
Competency 13: Legal and Ethical Requirements

Competency 11

Family Involvement

LESSON PLAN FOR COMPETENCY 11

STATE STANDARDS: STANDARD 4, COMPETENCY 11

Competency 011: The teacher understands the importance of **family involvement** in children's education and knows how to interact and **communicate** effectively **with families.**

STATE TEACHER PROFICIENCIES

Competency 011

The teacher understands the importance of family involvement in children's education and knows how to interact and communicate effectively with families.

The beginning teacher:

- Applies knowledge of appropriate ways (including electronic communication) to work and **communicate effectively with families** in various situations.
- **Engages families,** parents, guardians, and other legal caregivers in various aspects of the **educational program.**
- **Interacts appropriately** with all families, including those that have diverse characteristics, backgrounds, and needs.
- **Communicates effectively** with families on a regular basis (e.g., to share information about students' progress) and **responds** to their concerns.
- Conducts **effective conferences** with parents, guardians, and other legal caregivers.
- Effectively uses **family support resources** (e.g., community, interagency) to enhance family involvement in student learning.

TEACHING OBJECTIVES

At the end of the lesson, the student should be able to:

- Design a plan for developing a positive relationship with parents.
- Design a plan for communicating with parents.
- Describe effective communication methods of handling a parent conference including electronic methods.
- Describe how a teacher might respond to nonresponsive parents.
- Describe how a teacher might respond to hostile parents.
- Suggest ideas for learning about the community.
- Elaborate ideas for utilizing the strengths within the community.

INTRODUCTION/FOCUS

Perhaps nothing strikes fear into the heart of the brand new teacher quite like the ominous call from a parent who would "like a conference about Little Johnny at your earliest convenience." Even worse is if the call for a conference came through your principal! Suddenly, you're back in high school and feel like you're being called into the principal's office for some egregious offense.

Good communication skills have already been discussed in Competency 7, but communicating a lesson to students and communicating with parents are two different skills.

TRANSITION: This competency requires that the teacher understand both the importance of including parents in the educational processes of their children and taking a proactive stance when it comes to communicating with parents.

Research shows that parent involvement in a child's education increases student success. These lucky children:

- have better attendance, so they make better grades;
- better grades lead to higher motivation and higher esteem;
- higher self-esteem diminishes the allure of drugs and alcohol;
- all of these things lead to higher graduation rates;
- and higher graduation rates lead to increased higher education enrollment.

INSTRUCTIONAL INPUT AND GUIDED PRACTICE

What we need to know about family involvement

The Instructional Input in this lesson plan will contain *guided practice* in the form of questions placed throughout the chapter. References to web sites will also serve as guided practice as you research topics to gain further knowledge and information and application.

BEGIN AT THE BEGINNING

At your first faculty meeting, your principal may stress the importance of communicating with the parents of your students. He or she is likely to stress that calling a parent early in the semester with "good news" will soften a later call if necessary that might be "bad news." In your busy day, however, making time to call parents is sometimes the "last straw." As a result, when a problem arises, truly the first contact you will have with a parent is a difficult situation. You will have to be the judge about how to approach parents, but the principal's advice is sound.

State Proficiencies #1 and #4 State That the Teacher:

- Applies knowledge of appropriate ways (including electronic communication) to work and communicate effectively with families in various situations.
- Communicates effectively with families on a regular basis (e.g., to share information about students' progress) and responds to their concerns.

Most school districts today have professionally designed web sites; most districts also have a link to parents. For example, the Dallas Independent School District (*www.dallasisd.org*) has a link entitled "for parents." There are approximately thirty additional links that range from calendars to finding tutors for your children. Even small districts like Beeville ISD (*www.beevilleisd.net*) has a "BISD Parent Connect" link that takes parents to almost as many additional links as DISD.

Past the district level, however, is the teacher who must also do everything within his/her power to communicate effectively with the parents of their students. Following is a list of ways teachers can establish connections with their parents:

1. Encourage parents to join the PTA
2. Encourage and inform parents about volunteer opportunities at school

3. Parent-teacher conferences
4. Telephone calls (good first, please)
5. Establish a web presence on the school's web site
6. Post homework on the web site
7. Send home notes in an established pattern: for instance, on Friday, send a folder home with all things that are due and announce what children will be doing the next week.

The Classroom Environment Connection

Competencies 5 and 6 focus on establishing a **good working environment** within the classroom. When that positive environment exists, both of these competencies translate into good working relationships between the teacher and the community.

1. The teacher needs to learn how to respond to nonresponsive parents. It is not enough to say, "Well, parents just won't respond. So . . .".
2. Teachers must always keep in mind that occasionally there will be hostile and confrontational parents, so they must learn some basic conflict resolution techniques.

Whatever pattern of communication you establish, it should be part of a plan that parents can count on. Overreaching in your plans can be just as detrimental as too little communication, so create your plan and then have a conference with the principal or department chair to ask for approval.

State Proficiency #2 States That the Teacher:

✦ Engages families, parents, guardians, and other legal caregivers in various aspects of the educational program.

Usually, it is easy to engage parents in the extracurricular activities of their children. For instance, booster clubs exist for speech teams and band, for basketball and football. However, academic areas, unless it is the Academic Decathelon, for example, usually have a harder time establishing support for classes. Still, teachers might initiate support by asking for volunteers to work with students on special projects. Ask parents to be speakers on subjects where they have expertise, making sure to establish objectives first.

State Proficiency #3 States That the Teacher:

✦ Interacts appropriately with all families, including those that have diverse characteristics, backgrounds, and needs.

Everyone has seen movies featuring amazing blond, beautiful teachers who brave inner city gangs and ne'er do wells to reach their students. While participating in a community doorbell ringing project is desirable, often profitable in terms of attendance, and encouraged, teachers must be aware of dangers and misinterpretation of intent. Past that, many children of minority cultures are reticent to come to school and participate. Asking someone to go with you to visit a parent and help you interpret will go a long way to gaining the necessary help for your students.

State Proficiency #5 States That the Teacher:

✦ Conducts effective conferences with parents, guardians, and other legal caregivers.

Perhaps nothing scares a new teacher quite as much as a parent-teacher conference. The following in-depth discussion covers skills a teacher should practice from Day 1 in the classroom.

Several kinds of issues may arise that necessitate conferences with parents. For example, students who are frequently absent will need a great deal of parent-teacher support and cooperation. Failure to do homework is another frequent situation requiring a parent conference. You may learn upon visiting with parents that this child is viewing too much television, playing too many video games, or simply staying up too late talking on the telephone.

Document! Document! Document!

This may be a good place to interject the word and advice "Document, Document, Document!" This command means you need to write, in an organized fashion, any encounter with a student that you believe might later lead to a parent conference. Your documentation should include:

+ The day's date, and
+ a clear statement of everything that happened
    ◇ include your words and
    ◇ the student's words (even if it includes profanity)
+ Keep a readily-accessible file for documentation

> **NOTE**
> Understand that your private notes are just that—private, so keep them secure and away from accidental "prying" eyes. No one can demand to see your notes UNLESS the conflict grows into the legal system in which case they can be subpoenaed. In the unlikely event that may happen, make sure your language is clear and concise and as emotionless as possible. Sort "fact" from "fiction" and deal with fact. Leave the fiction alone.

Later, you will be very glad you have documentation of the event. Sometimes students tell parents half-truths, so angry parents come to you based upon their child's version of events, and if you are not prepared, you may find yourself being defensive. Defensiveness is to be avoided at all costs!

You may be told by other teachers that it "does no good" to telephone parents (besides "They all work, and you just waste your time trying to get them") which feeds into the somewhat predominant thinking that parents just don't care about their children. While the noncaring parent certainly exists, he/she must prove that he doesn't care before you believe it to be true.

The research of James Comer in the 1990s reveals that some parents are reluctant to become involved in the education of their children for several reasons:

+ Because some parents have had negative experiences in school, they want to stay way from schools.
+ They may avoid schools if they never graduated from high school.
+ Some parents believe that they would be perceived as inept or as meddling.
+ Some parents do not have enough skill to follow channels to see the principal.

Usually, the nonresponsive parent is one who may be single and/or overworked and stressed. She/he doesn't want "trouble" at school any more than you want "trouble" with a parent. Remember, too, your role is to teach the child—no matter what—so look for the win-win solutions.

On the other hand, once parents become involved in the education of their children and feel valued as a contributor, many benefits accrue:

+ Students show improved grades, attendance, test scores, and the ability to handle more complex, higher cognitive academic tasks.
+ Students have reduced suspension and referral rates for discipline problems.

Those two benefits compose the basis for a win-win situation.

Dealing with the Angry Parent

I read somewhere that today's parents are too busy to parent, but they're not too busy to be the heroes against the oppression of schools! Whether that be true or an exaggeration, I don't know, but dealing with angry parents is not a good situation to be in. That is why you should learn a few rules:

- Less is more: Let the parent talk; keep your opinions to yourself.
- When it is time for you to speak, have your documentation of the event at hand (grades, progress reports, a child's note, etc.).
- Sort "fact" from "fiction" and deal exclusively with fact. Leave the fiction alone.
    a. I'll admit that is easier said than done, and most teachers do not get enough practice to get really "good" at such scenes.
- Prepare emotionally for a conference by thinking about the situation clearly. Choose your words carefully and stay professional and calm.

Note: Teachers normally use professional educational terms to discuss issues, and parents might perceive this practice as teachers talking down to them. Judge the situation and adjust your speech accordingly. Do not use jargon to intimidate anyone.

Likewise, never underestimate the parent who is involved and who does his homework prior to coming in to see you. Knowledge is power for both the parent and the teacher!

- Show understanding of the parents' position.
- Sometimes, parents will end the conference thanking you for caring about their child.
    a. In the end, a parent may even tell you that they understand where you are coming from; when that happens the door is open to finding a way to work with the parent and the child.
    b. If you expect the worst, ask the principal to join your conference, although do not let it appear like you are "ganging up" on the parent.
- Finally, value the parent's contribution and conclude on a positive note.

Rules! Rules! Rules!

Every teacher develops a classroom discipline plan (C6). That plan should be in strict accord with the school's policy, which can be found online or in printed form.

Usually the last resort for dealing with discipline is to refer the student to the office for suspension, study hall, or expulsion. Each step of discipline in the classroom should be carefully documented with the date, time, and occurrence as described previously.

It is inevitable that at some time during a teacher's career, it will become necessary to send a child to the office for a severe offense. In that case, use the following guidelines to work through the problem because it is likely that you will be called into the principal's office to talk to the parent.

- Know district policies about referring students to counselors or professionals who specialize in behavioral problems.
- Some schools have Student Assistance Programs (SAP) and Student Assistant Counselors (SACs).
- Know district policies about referring students to the principal and follow those guidelines to the letter.

Whatever the event or however it unfolds, be sure to exhibit professional and confidential behavior. Never, but never speak to other students about the behavior of any child.

Remember, the overarching goal of education is to educate the student by whatever means possible, so the teacher should strive to develop a positive relationship with parents.

> **QUESTION**
> How does a teacher establish a positive relationship with parents?
>
> *Your Answer:*

If you answered that this relationship is developed through open and free communication between teacher and parent, you are on the right track. Like everything else in teaching, you must plan that communication. You must also exude that you are a fair teacher. You must find creative ways of demonstrating that fairness and openness to parents.

State Proficiency #6 States That the Teacher:

✦ Effectively uses family support resources (e.g., community, interagency) to enhance family involvement in student learning.

Initially, the teacher can do several things as she prepares to teach in a particular school. She can learn about the community by:

Touring the school's community and doing an environmental scan;

Find out who is responsible for setting up school district–community programs.

A teacher can research the parent-teacher organizations such as PTA and determine what role it plays in the school.

Read the "School's Report Card" (AEIS Report/TEA) in a knowledgeable way and understand the role that you play in that report.

Then, the teacher can utilize the strengths of the community by:

Identifying the organizations that connect to the school;

Learning the steps involved in bringing the community resources into the classroom;

Identifying the major problems in the community; and finally,

Learning how organizations and programs assist in the learning process.

Some school districts participate in a district-wide plan for character development. One such program is "Character Counts," which focuses on the character traits of "trustworthiness, respect, responsibility, fairness, caring, and citizenship." The "Six Pillars of Character" will work nicely into the six six-week grading periods. Teachers can encourage parents to reinforce these traits at home as they are introduced at school. More can be found about this outstanding example of building character at *www.charactercounts.org*.

INDEPENDENT PRACTICE AND MODELING (HOMEWORK)

1. **Scholar's Vocabulary:** Using the State-produced list of proficiencies preservice teachers should have related to Competency 11, highlight terms you wish to place in your interactive glossary. You should have a minimum of five terms from C11. (See the model in the Appendices.)

2. **Reflective Writing:** Using the eleven-sentence model in the appendices, write a reflection on Competency 11.

3. Research a large independent school district online and investigate the parent connection the ISD hopes to make. Access a large ISD's web presence and click on its community link.
   a. Cut/paste the mission of the ISD regarding parents.
   b. List the opportunities parents have to be involved with the school; Evaluate how effective/sincere the web site is in integrating parents into the school.

4. Obtain a copy of a discipline referral form for an ISD. Using an event that happened during one of your classroom observations, fill out the form as accurately as possible.

CLOSURE/FOLLOW-UP

Parent-teacher communication serves some very important purposes. Some of them might be:

+ to discuss a child's learning problems;
+ to ward off failure;
+ to discuss class plans for the year;
+ to find opportunities to assist the teacher; and
+ to create rapport between home and school.

Of all the reasons for establishing open lines of communication with the homes/parents of your students, the most important reason is their welfare and achievement.

Remember that the children who are read to in early childhood by parents who set high expectations are usually successful. The more you can do to encourage parents to check homework, read aloud, provide a variety of reading materials, and talk to children about expectations, the easier your job will be.

ASSESSMENT

Competency 11 mandates that the preservice teacher learn about the community and about the parents of the students she will teach.

Ask yourself whether you have mastered these objectives.

+ **Objective 1:** Did you design a plan for developing a positive relationship with parents?
+ **Objective 2:** Did you design a plan for communicating with parents?
+ **Objective 3:** Can you describe effective communication methods of handling a parent conference?
+ **Objective 4:** Write some sample responses for dealing with nonresponsive parents.
+ **Objective 5:** Create a scenario of a meeting with a hostile parent and describe how a teacher might respond.
+ **Objective 6:** Suggest ideas for learning about the community.
+ **Objective 7:** Elaborate ideas for utilizing the strengths within the community.

Competency 11 Family Involvement

PRACTICE QUESTIONS

Now assess your learning by answering these questions. Answers are given in the Appendices.

1. You have an angry father who enters the school because his son has called home three times already asking Daddy to bring his walking shoes for a field trip. He is rude to his son's teacher and tells him that he should send notes home to the parents about field trips. This is his second trip to the school to bring a field trip slip and now walking shoes, and he is tired of taking off of work to come to the school. How should the teacher deal with the hostile parent?
    a. Tell the parent to talk to his child to find out what he is doing.
    b. Ask a neighbor teacher to witness the situation just in case it gets out of hand. Document the situation while the father is still there.
    c. Tell the parent you understand his dilemma, but you have over 280 students to deal with each day, and you cannot be sure every child takes messages home.
    d. Follow the school's handbook as closely as possible regarding field trips. Try to diffuse the situation by remaining calm.

2. Mrs. White calls a parent to discuss trouble she is having with a parent's child. She begins the conversation by saying, "I think there is something wrong with your child." What should Mrs. White have said to this parent in place of what she did say?
    a. "Your child is a disruption in my class. Every day I intervene in potentially serious occurrences. Could you please talk to him and ask him to behave?"
    b. "Your child will have to be removed from my classroom if his behavior does not change."
    c. "Your son and I have different ideas about classroom behavior. Could you come to school so that we might all three discuss this situation and resolve it?"
    d. "Your child has a behavior problem that we need to discuss as soon as possible."

3. Mrs. Smith is a new teacher and is trying to become familiar with the parents of students. What is the best thing she can do to meet the parents of her students?
    a. Send a note home with the students inviting parents to come visit with her during her conference period.
    b. Call all of the parents during her office time to visit with them.
    c. Invite everyone to an open house the first month of school.
    d. Invite the parents to visit the classroom for a day.

4. A teacher should let the parents know that they can:
    I. be reached at specific times or in specific ways.
    II. be contacted directly as questions or concerns arise.
    III. take over any responsibilities that the parent does not have time for.
    IV. visit with her at any time.
        a. I, II, III.
        b. I, III, IV
        c. II, III, IV
        d. I, II, IV

5. What are some things that parents could to do help both the teacher and the student/child?
    I. Set a good example.
    II. Emphasize the need for competition.
    III. Provide resources at home for reading and learning.
    IV. View drinking by underage youth and excessive partying as a serious matter.
        a. I, II, III
        b. I, III, IV
        c. I, II, IV
        d. II, III, IV

6. Derrick is an eleventh grade student who is juggling student council, FFA, and a part-time job after school and on some weekends. His grades have been suffering since he's taken on these new responsibilities. Derrick's father calls his teacher to show his concern with these issues regarding Derrick. It would be most appropriate for the teacher to:
    a. ask Derrick and his father to meet with her to discuss possible options for balancing Derrick's school and job responsibilities.
    b. set up appointments with community resources to assist the father.
    c. assure Derrick's father that the school staff will keep Derrick's class involvement minimized.
    d. set up an appointment with the father and the school counselor to provide advice and support.

7. Paul, a twelfth grader at AHS, is a popular football player. He is smart, cute, and is planning on being Valedictorian, but a girl is also vying for the top position in the class. Toward the end of the year he does not turn in a homework assignment. He knows that he must take responsibility for the grade and take an "O" for the assignment. He does not seem that upset by this, but his mother shows up at the school yelling and screaming at the teacher, principal, and even the superintendent. She cannot believe that they will not forgive Paul this one assignment and let him make it up or that they will not even change the grade. As a teacher how would you handle this situation?
    a. Ask the parent to read the homework policy and then she will understand.
    b. Calmly explain that Paul knew what his responsibilities were, and show her how this "O" will or will not affect his grade and his position in the class.
    c. Let Paul turn in the assignment late since he has been a stellar student.
    d. Let the principal and superintendent handle the problem; it is clearly out of the teacher's realm of responsibility.

8. Erin has been having behavior problems in English class for the first part of the semester. Mrs. Williams has had several conferences with Erin's mother concerning these behavior problems. During the last part of the semester though, Erin has been a model student. Mrs. Williams would like to let Erin's mother know this. What would be the best way to communicate this good behavior to Erin's mother?
    a. Send a note explaining this behavior.
    b. Schedule a conference with Erin's mother.
    c. Telephone the parent.
    d. Do nothing; Erin's grades reflect the change.

9. You saw Oscar hit Steve, a student of yours. Steve than chased the student and proceeded to throw Oscar on the ground and begin a fight. You sent both students to the office and documented the event. When Steve's mom got a copy of the referral from the office, she was upset at the way you worded the office referral because it made Steve look guilty. She wanted it changed; she had no problem with the punishment just the wording. What should you do?
   a. Do not change the document; explain to the parent that you reported your observations honestly.
   b. Agree to rewrite the referral moderating the words to show that Oscar was primarily at fault.
   c. Tell the parent that you will change the referral and then do nothing. The parent would not get a second, revised copy from the office.
   d. Explain to the parent that the principal had already seen the referral, acted upon it, and sent it to the parent; therefore, the document became an official state document. You were powerless to change it.

10. During a test, you observe Billy cheating by accessing notes he carefully placed on the floor beside his desk. Your policy is to take up the test and give a zero. Billy goes home and tells his parents that you accused him of cheating and gave him a zero. Understandably, Billy's parents are quite upset and want to have a meeting with you. At the meeting they tell you that their son does not cheat and that you will allow him to have a retake, or else they will go to the superintendent who is a friend of theirs. What should you do?
    a. Allow Billy to have a retake.
    b. Allow Billy to have a retake, but the highest grade he can get is a 70.
    c. Have a meeting with the parents, the principal, and Billy and explain to them what happened and that the grade sticks.
    d. Tell the parents that they do not have the whole story. Produce the cheat sheet and reiterate that you will not allow a retake.

11. Mr. Jones takes his fifth grade class to the Panhandle Plains Museum to see the dinosaur display. This is an example of:
    a. school-business relations.
    b. school-parent relations.
    c. school-civil service relations.
    d. school-parent sponsor relations.

12. Mrs. Smith invites a Wall Street stockbroker to her twelfth grade classroom to explain how Wall Street trading affects day-to-day life. The type of class you would want this in is:
    a. government class.
    b. economics class.
    c. math class.
    d. geography class.

13. Sgt. Remington is invited to come into Mrs. Meyers' fourth grade class to discuss home safety. The topics that Sgt. Remington can discuss include:
    a. playing with matches.
    b. gun safety.
    c. talking to strangers.
    d. All of the above.

14. Mr. Wallick, who is a twelfth grade health teacher, might invite which persons from the community to talk with the class?
    a. Medical personnel to talk about STDs
    b. Substance abuse counselor to talk about drugs
    c. Cancer survivors to talk about smoking
    d. All of the above.

15. Miss Moore's homeroom mothers want to start a class fundraiser to get the first grade classroom a multimedia system. Is this a good or bad idea?
    a. It's a bad idea because it shows favoritism for her classroom.
    b. It's a bad idea because her students are too young to benefit from the complicated plan.
    c. It's a good idea to have computers accessible to the children at an early age to promote computer awareness.
    d. It's a good idea because parents will be doing most of the work.

CAREER PLANNING

Teachers who do a great job of communicating with parents might work toward a media communications position. Keep in mind, the Superintendent usually handles media in small districts, but in larger districts, there will often be an entire office devoted to media relations. Assistant Principals also spend a greater part of every day working with parents. Individuals who like conflict management and handle conflict well are suited for these positions.

MATERIALS NEEDED

Internet, school handbook(s), teacher interview

SUGGESTIONS FOR ADDITIONAL ASSIGNMENTS

1. Make a mock telephone call to one of your cooperative learning group members and explain to that "parent" why you are requesting a meeting.
    a. Create a method for keeping records of telephone calls.
    b. Record the results of that telephone call.
    c. "Meet" with the parent.
    d. Record your reactions.
    e. Share your answers/recordings within your group.

2. Design a comprehensive plan for communicating with parents that you would be comfortable with. You may wish to include web, paper, telephone, and person-to-person methods.

3. Refer to the student handbook of an ISD, and investigate an ISD protocol for reporting grades. Then, access this web site for *Education World*: http://www.educationworld.com/a_tech/tech/tech101.shtml

    Education World provides many free and interactive templates. Choose one letter, one progress report, and one other template of your choosing to work with. Individualize each of these documents.

4. Visit an educational bookstore and shop the aisles to find creative ways to communicate with parents. Document your "wish" list with photos of creative ideas you would like to use.

5. Research the role of Parent-Teacher Organizations today. Some of these organizations might be Parent-Teacher Association, Parent-Teacher Organization, or Parent-Teacher-Student Association. Write a short reflective essay over the role of PTAs today.

6. If your local ISD has an active PTA, interview the President to discover ways that the organization works with the school to promote children's educational welfare.

7. Investigate an ISD that uses web sites, and visit with a teacher to find out how the process works. Write a brief essay discussing the pros/cons of creating a class web site.

8. Interview a juvenile probation officer regarding the local issues within the schools.

9. Identify organizations such as CASA and Junior Achievement to discover what they do and how their resources might be a positive influence in the ISD.

10. Design a communication plan for teacher and family.
    a. Template, technology, newsletter

11. Pretend it is open house in the fall, and you are about to meet with your parents for the first time. Write your speech to parents and tell them how you will engage families this year.

12. Family support resources abound in every community. Find someone associated with Family Protective Services to interview. Write your essay in a Q&A format focusing on the school-FPS connection.

13. Check to see if your community has a Court Appointed Special Advocate (CASA) program. This organization focuses on abused and neglected children who become part of the court system. Interview an individual who is associated with CASA, then write a report that demonstrates how CASA assists school children.

14. What is conflict management? Use the Internet to find information on conflict management protocol and create a list of interventions that might be useful to you in the classroom.

Competency 12

Professional Knowledge and Skills

LESSON PLAN FOR COMPETENCY 12

STATE STANDARDS: STANDARD 4, COMPETENCY 12

Competency 012: The teacher enhances **professional knowledge and skills** by effectively interacting with other members of the educational community and participating in various types of professional activities.

STATE TEACHER PROFICIENCIES

Competency 012

The teacher enhances professional knowledge and skills by effectively interacting with other members of the educational community and participating in various types of professional activities.

The beginning teacher:

- Interacts appropriately with other professionals in the school community (e.g., **vertical teaming, horizontal teaming, team teaching, mentoring**).
- Maintains supportive, cooperative **relationships with professional colleagues** and collaborates to support students' learning and to achieve campus and district goals.
- Knows the roles and **responsibilities of specialists** and other professionals at the building and district levels (e.g., **department chairperson, principal, board of trustees, curriculum coordinator, technology coordinator, special education professional**).
- Understands the value of participating in **school activities** and contributes to school and district (e.g., by participating in decision making and problem solving, sharing ideas and expertise, serving on committees, volunteering to participate in events and projects).
- Uses **resources and support systems** effectively (e.g., mentors, service centers, state initiatives, universities) to address **professional development** needs.
- Recognizes characteristics, goals, and procedures associated with **teacher appraisal** and uses appraisal results to improve teaching skills.
- Works productively with **supervisors, mentors,** and other colleagues to address issues and to enhance professional knowledge and skills.
- Understands and uses **professional development resources** (e.g., mentors and other support systems, conferences, online resources, workshops, journals, professional associations, coursework) to enhance knowledge, pedagogical skills, and technological expertise.
- Engages in **reflection** and **self-assessment** to identify strengths, challenges, and potential problems; improve teaching performance; and achieve professional goals.

TEACHING OBJECTIVES

At the end of the lesson, the student should be able to:

- Explain the function of the local school board.
- Differentiate among the several professional educational organizations.
- Discover specialized professional organizations.
- Articulate several purposes for belonging to a professional organization.
- Discover professional learning goes far beyond college graduation.
- Demonstrate what it means to be a reflective practitioner through reflective writings.
- Recalling the "Career Planning" sections in each chapter, explain the teacher roles within the school.
- Describe site-based management and explain how a school with site-based management might factor into your obtaining a position.
- Describe the following teacher roles within the school:
    ◇ Resource evaluator
    ◇ Curriculum worker
    ◇ Specialist
    ◇ Transmitter of values

C12 KEY WORDS: PROFESSIONAL DEVELOPMENT

Terms associated with professional development

Professional Development	Inservice Training	School Board
Hierarchy	Preservice	Lifelong Learners
Salary Schedules	Texas Teacher Retirement System	ISD
Paraprofessional	Student Teaching	SBEC
NTE	ETS	PDAS
TEA	TheCB	

INTRODUCTION/FOCUS

Have you ever heard the teacher *put-down* "Those who can, do; and those who can't teach"? That anyone would even think that thought much less say it out loud is distressing because what job could possibly be more important that teaching tomorrow's leaders? You may also have heard more uplifting statements such as, "If you can read, thank a teacher," or "Every doctor/lawyer/accountant had teachers." I prefer to think that professionals in the field of teaching have an innate sense of their worth and their importance to society.

Aristotle had it right when he said, "Teachers, who educate children, deserve more honor than parents, who merely give them birth; for the latter provide mere life, while the former ensure a good life." Aristotle wasn't attempting to demean parents when he used the phrase "mere life"—he was trying to show the comparison between the physical event of birth and the spiritual blessing of fruitful living. "Mere life" implies meeting basic needs, while educating children ensures a good life or quality of existence. If you take the time to ask a lot of teachers if they feel "honored" to be teachers, you will hear them say they take great pride in influencing future generations—that there is no greater payment than seeing children grow day by day.

This competency stresses the importance for educators to be part of a team—a team composed of parents, children, school personnel, and personal families. These interpersonal connections demand that a future teacher understand and engage in ongoing professional development and lifelong learning. The following quote from *The Law of Accelerating Returns* demonstrates how rapidly information is increasing and, thus, how important it is for teachers to stay abreast of change.

> "An analysis of the history of technology shows that technological change is exponential, contrary to the common-sense 'intuitive linear' view. So we won't experience 100 years of progress in the 21st century—it will be more like 20,000 years of progress (at today's rate). The 'returns,' such as chip speed and cost-effectiveness, also increase exponentially. There's even exponential growth in the rate of exponential growth."
>
> *Kurzweil (2001) essay* The Law of Accelerating Returns

TRANSITION: Some say knowledge doubles anywhere from every year to every seven years, and we laughingly refer to *information overload* or to *TMI* (too much information) from time to time. As might be expected with knowledge increasing exponentially, teacher professional development is a necessity to maintain credibility and relevance in the classroom.

INSTRUCTIONAL INPUT AND GUIDED PRACTICE

What we need to know about professional development

The Instructional Input in this lesson plan will contain *guided practice* in the form of questions placed throughout the chapter. References to web sites will also serve as guided practice as you research topics to gain further knowledge and information and application.

QUESTION
What is Professional Development?

Answer: **Professional development** refers to skills and knowledge attained for both personal development and career advancement. Professional development encompasses all types of facilitated learning opportunities, ranging from college degrees to formal coursework, conferences, and informal learning opportunities situated in practice. It has been described as intensive and collaborative, ideally incorporating an evaluative stage.[1] There are a variety of approaches to professional development, including consultation, coaching, communities of practice, lesson study, mentoring, reflective supervision, and technical assistance.[2]

Accessed Wikipedia 7/14/10
http://en.wikipedia.org/wiki/Professional_development#cite_note-0 for both {1} and {2}.

BEGIN AT THE BEGINNING

Introduction to Professional Development

The definition of professional development provided gives a comprehensive description of the activities one may engage in to increase or further develop professional skills. Those activities (and others) are bulleted here for emphasis:

- personal and career advancement
- college degrees
- formal coursework
- conferences
- informal learning opportunities situated in practice
- intensive and collaborative
- incorporating an evaluative stage
- consultation
- coaching
- communities of practice
- lesson study
- mentoring
- reflective supervision
- technical assistance

Once an individual graduates from college and becomes certified to teach, one begins to understand the importance of ongoing development.

> **QUESTION**
> I thought when I finished college, my "school work" would be complete.
> Am I expected to pay for additional development?
>
> *Your Answer:*
>
> NOTE: In the State of Texas one is expected to accumulate Continuing Education Units (CEUs) to keep the teaching certificate current; while there are choices to be made in what kind of professional development you want to attend, you must renew your certificate every five years.

If you want to continue your formal education (see the Career Planning section in each chapter) with a graduate degree, you will probably have to pay for the costs associated with that degree. Some districts may offer a reimbursement plan, but more often, there will be a pay increase once the degree is granted. Many local chapters of professional organizations, such as Delta Kappa Gamma and Phi Theta Kappa, offer scholarships for students who wish to obtain additional formal education.

School districts often provide professional development opportunities for teachers at the beginning of each semester during the **inservice** days. Teachers must participate in these activities and often will have a say in what is to be learned or who the presenters will be. Inservice training will often provide professional development hours toward certificate renewal.

Local universities and colleges will also offer many educational opportunities, so bookmark the websites and keep abreast of offerings semester by semester. For example, there may be a local Teachers of English chapter at the university or a science conference geared towards public school pedagogy. Most universities have a strong interest in reading and promote reading through national (IRA) and state (TSRA) organizations of reading. These opportunities provide excellent additional opportunity for bolstering your academic credentials.

Finally, do not forget about adding an additional certification area to your resume. One can undergo the lengthy process of becoming a nationally certified teacher (NTE) or simply take an additional six college credit hours to receive an ESL or special education endorsement.

Preservice teachers are those who are in training to become teachers. They often participate in many professional development opportunities, such as attending lectures or student organization meetings, as part of their training. As noted in the introduction of this textbook, this course is aligned with the Pedagogy and Professional Responsibilities (PPR) standards set by the State. In learning the PPR competencies, you are getting the foundation for all of your future professional development as a teacher.

Foundational to the profession of teaching are several questions. Why do I want to teach? What do I believe about teaching as a profession, and what are the characteristics of good teachers? Following is an outline of some of the major reasons individuals decide to pursue teaching as a career.

> **QUESTION**
> Why Teach? On the table of contents page of your ePortfolio, you have an opportunity to write "My Motivation to Teach."
>
> Why do you want to teach?

Many teachers say they teach because they like children. Others say they teach because they desire to help children learn and they love that *light bulb* that goes off ever so often! Still others say they teach because they want to help children become good citizens. Finally, some say they teach because of a former teacher!

Even though monetary rewards have never been associated with teaching, teacher salaries have been rising steadily over the last several decades. Teachers also, for the most part, like the environment of the schoolhouse and state that their working conditions are usually very good.

Guess at what you think your first year's salary will be when you get that first contract? _____

Now access the following web site to compare what you think the salary will be to what the actual salary will be: *www.tea.state.tx.us*. Once you get to the TEA's home page, scroll down the alpha order list to "salary schedules" to find current salaries. You might also be interested in going to the web site of an independent school district were you would want to teach to compare that ISD's salary schedule with the State's schedule.

What Does a Teacher Do?

Even though you have observed teachers throughout your educational life, you may not know all the things a teacher does. Following are a few of the activities that make up a teacher's professional life.

> **STUDENT QUESTION**
> What does a teacher do?

Teachers have many jobs—some of which are very apparent to students, but many of which are not so visible. Teachers do paperwork:

- Grade papers
- Fill out grade reports
- Fill out progress reports
- Plan for lessons
- Make copies
- Prepare bulletin boards
- Prepare reports for the main office
- Set up and maintain a grade book
- Make overheads
- Post children's work around the room and in the hallways
- Take attendance and make reports
- Take lunch money and account for it
- Keep discipline records documented
- Sign in and out of the building
- Order equipment and supplies

All of these tasks do not require the same amount of time, but all of them are important. A teacher's records are very important, and accuracy is a must. The principal might even say, "When you evacuate the building in case of a fire, get the kids out, then get your gradebook, and leave everything else behind!" Today, teachers may not even have a paper copy gradebook, so grades are automatically registered on a computer. Even though the ISD probably provides for periodic back up of files, you should learn to back up your own files in a timely fashion to prevent irreplaceable loss.

The Teaching Process

Of course, you know that teachers teach, but what, exactly, goes into the teaching process? Following is a partial list of activities involved in teaching.

Teachers teach:

- Consult or write curriculum guides
- Prepare semester/unit plans
- Prepare all materials needed for each plan
- Secure all technology needed for lessons
- Write tests
- Evaluate tests
- Decide if students need re-teaching
- Decide if students need enrichment
- Prepare lessons for inclusion students
- Mentor students individually

Teachers organize:

- Pick up mail daily
- Keep records on students
- File plans and student work
- Consult with other teachers about lessons
- Plan for semesters and units as a whole
- Serve on committees
- Supervise extracurricular activities

Teachers communicate:

- With students
- With parents
- With other teachers
- With administration
- With community members
- By maintaining web sites

Within these many activities, four terms related to the teaching process are very important: vertical teaming, horizontal teaming, team teaching, and mentoring.

Vertical teaming refers to the K–12 vertical structure of education. English teachers from the 6–7–8 grades, for example, may work with the high school English teachers to be sure they are teaching sequentially.

Horizontal teaming refers to grade-level teaming. For example, all the third grade teachers may meet once a week to write lesson plans, or all the third grade teachers across a school district may meet for the same purpose.

Team teaching involves two teachers, usually of two different disciplines, who teach the same group of students in a thematic way. For example, the American History teacher and the American Literature teachers may "team" to teach periods in American history/English at the same time.

Mentoring is an ongoing event through which experienced teachers may pair with new teachers or teachers mentor students through student organizations or in small study groups.

The Professional Development and Appraisal System (PDAS)

Each year teachers must be evaluated by a State-approved instrument called the PDAS. Following is information from Region 13's web site describing this process. Access this web site to learn more about how you will be evaluated *http://www5.esc13.net/pdas/*.

Professional Development and Appraisal System (PDAS) Introduction

PDAS remains in place as the State's approved instrument for appraising its teachers and identifying areas that would benefit from staff development. Cornerstones of the process include a minimum of one 45-minute observation and completion of the Teacher Self-Report form. PDAS includes 51 criteria within eight domains reflecting the *Proficiencies for Learner-Centered Instruction* adopted in 1997 by the State Board for Educator Certification (SBEC). The domains are:

1. Active, Successful Student Participation in the Learning Process
2. Learner-centered Instruction
3. Evaluation and Feedback on Student Progress
4. Management of Student Discipline, Instructional Strategies, Time/Materials
5. Professional Communication
6. Professional Development
7. Compliance with Policies, Operating Procedures, and Requirements
8. Improvement of All Students' Academic Performance

Included in the appraisal system are Instructional Leadership Development (ILD) and Administrator Appraisal.

PDAS requires that new teachers and teachers new to a district receive an orientation. In addition, the *PDAS Teacher Manual* is to be given to ALL teachers (see *Letter to the PDAS Trainer Addressed*).

Teacher Characteristics

Another important self-assessment list includes characteristics usually attributed to good teachers.

QUESTION
What are the characteristics of a good teacher?

Teachers have many wonderful characteristics that are geared toward interpersonal relationships and organizational skills. It should be noted that "good teachers" are set apart from "teachers." When teacher recruiters talk about teaching, they usually talk about the need for "good teachers." As you can see from the following short list of characteristics, good teachers must be multitalented.

Good teachers are usually:

- Good communicators:
  - Encouragers
  - Challengers
  - Respectful
  - Passionate about teaching
  - Enthusiastic
- Champions for children:
  - Knowledgeable about human development
  - Know something of educational psychology

- Are patient
- Are sensitive to diversity
- Are available
- Are mentors
✦ Models for high expectations:
  - Initiators
  - Practical
  - Supportive
  - Creative
  - Inclusive
✦ Lifelong learners:
  - Learn for the sake of learning
  - Prepared
  - Thinkers
  - Questioners
  - Listeners

For more information on good teaching, go to this website: *http://www.bygpub.com/* and scroll down to "teaching."

How Does One Become a Teacher?

The process for becoming a teacher is unique to each state. In the State of Texas, the best resource for studying how to become a teacher is the Texas State Board of Education (SBEC) web site: *http://www.sbec.state.tx.us*.

At this web site, in the left-hand column, click "State Board for Educator Certification." Click "Educator Certification." In the left-hand column, click "Certification Information." Click "Certification Information Home." Then click "Becoming a classroom teacher in Texas." You can click on several other links that clarify the process. Click on "Testing/ Accountability." Then click on "Educator Testing," and click on "Study Guides & Preparation Manuals." Click on "TExES" (Texas Examinations of Educator Standards) to access information about the competency examinations required in the State of Texas before one can become certified. At the end of this chapter is an interactive assignment that will allow you to answer this question completely for becoming a teacher in Texas.

> **QUESTION**
> What is involved in teacher training?

Teacher Training in Texas

Teacher training in the State of Texas is varied, but many opportunities for certification exist. When an individual graduates from high school, he can begin his education training in community college with the Associate of Arts in Teaching, or he can go directly to a four-year program at a university. Teacher programs vary from university to university, but there are many similarities in the programs as well. Most universities see their mission in teacher training as very important and strive to make sure every candidate successfully completes the program.

Your choice of university should be based on a good match between you and the training you hope to obtain. All universities do not offer all teacher certifications, so before you transfer or enter a university program, you should access the university web site to determine if the desired degree is offered at that site. To find out about the programs offered at universities, you can also go to accredited programs from the SBEC web site *http://www.sbec.state.tx.us* and click on "Educator Certification." Then click on "Career and Technical Education." Click on the "Specific Requirements for Standard Career and Technical Education Certificates Based on Experience and Preparation in Skill Areas" link. Then click on the "approved educator preparation program" link to see a list of accredited programs. Most colleges of education will have their own web site that will give you important information about each program, such as required tests and scores and GPA requirements.

Certification Requirements

At the end of your teaching program, you will be required to obtain certification to teach. Go to *http://www.sbec.state.tx.us* and click on "Certification Requirements" to find out more about this process. All preservice teachers will take a minimum of two tests: one in the Pedagogy and Professional Responsibilities (PPR), which is grade-level specific and one for the content certification.

> **NOTE**
> Community Colleges in Texas offering the AAT focus on the Pedagogy and Professional Responsibilities curriculum.

Generally, in the State of Texas, a student completes the first two years of college in a core of courses that resemble many of the courses he has had in high school. Once the student begins the Junior/Senior years, the education focus becomes intensive. Students must generally take courses to develop professional skills, methods courses to help them apply the theory they learn in the professional development courses, and finally, they student teach. All through the program, students will be required to complete many field experience hours at elementary, middle, and secondary schools.

> **NOTE**
> There may be exemptions from student teaching if the student works as a paraprofessional in an ISD. There may also be tuition exemptions for paraprofessionals. Check with individual ISDs to determine the extent of benefits and local requirements for becoming a paraprofessional. Generally, the AAT will suffice as direct entry to become a paraprofessional at any ISD.

It should be noted that many of the states that require competency testing (not Texas) require the National Teacher Examination (NTE). Access information on that test on the Educational Testing Service (ETS) web site: *http://www.ets.org/praxis/*.

> **QUESTION**
> Where else can I find other sources for information on teaching?

Professionals in the State of Texas

Understanding the teacher's relationship with the State of Texas becomes very apparent as a student begins the advisement process for becoming a teacher in the state. Graduation rules regarding the number of hours a student must have to matriculate have changed significantly in the past few years; therefore, there is little or no room in the degree plan for elective or extraneous hours. Students wishing to be teachers must resolve early on to get good advisement and to access a schedule of the rotation of classes.

The web sites related to various state teacher sites are often complex and difficult to navigate for the novice, but you must learn to navigate them to get the most out of your future career as a teacher. You already know about the State Board for Educator Certification (SBEC), but you should also know about the Texas Education Agency (TEA) and the Coordinating Board (TheCB).

The Coordinating Board's Mission Statement

The Texas Higher Education Coordinating Board's mission is to work with the legislature, governor, governing boards, higher education institutions, and other entities to help Texas meet the goals of the state's higher education plan, Closing the Gaps by 2015, and thereby provide the people of Texas the widest access to higher education of the highest quality in the most efficient manner.

This statement can be accessed on the web site: *www.thecb.state.tx.us* along with multiple links to important information.

The Texas Education Agency's Mission Statement can be accessed at *www.tea.state.tx.us*.

The mission of the Texas Education Agency is to provide leadership, guidance, and resources to help schools meet the educational needs of all students.

When you become a teacher in Texas you will also become part of the **Texas Teacher Retirement System (TRS),** so that is one additional web site you will access from time to time at *www.trs.state.us.tx*. While retirement is the last things on a beginning teacher's mind, it is important to realize that your salary and your years of experience as a Texas educator factor into your ultimate retirement. You should make sound retirement decisions beginning with your first year of employment.

Professional Organizations

Once you are hired as a classroom teacher, one of the more difficult decisions you will be asked to make is to join a professional organization during the first week of teacher inservice. Several professional organizations will make a "pitch" for your membership, and all you will be able to think about is the cost and what your first paycheck is likely to be. It will be a difficult decision, but one that all teachers should consider carefully.

Professional organizations have been around for a long, long time. There are specific characteristics that define a profession, but you may not be aware of what they are yet. One of those characteristics is that the "profession" has organizations (national, state, or local) that promote and serve the interests of its members. Some of the professional organizations that you will hear from include the Texas Classroom Teachers Association (TCTA), Association for Teachers and Professional Educators (ATPE), and the National Educational Association (NEA). Later in the Assessment section of this lesson plan you will find an opportunity to research these organizations through their web sites.

Is Teaching a Profession?

> **QUESTION**
> Name several jobs you believe to be professions.
> Do you think teaching is a full profession or not? Why?

One important question that arises from time to time is the topic of professionalism. Most teachers call themselves *professionals,* but some people outside the profession do not think of teaching as a full profession.

The following practice #3 is designed to help you think through your personal conceptions of whether teaching is a profession or not.

Renewing Your Teaching Certificate

The emphasis on this competency is professionalism and professional growth to ensure that teachers become **lifelong learners** themselves. One last thing educators must know is that every five years educators must renew their certification.

232   Competency 12   Professional Knowledge and Skills

The Texas Education Agency has in place several requirements that all certified educators must adhere to:

- Hold a valid Standard Certificate that has not been, nor is in the process of being, sanctioned by TEA;
- Successfully undergo a national criminal background check by submitting fingerprints for review;
- Not be in default on a student loan or in arrears of child support;
- Complete the required number of clock hours of Continuing Professional Education (CPE);
- Pay the appropriate renewal fee;
  - NOTE: Please note that educational aides are not required to complete any CPE hours for certificate renewal.
- The CPE requirements for each class of certificate are as follows:
- Classroom teachers must complete 150 clock hours every five years;
- Counselors must complete 200 clock hours every five years;
- Learning resource specialists and school librarians must complete 200 clock hours every five years;
- Reading specialists must complete 200 clock hours every five years;
- Educational diagnosticians must complete 200 clock hours every five years;
- Master teachers must complete 200 clock hours every five years; and
  - Superintendents, principals, and other professional personnel must complete 200 clock hours every five years.

INDEPENDENT PRACTICE AND MODELING (HOMEWORK)

1. **Scholar's Vocabulary:** Using the State-produced list of proficiencies preservice teachers should have related to Competency 12, highlight terms you wish to place in your interactive glossary. You should have a minimum of five terms from C12. (See the model in the Appendices.)

2. **Reflective Writing:** Complete your reflective writing assignment for Competency 12 by using the eleven-sentence model.

3. Using the following "T" chart, in the first column, list as many professional jobs as you can think of. Then, in the second column, list jobs that you believe are non-professional in nature.

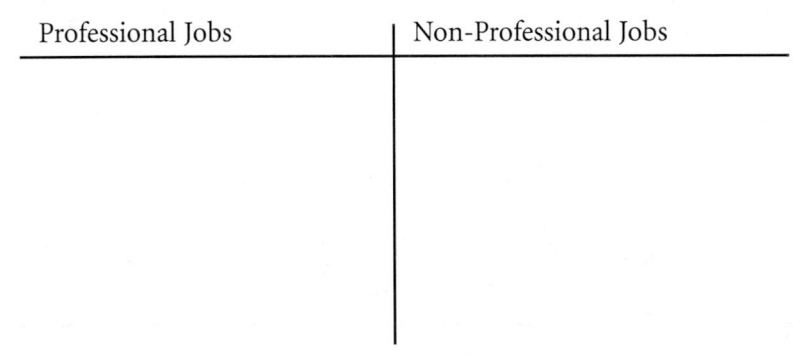

Professional Jobs	Non-Professional Jobs

Why are the jobs in the first column professional?

Why are the jobs in the second column non-professional?

Using your rationale from the two descriptions, what is the difference between a professional and a non-professional job?

4. Google and define the word *professional*; then, using several of the web sites provided, construct a list of characteristics for professionals.

Characteristics of a Professional

1.
2.
3.
4.
5.

6.
7.
8.
9.
10.

After you complete this list, compare it to your "T" Chart. What did you miss when you were brainstorming and filling out your "T" Chart?

5. Research the following educational organizations and list the membership requirements, dues, member benefits, and legislative activity according to each of these organizations: Texas Classroom Teachers Association (TCTA); Association of Texas Professional Educators (ATPE); National Education Association (NEA), and the Education Society of Midland College. Are students allowed to join any of these professional organizations before they graduate and become teachers?

TCTA: *http://www.tcta.org/*

ATPE: *www.atpe.org/*

NEA: *www.nea.org/*

EdSoc: *www.midland.edu*

After reading through much of the online information, do you believe it is important to belong to one of these organizations? Why or why not? What is the biggest drawback? What is the greatest advantage?

6. Access this web site: *http://thestatecolumn.com/state_politics/texas.php* and choose one current news article (you may need to start from *http://thestatecolumn.com* and click on "Texas") that will affect you as a teacher (e.g., today, the governor speaks about the future of electronic textbooks in classrooms), and write a brief position paper on the idea discussed.

CLOSURE/FOLLOW-UP

Throughout this study, you have had the opportunity to think about the concept of a professional and what sets a professional apart from the remainder of the working people in society. By now you should have a clear idea of your opinion of whether and under what circumstances teachers are or are not professionals. Then, you have had opportunity to consider carefully the many professional educational organizations that exist and reflect upon why those organizations exist and whether or not you feel you should join.

Whether you believe teaching is or is not a profession is almost irrelevant. In the end, it really boils down to the individual teacher who may or may not choose to behave professionally when dealing with each other, the community, parents, and/or students. You must develop a personal vision/concept of professional behavior and then decide whether you are up to the challenge. Then, you must keep up to date with educational news and happenings and perform accordingly and consistently.

ASSESSMENT

Ask yourself whether you have mastered these objectives.

- **Objective 1:** List several professional educational organizations.
- **Objective 2:** Name the professional organizations for your area of specialization.
- **Objective 3:** Articulate several purposes for belonging to a professional organization.
- **Objective 4:** Show your understanding of lifelong learning by describing how professional learning goes far beyond college graduation.
- **Objective 5:** Demonstrate what it means to be a reflective practitioner through reflective writings.
- **Objective 6:** Recalling the "Career Planning" sections in each chapter, explain the teacher roles within the school.
- **Objective 7:** Describe a site-based management team and explain how a school with site-based management might factor into your obtaining a position.
- **Objective 8:** Describe the following teacher roles within the school:
  - Resource evaluator
  - Curriculum worker
  - Specialist
  - Transmitter of values

PRACTICE QUESTIONS

Now assess your learning by answering these questions. Answers are given in the Appendices.

1. Mrs. Jameil went to a workshop that taught self-reflection and self-evaluation. In this workshop, she discovered how to reflect upon her teaching after each day and in return to write better self-evaluations. She also learned that she could visit other teachers' classes and invite other teachers into her classes. This workshop helped Mrs. Jameil grow personally and change professionally. Mrs. Jameil is clearly focusing on her growth in which of these areas?
   a. Site-based management stressing teamwork
   b. Effective schools research stressing high expectations
   c. Teacher as professional stressing professional growth
   d. Teacher roles within the school stressing improved scores for students

2. The concept of *academic engaged time,* sometimes called *time on task,* refers to the amount of time devoted to instruction and learning. What does either of these phrases involve?
   a. The time allocated or planned for instruction
   b. The time actually spent on instruction
   c. The time the student is actively engaged in learning
   d. All of the above.

3. Key decisions that are made in the schools and involve teachers, parents, and possibly other community members fall under which scope?
   a. Teacher as professional
   b. Teacher roles within the school
   c. Effective schools research
   d. Site-based management

4. Sometimes professional behavior involves common sense. Since male teachers are targeted for most sexual harassment complaints, how can a male teacher or any teacher for that matter help avoid a complaint?
   I. Avoid being alone with a female student.
   II. Avoid looking over a female student's shoulder to check work.
   III. Avoid touching, even a pat on the back.
   IV. Avoid saying or listening to any questionable jokes.
      a. I and IV
      b. I, II, and IV
      c. I, III, and IV
      d. I, II, III, and IV

5. You are a member of a professional teacher organization, and you are upset at the lack of health benefits for teachers. Which of the following should you **not** help your organization do?
   I. Organize a teacher rally in Austin
   II. Organize a strike
   III. Circulate a petition to teachers, making the problem clear
   IV. Write letters to legislators
      a. II
      b. III
      c. II and III
      d. You can do all of these.

6. Mr. Bingham is a new teacher and feels that he is a very capable classroom manager, so he does not anticipate any real problems with students or teachers. He decides that paying serious money for liability insurance through a professional organization is not necessary. What is the flaw in his thinking?
   a. There is no flaw in his thinking. He is capable of handling students. He had no problems during student teaching.
   b. Although he may be capable of handling students, he needs to be insured in case something extraordinary happens. You do not have to be "guilty" of anything to be accused.
   c. The only flaw in his thinking is that he is capable of handling his students.
   d. There is no flaw in his thinking; money is particularly important to new teachers, and belonging to a professional organization is quite expensive.

7. The principal, Mr. Nottingham, has just notified Ms. LaFever that a student has accused her of sexual harassment, so she is under investigation by the district. She is being placed on temporary suspension with pay. It seems two of her male students have accused her of flirting and making threats about their grades going down. Ms. LaFever panics because she did not join a professional organization; therefore, she has no liability insurance. Now, she fears, she is in danger of losing her job. Since the case is in its infancy, it has not gone to court. She knows she is innocent, but she still must hire a lawyer. She asks the principal if the district will cover those legal costs because she is innocent. While she does not yet know what the boys are claiming, she is certain that there is no evidence to support the boys' case. What should she have done to prevent this situation?
    a. She should have only paid attention to the girls because boys will make up stories to get attention especially with cute, young teachers.
    b. She should have joined a professional organization; although an organization could not have prevented the suit, it could help her through this difficult time.
    c. This situation is out of her control; she needs to go to the superintendent immediately and ask for financial help from the district; after all, she is innocent.
    d. She should wear very conservative clothing; the boys targeted her because she dressed provocatively.

8. Mr. Warren is the eleventh grade math teacher at Vanderbilt High School. He is excited about teaching and especially about the great hours. When he arrives for orientation, he discovers that he has to sponsor the math honor society and the math team. These extra activities will force him to stay after school several times a week, and he planned on private tutoring for extra money. He asks to withdraw from these extra responsibilities, but the principal denies the request. Who is correct in this situation, the principal or Mr. Warren and why?
    a. Mr. Warren. A teacher should only have to teach classes he agreed to teach when he accepted the job.
    b. Mr. Warren. He asked about extracurricular activity before the school year started and was told he would not have any responsibility for outside supervision. After all, he is a new teacher and needs to settle in before taking on more responsibilities.
    c. The principal. He can't find sponsors among the math faculty for math organizations because the teacher who was sponsoring is having a baby and is on bed rest.
    d. The principal. Mr. Warren should realize that there is a line in most teacher contracts that says "Will perform duties as assigned."

9. Jackie Q. comes to English class appearing to be stoned completely out of her mind. This is not the first time she has appeared to be out of control although Mr. Bell, her teacher, did not document the previous events. Mr. Bell now notices the unusual behavior and fears the worst—drug abuse. Furthermore, Mr. Bell has observed her with the wrong crowd at football games. What should he do with his suspicions of possible substance abuse?
    a. Ask her to stay behind after class and then discuss his suspicions with her. Ask her to stop her negative behavior.
    b. Call her parents and ask them to meet to talk about Jackie's problems.
    c. Ignore Jackie's problem and his suspicions because his suspicions could be wrong. Keep observing but begin documenting.
    d. Express his concerns to the appropriate school personnel to get Jackie on the school's radar for possible counseling to address her problems.

10. An English teacher, who has never taken a college course in drama, suddenly finds herself the new one-act play coach. The principal explained to her that because she was an outstanding English teacher who incorporated the study of drama in her class, this was a perfect fit for her. The teacher recognized a "snow" job when she saw it, but she saw the principal would not change her mind. This teacher teaches a full load but has never undertaken any extracurricular activities. What is her best course of action? She should:
    a. retire at mid-semester; she thinks the assignment is above and beyond the call of duty and she is tired.
    b. falsely tell the principal that her husband has taken a job in another city. After he appoints another sponsor, she will tell him the job fell through.
    c. ask the principal to assign another teacher to help her so the one-act play competition can be a cooperative venture.
    d. ask the principal if this is an ongoing thing or a temporary appointment before she adjusts to the new position and learns all about acting.

CAREER PLANNING

Students who plan on spending a career in education and like the concept of influencing and managing education in an administrative capacity may look to any of the web sites mentioned in this chapter to find opportunities for employment with the State of Texas. These offices are all located in Austin, Texas. These jobs require a high level of expertise, sometimes including a Ph.D. Be sure to look at the Master Teacher requirements.

MATERIALS NEEDED

Internet, pen, paper

SUGGESTIONS FOR ADDITIONAL ASSIGNMENTS

1. Attend a school board meeting

    Find a school board meeting to attend in your community. Research dates and times for meetings. Dress professionally and arrive promptly and sign in (if there is a place to sign in) and take a copy of the agenda. Introduce yourself to any administrator who happens to be there. Explain that you are there as an observer as part of an education class assignment. Take a seat (eat/drink if offered).

    ✦ Listen as the meeting unfolds.
    ✦ Make notes on your agenda—sides/back
    ✦ After the meeting is over, you may privately ask questions to a board member or administrator. Do not speak aloud in the meeting.
    ✦ Thank you is always appropriate as you leave.
    ✦ Write a two-page reflection about your experience after researching online what a school board is and who its members are. Find out which board member is your district representative.
        ◇ What did you learn about the membership of the school board?
        ◇ Were you received cordially? With suspicion?
        ◇ What is the role of the superintendent?
        ◇ Who else was in attendance? Media? Teachers? Parents? Students? Why were they there?
        ◇ Was there any controversy? About what? What was the resolution?

◇ What did you learn about "gifts" to the district? (if anything)
◇ What did you learn about employment practices?

2. Join the Education Society at Midland College (or at your college; if there is not an educational organization, form one).

3. Find a professional organization related to the area you want to teach. For example, if you want to be a reading teacher, research professional reading organizations (mentioned previously in the lecture); if you want to be a special education teacher, research professional organizations devoted to exceptional children.

    Write a one-page (double-spaced) essay focusing on the many benefits/values of belonging to a professional organization closely related to your area of study. Provide a copy of the home page of your organization as well as a copy of the Code of Ethics for that same organization.

4. Contact the TSTA office and obtain a copy of "A Good Start" or some other first-year teacher booklet. Analyze the contents in light of other competencies.

5. Become acquainted with the professional organizations related to education: American Association of University Women (AAUW), Texas Student Education Association (TSEA), Council for Exceptional Children (CEC), Reading Council, Kappa Delta Pi, Phi Delta Kappa, and Delta Kappa Gamma. How does one become a member? Why should one become a member?

    (Web sites for each of these are given under "Professional Resources.")

    Obtain a copy of the "Survival Guide," a publication of the Texas Classroom Teacher's Association (available online at *www.tcta.org*). Scroll down the list to find "new teachers" and find out what you need to know to survive.

6. Effective schools research outlines the practices of schools that are successful. Read the areas of this research that directly pertain to professional leadership. Analyze the research on educational leadership and write a summary statement about your leadership skills and evaluate whether you might be up for the challenge at a future time.

7. Define the following terms: Vertical teaming, horizontal teaming, team teaching, mentoring. How do you think a principal's leadership factors into setting up these kinds of school-based cooperative learning teams?

8. Locate an Independent School District's Mission. Copy it at the head of your paper and describe its content in light of its support for professional development of employees. Dig deeper into the web site to see if there is other information given on professional development. Evaluate whether you believe this district is truly devoted to the professional development of its teachers and support staff.

9. Interview a teacher to discover the roles each of these individuals play in the success of a school's academic programs.
    a. Chairperson of a department
    b. Principal and assistant principal(s)
    c. Board of trustees
    d. Curriculum coordinator
    e. Technical coordinator
    f. Special education professional

10. Read through a week's worth of local newspapers to see how visible school activities are. Are there special contents in the newspapers devoted to students and teachers? Who provides the information to the news media regarding school events?

11. Review the Texas Education Agency rules for recertification every five years. Which of these areas appeals to you the most for your future growth? Why?

12. Review your local Region Service Center or ISD web sites to find out more about the professional development and appraisal system. As you survey the "domains" upon which you will be evaluated, identify the relationships among these domains and the competencies under which you are being trained. In a brief essay, write the similarities you identify and any discrepancies you might discover.

13. The Region 13 web site refers to a self assessment and a learning plan. Find a copy of a self-assessment/learning plan and reflect (write) upon the concept of completing the circle of your training—from preservice to inservice.

14. Review the GOALS 2000 program endorsed by President George HW Bush. (#1) at *http://www2.ed.gov/G2K/GoalsRpt/index.html*. In light of the past ten years, what progress has been made toward GOALS 2000? Do you believe it is the role of government to promote/pass into legislation the goals for American education? Why or why not? Write a position paper on the following points:

    Discuss point 1: School Readiness. Is this possible? How?

    Discuss point 2: School completion. Is this possible? If not year 2000, when?

    Discuss point 3: Student achievement and citizenship: competency testing. How will achieving this goal help U.S. citizenship?

    Discuss point 4: What do you believe the State's role in mandating professional development will be?

    Discuss point 5: Mathematics and Science: Is this possible? How?

    Discuss point 6: Adult literacy and lifelong learning: Possible?

    Discuss point 7: Safe...schools. How?

    Discuss point 8: Parental participation. What will your role be?

After you have completed the position paper based on Goals 2000, research the Obama administration's move toward nationalization of public education. Is this desirable? Why or why not?

Competency 13

Legal and Ethical Requirements

LESSON PLAN FOR COMPETENCY 13

STATE STANDARDS: STANDARD 4, COMPETENCY 13

Competency 013: The teacher understands and adheres to **legal and ethical requirements** for educators and is knowledgeable of the **structure of education** in Texas.

STATE TEACHER PROFICIENCIES

Competency 013

The beginning teacher:

- Knows **legal requirements** for educators (e.g., those related to special education, students' and families' rights, student discipline, equity, child abuse) and adheres to legal guidelines in education-related situations.
- Knows and adheres to legal and ethical requirements regarding the use of educational resources and technologies (e.g., **copyright, Fair Use, data security, privacy, acceptable use policies**).
- Applies knowledge of **ethical guidelines** for educators in Texas (e.g., those related to confidentiality, interactions with students and others in the school community), including policies and procedures described in the **Code of Ethics and Standard Practices for Texas Educators**.
- Follows procedures and requirements for **maintaining accurate student records**.
- Understands the importance of and adheres to required procedures for **administering** state- and district-mandated **assessments**.
- Uses knowledge of the structure of the **state education system**, including relationships among campus, local, and state components, to seek information and assistance.
- **Advocates** for students and for the profession in various situations.

TEACHING OBJECTIVES

At the end of the lesson, the student should be able to:

- Draw a diagram of the hierarchy of the legal system/education in the United States.
- Draw a diagram of the hierarchy of public education administration in a Texas school district.
- Draw a diagram of the hierarchy of the educational structure in Texas.
  ◇ Summarize the importance of following the chain of command.
- Define the roles of the school board and superintendent.
- Have you dDemonstrated your through usageability to use the Texas Education Agency and State Board of Education and The Coordinating Board web sites with assurance? by documenting five places on each site which you have visited and what you found there.
- Explain how public education in the State of Texas is financed.
- Find a Family Educational Rights and Privacy Act (FERPA) policy in and ISD's handbook.

C10 KEY WORDS: LEGAL AND ETHICAL REQUIREMENTS

Terms associated with legal and ethical requirements

Busing	
Cultural Difference Theory	De facto Segregation
De jure Segregation	Desegregation
Separate but Equal	Second-generation Segregation
Sex Discrimination	Chain of Command
Sex-role Stereotyping	No Child Left Behind
Compensatory Education	Title 1 Title IV Title VI Title IX

Competency 13 Legal and Ethical Requirements   243

Court Cases and Legal Issues Impacting Teacher Education
Brown vs Board of Ed of Topeka
Plessy v. Ferguson
Civil Rights Act of 1965

INTRODUCTION/FOCUS

News Item: Teacher fastens student to chair with duct tape!

News Item: Teacher hangs President Obama in effigy in class!

News Item: Teacher admits improper relationship with sixth grader!

These paraphrased titles of actual news stories are alarming and, at first glance, one wonders how anyone could be foolish enough to tie a student to a chair with duct tape much less hang a sitting President in effigy! One doesn't have to read newspapers or listen to the nightly news very long before stories like these are made public.

PROFESSIONAL DEVELOPMENT
The privilege of teaching carries with it the responsibilities of law and ethical behavior.

This competency deals with the **legal and ethical requirements** for educators and being knowledgeable of the **structure of education** in Texas.

TRANSITION: With the twin topics of law and ethics in mind, the last chapter for the last competency in the fourth Standard, Competency 13 deals primarily with the Teacher and the State of Texas.

INSTRUCTIONAL INPUT AND GUIDED PRACTICE

What we know about the legal and ethical requirements

The Instructional Input in this lesson plan will contain *guided practice* in the form of questions placed throughout the chapter. References to web sites will also serve as guided practice as you research topics to gain further knowledge and information and application.

BEGIN AT THE BEGINNING

The United States Constitution gives rights to states to educate its citizens. This one privilege is the source of major debate at this time in America. Certain entities believe that national standards for teacher certification and for student achievement should be a function of the federal government.

State Control or National Control of Education?

One of the reasons given for wanting to nationalize education is that, frequently, teachers move from state to state and discover that they must take college coursework and more tests to be certified in the new state. In Chapter 12, you learned about becoming a teacher in the State of Texas; you should know that training and certification is left to the individual states by virtue of the U. S. Constitution, Amendment 10:

> "The powers not delegated to the United States by the Constitution, nor prohibited by it to the States, are reserved to the States respectively, or to the people."

State Proficiency #1 States That the Teacher:

✦ Knows legal requirements for educators (e.g., those related to special education, students' and families' rights, student discipline, equity, child abuse) and adheres to legal guidelines in education-related situations.

The Introduction to the Teaching Profession course does not deal in depth with special education; those topics are left for the advanced course EDUC 2301—Introduction to Special Populations. What is important to know about special education at this point is that Federal Law trumps State Law where special needs students are concerned. At this time, states have the sovereign right to control education within their boundaries. The notable exceptions, however, are Individuals with Disabilities Education Act (IDEA) and issues related to special education.

Civil Rights Act 1965

The effects of the Civil Rights Act of 1965 are felt throughout every State's educational system. You may have believed heretofore that the Civil Rights Act involved Rosa Parks refusing to give up her seat to a white man on a bus several years ago, and you would be right insofaras the onset of the Civil Rights Movement. That one act by a frail woman is usually credited for initiating the Civil Rights Act. What you may not know is that Rosa Parks' act reverberated throughout all public systems in America—the educational system was no exception.

Prior to the passage of this 1965 Civil Rights legislation were several other cases dealing with the concept of **separate but equal.** As early as 1896, *Plessy vs Ferguson* (163 U.S. 537) "separate but equal" was declared constitutional by the Supreme Court. Put simply the phrase "separate but equal" means that people can be segregated legally (kept separate) if equal opportunity exists. Clearly the court believed that concept to be constitutional, and separate but equal was practiced across the land.

Soon, "access and equity" became two of the most critical issues in public education and ultimately led to the landmark case of *Brown vs Board of Education* in Topeka, Kansas, in 1954 (347 U.S. 483). In this case, the Supreme Court declared that separate schools for black and white children did, in fact, deny black children equal education and therefore, on the grounds of inequity, separate schools were declared unconstitutional. This one case effectively overturned many cases going all the way back to *Plessy vs Ferguson* in 1896.

As a result of the Civil Rights Act of 1965, the twin concepts of **access and equity** went under the microscope and through the years came to include other groups of children who had not been previously served well—the special needs children. Separate but equal would not suffice any longer for ignoring the special needs of this large group of children.

Throughout these some 45 years since 1965, the law of the land has morphed into several public laws, each of which attempts to create a fair and just educational environment for children with disabilities The first such law was PL 94.142 in 1984–85. A special provision within that public law was Section 504. This section dealt specifically with discrimination:

> "No otherwise qualified handicapped individual . . . shall, solely by reason of his handicap, be excluded from the participation in, be denied the benefits of or be subjected to discrimination under any program or activity receiving Federal financial assistance."

Following, in 1975, was the Individuals with Disabilities Act (IDEA), which was tweaked in the Individuals with Disabilities Improvement Act (IDEIA) of 2004. Read more about the development of special education services on this web site: *http://idea.ed.gov/explore/home*. Public Law 105-17 can be downloaded at this web site: *http://www2.ed.gov/offices/OSERS/Policy/IDEA/the_law.html*

Furthermore, the No Child Left Behind Act of 2001 (NCLB) has placed certain regulations and limitations upon the classroom teacher as well. The web site http://ed.gov/nclb/landing.jhtml contains more detailed information about NCLB.

Competency 6 deals primarily with student discipline, but there are legalities attached to discipline that preservice teachers should be aware of as well.

Child Abuse

The National Child Abuse Prevention Treatment Act (NCAPT) (1974) identified child abuse and neglect as state crimes defined by state laws. If a teacher has reason to **suspect** a child of being abused or neglected, he has an obligation to report that abuse to the appropriate state authorities. The NCAPT also specifies that sexual or racial harassment must be reported as well as infractions dealing with weapons and alcohol and drugs. Some common indicators that a teacher might use to determine whether to make a report or not include: a child with bruises, welts, cuts, or burns; a child who has difficulty sitting or walking; frequent delinquency; or consistent hunger.

The teacher should document the observations and provide them to the principal and/or a counselor taking care to provide detailed information about time and date. While this documentation may be called into court should the case progress to that degree, the initial report is made anonymously. The teacher who brings abuse issues to the notice of authorities with *reasonable cause* is protected from lawsuits.

State Proficiency #2 States That the Teacher:

✦ Knows and adheres to legal and ethical requirements regarding the use of educational resources and technologies (e.g., copyright, Fair Use, data security, privacy, acceptable use policies).

While some of these issues were discussed in the chapter on technology, it is appropriate to mention them here.

Copyright

> The Congress shall have the Power . . . To promote the Progress of Science and useful Arts, by securing for limited Times to Authors and Inventors the exclusive Right to their respective Writings and Discoveries . . .
>
> —*The United States Constitution, Article 1, Section 8, Clauses 1 and 8*

Copyright laws are usually introduced to students writing term papers in English or History classes. "Do not plagiarize!" is the charge. Helping students understand what constitutes plagiarism and what constitutes free idea exchange is a difficult task for teachers. That task is even more difficult with the advent of so much print media that is so easily accessed on the Internet.

Generally, the terms one needs to know are **public domain** and **fair use**. Included in the public domain are items including poetry, novels, music, and such written over 75 years ago. The standard for judging whether something is copyrighted or not comes under the heading of fair use. According to the U.S. Copyright Office, there are four factors in determining whether something is used "fairly" or not:

1. The purpose and character of the use, including whether such use is of commercial nature or is for nonprofit educational purposes;

    ✦ What exactly does "educational use" mean? It usually means that a teacher makes a "spontaneous" decision to use a work "temporarily."

2. The nature of the copyrighted work;

    ✦ What exactly does "educational use" mean? A teacher may copy paragraphs from a copyrighted source, whereas copying an entire chapter is probably not fair use.

3. The amount and substantiality of the portion used in relation to the copyrighted work as a whole; and

    ✦ What exactly does "educational use" mean? A teacher might duplicate short excerpts from a longer work which does not constitute the entire work.

4. The effect of the use upon the potential market for, or value of, the copyrighted work.
   + What exactly does "educational use" mean? If there will be no reduction in sales, fair use is usually implied.

If the work is copyrighted, you must obtain permission of the author (various means) to obtain permission. It is to be emphasized that ignorance of copyright laws is not excusable. Several lawsuits have been filed against teachers for breaching this important concept. Fines can run up to $100,000 for each infringement.

Check with your school district about district policies regarding copyright laws.

Finally, students must know that certain "copying" of materials is prohibited:

1. copying computer software (such as Windows®);
2. copying movies or purchasing bootlegged versions of a movie; and
3. copying music.

For further information, refer to this web site: *http://www.copyright.gov/fls/fl102.html* and to *http://www.templetons.com/brad/copymyths.html* for more information on fair use.

Privacy

> **Question**
> What kinds of records are involved in the Family Educational Rights and Privacy Act (FERPA)?

FERPA, otherwise known as the Buckley Amendment, applies to ***all*** school records not just students' files. This means that all public educational institutions including community colleges and universities as well as public schools are bound by this law. Some important points to remember about this law are:

1. Parents (or guardians) must be informed about their rights regarding a child's records.
   a. Schools may give out names and addresses.
2. Parents have the right to inspect and review records.
   a. Outsiders do not have this right.
   b. Does not entail the right to copy records.
3. Parents can challenge the accuracy of the records.
4. The law protects the confidentiality of the records.
   a. Cannot post social security numbers in conjunction with grades.
5. The law provides an avenue for complaints.

What about the teacher's rights in relation to FERPA? A teacher who has a legitimate educational interest in the child may access the records of a child. For example, if a teacher wants to have a child tested for a learning disability because of work completed in class, she may work with the counselor and view the child's records to determine if he has been tested before.

State Proficiency #3 States That the teacher:

✦ Applies knowledge of ethical guidelines for educators in Texas (e.g., those related to confidentiality, interactions with students and others in the school community), including policies and procedures described in the Code of Ethics and Standard Practices for Texas Educators.

Confidentiality falls under the FERPA discussion in the previous section as well as that of data security which follows. Teachers should assume that all student records are confidential and be very reticent to give anyone information without understanding exactly what the penalties are.

Naturally, teachers have many interactions with students and the community at large. As teachers go about their day-to-day lives inside and outside of the classroom, they should be very sure that they do not inadvertently give out information that should be kept private. The best caveat is "If in doubt, keep it to yourself!"

A complete copy of the Code of Ethics and Standard Practices can be found at this web address: *http://www.sbec.state.tx.us/SBECOnline/default.asp*

As you can see from this descriptive list of legal Standards, teachers must understand that they accept a job of public trust when they enter the classroom. That trust cannot and should not be broken for any reason.

State Proficiency #4 States That the teacher:

✦ Follows procedures and requirements for maintaining accurate student records.

Keeping student records: **Data Security**

The Buckley Amendment also provides for the security of educational records. The standard applied to educational records is on a "need to know" basis. Before assuming that someone has the "right" or "authority" to view records, ask "Does the teacher/counselor, etc., have a legitimate educational need to view records?"

Schools and teachers must maintain accurate records and keep them safe and secure from people who do not have a legitimate need to know.

Additionally, teachers must be careful to keep all student records secure at all times. Leaving records unattended on a desk is inviting prying eyes and future problems with privacy.

State Proficiency #5 States That the teacher:

✦ Understands the importance of and adheres to required procedures for administering state- and district-mandated assessments.

Administering State Assessments

The accountability for tests is not to be taken lightly. In fact the Texas Education Code (TEC), Chapter 39, Subchapter B specifically states that the superintendent of each school district is responsible for:

1. maintaining the integrity of the test administration process; and
2. ensuring that every test administrator receives at least annual training in these procedures as provided by the TEA through the education service centers.

This portion of the Code can be accessed at: *http://ritter.tea.state.tx.us/rules/tac/chapter101/ch101b.html*

State Proficiency #6 States That the teacher:

✦ Uses knowledge of the structure of the state education system, including relationships among campus, local, and state components, to seek information and assistance.

Hierarchy: local, state, federal governments

The hierarchy of educational systems is an important one to address. Sometimes new teachers do not know about the intricate hierarchical tiers of government that oversee their jobs at the local, state, and federal levels. Teachers can and do get into "trouble" when they ignore that hierarchy either through ignorance or a failure of memory.

PROFESSIONAL DEVELOPMENT

Teachers should be aware of the many laws that govern schools, be able to diagram the hierarchies that govern educational systems in the United States, and be able to describe the importance of following the **chain of command**.

The first hierarchy is the Hierarchy of Law. The local school board sets the local policy, but it cannot be in conflict with decisions made at the state level or at the federal level. For example, if the Supreme Court has ruled that black arm bands are an issue of free speech, a local school cannot bar students from wearing black arm bands to school.

Every so often a case comes up locally that works its way through the court system to the Supreme Court. **Tinker v. Des Moines Independent Community School District** of 1968 was one such case where a fifteen-year-old student wore a black arm band to school one day in silent protest of the government's role in the Vietnam War. Expelled by the principal, a lawsuit followed that worked its way through the courts all the way to the Supreme Court, which ruled the arm band was an expression of "free speech."

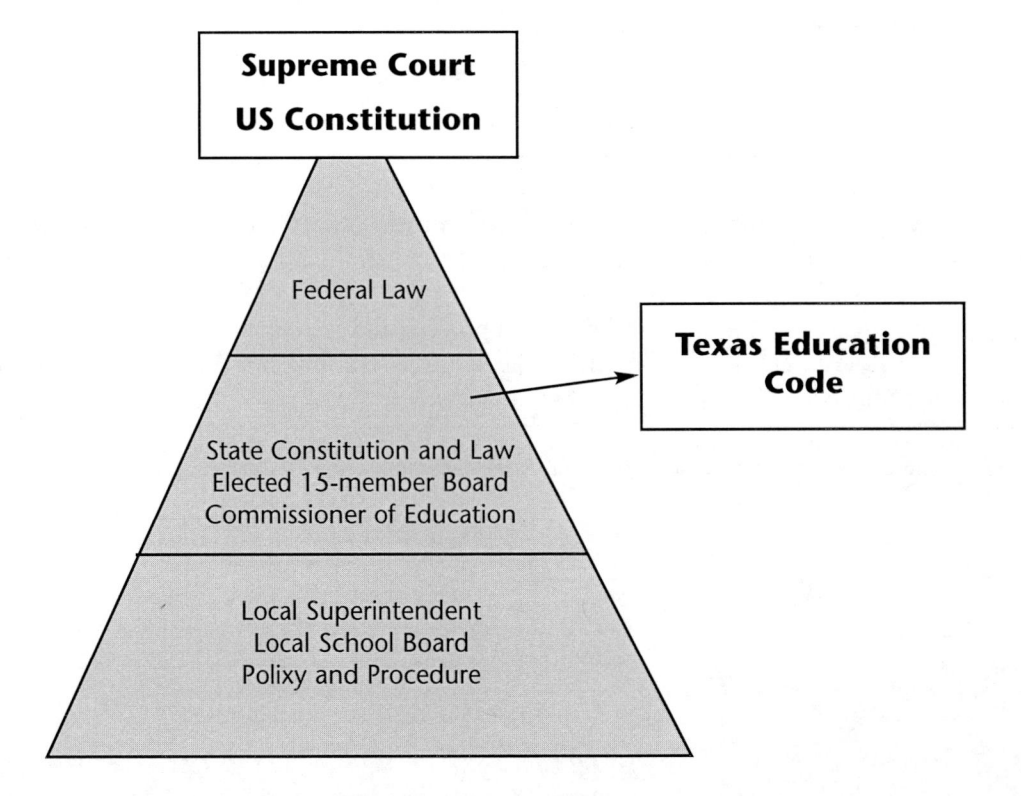

```
              Supreme Court
              US Constitution
                    ▲
                   / \
                  /   \
                 / Federal Law \
                /───────────────\
               /                 \  →  Texas Education Code
              / State Constitution and Law \
             /  Elected 15-member Board    \
            /   Commissioner of Education   \
           /─────────────────────────────────\
          /                                   \
         /        Local Superintendent         \
        /         Local School Board            \
       /          Polixy and Procedure           \
      ─────────────────────────────────────────────
```

Likewise, the Guns-Free Schools Act of 1994 was decided by the Federal Government:

"Except as provided in paragraph (3), each State receiving Federal funds under this chapter shall have in effect a State law requiring local educational agencies to expel from school for a period of not less than one year a student who is determined to have brought a weapon to a school under the jurisdiction of local educational agencies in that State, except that such State law shall allow the chief administering officer of such local educational agency to modify such expulsion requirement for a student on a case-by-case basis."

This Act in short requires schools districts that receive federal funding (and most do) expel any student who brings firearms to school. Many states, including most Texas school districts, have adopted a "zero tolerance" policy against firearms, weapons, drugs, and alcohol. This strict interpretation of the law has caused some ridiculous infractions—such as a second grader who brings a plastic knife in his lunch being expelled.

Harassment: a final issue that sometimes brings controversy is sexual and racial harassment. Some employees must undergo training and pass an examination on sexual harassment so institutions can cut down on the instances of behavioral issues that can arise under this umbrella. In short, teachers can be accused of sexual harassment if they require a "quid pro quo" for grades or if they create a hostile environment for students or peers. Again, documentation is key to filing any grievance or complaint.

Racial harassment has made headlines in the past few years in the form of intolerance for gender differences. In some instances, students have been murdered for their perceived gender preferences. Suffice it to say that any time a teacher observes harassment of any kind, it should be reported to the proper authorities. Indifference is not an option.

It is clear to see that the federal government and state government cross paths in many places, usually involving money and/or the law. A few distinctions between the two still survive, however, including the rights of states to set certification rules and regulations. In Texas, those rules and regulations are set by the State Board of Education. The State Board of Education hierarchy looks like this:

```
              /\
             /  \
            / State \
           / Board of \
          / Education  \
         /--------------\
        /                \
       /                  \
      /  State Commissioner \
     /----------------------\
    /                        \
   / Policy Setting Organizations: \
  /                                 \
 /       TEA, TheCB, SBEC            \
/-------------------------------------\
```

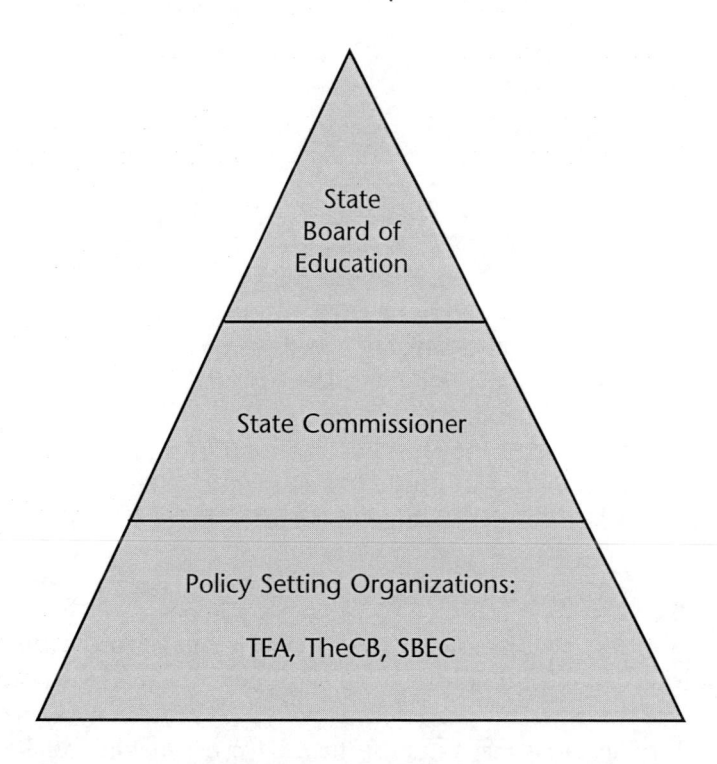

Like the local school board, the State Board of Education has a chief officer known as the Commissioner of Education. Now, you know that the State Board of Education is an elected body and as such conducts the State's official business of education. The SBOE administers the Permanent School Fund, sets passing scores for the TAKS, and oversees Adult Basic Education (ABE) programs among many other duties including setting policy much like the local board sets policy for local districts. The business of the State is administered through the Texas Education Agency.

On the other hand, the Coordinating Board conducts the business of higher education in Texas, and as such connects with public school education in many ways. The Readiness Standards and the Texas Success Initiatives (TSI), for example, constitute two places that schools and colleges and universities intersect, so higher education is very interested in what goes on in public schools.

There is a Commissioner of Higher Education who reports to a nine-member board that is appointed by the Governor of Texas.

The next hierarchy is the local school district hierarchy. It is clear that teachers are at the bottom of the hierarchy and seemingly a long way away from the State Board of Education much less the Supreme Court. Still, at the local level many problems occur, so teachers must work their way upwards when a grievance occurs.

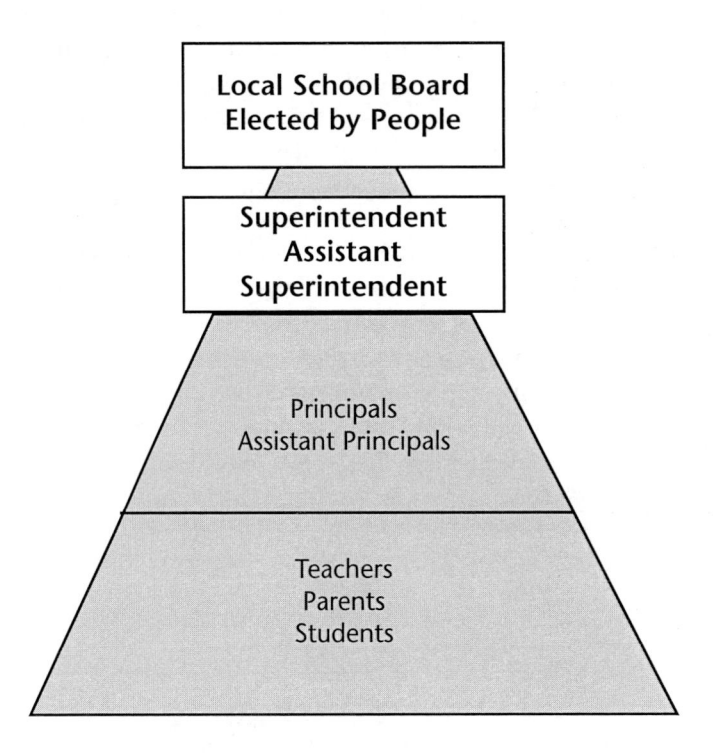

```
┌─────────────────────┐
│  Local School Board │
│   Elected by People │
└─────────────────────┘
    ┌──────────────┐
    │ Superintendent│
    │   Assistant   │
    │ Superintendent│
    └──────────────┘
       Principals
    Assistant Principals

         Teachers
         Parents
         Students
```

If a teacher is unfortunate enough to have a grievance against the school district, the teacher should definitely have become a member of a professional organization as discussed in Chapter 12. Professional organizations provide initial free counsel to teachers who find themselves in trouble and are very adept at identifying a true grievance and filing the same if warranted.

One frequent problem that arises is the breaking of a contract. If a teacher misses a timely deadline for submitting a resignation, the school district can hold the teacher to the contract. Obviously, there would be some reasonable excuses for a late resignation, but last-minute change of heart would not be one of them!

DUE PROCESS

Most people have heard of due process as it relates to search and seizure—usually these cases are on the 10 p.m. news and involving contraband of some sort. What new teachers may not realize is that due process applies to them as well as to students. Due process is for everyone's protection—especially for those who might feel threatened by arbitrary decisions made against them. Likewise, neither teachers nor administrators can arbitrarily search a student's backpack or locker because she suspects contraband of being there.

LIABILITY

When teachers hear about the application of law in the educational setting, they often ask if they are liable. The answer is usually *no* if the teacher has acted within the scope of his duties and follows school procedure and policies. The terms *negligence* and *reasonable* are applicable to all teachers. Answer the question "Would a *reasonable* person have done the same thing under similar circumstances?" If the answer is "Yes," then, the teacher would not be liable.

In conclusion, one of the most difficult transitions to make in becoming a teacher is learning to operate well within a hierarchy. A hierarchy is defined as levels of power. In teaching, the hierarchy is like this:

- School Board
- Superintendent
- Principal
- Assistant Principal
- Teacher
- Student
- Parent

The teacher must remember that no matter what the problem, the school system has a prescribed way of approaching its solution. In other words, the teacher must follow the hierarchy of power. Often, the teacher can go straight to the principal, but the teacher would never go directly to the superintendent or to the school board.

COMPENSATORY EDUCATION

Compensatory Education is a broad topic, but students have undoubtedly heard of Title IX (providing equal athletic access to females). Other "Title" programs are identified in the following paragraphs.

The purpose for compensatory education is to provide the educational means for success for children and/or any other Local Education Agency's (LEA) students who are at risk of dropping out of school. The need for compensatory programs is established by student performance data from the Texas Assessment of Knowledge and Skills (TAKS) tests as well as other data provided by school districts which identifies groups of students.

Title Programs are established by the federal government. Several that have significance to educational systems include:

Title 1: Improving the Academic Achievement for the Disadvantaged. The federal government, through monetary contribution to individual states that apply for funding, tries to ensure that all children have an equitable education. More information can be found at this web site:

http://www2.ed.gov/policy/elsec/leg/esea02/pg1.html

Title IV: 21st Century Schools: The purpose for Title IV is to bring awareness to and support programs for violence prevention in schools. More information about Title IV can be found at this web site:

http://www2.ed.gov/policy/elsec/leg/esea02/pg51.html

Title VI: Innovative Education Program Strategies: Title VI provides support for innovative programs in technology, educational materials, reform projects, programs for at-risk children, literacy programs, gifted-talented programs, reform linked to Goals 2000, and school improvement programs. For more information see this web site:

http://www2.ed.gov/pubs/ArtsEd/part3.html

Title IX: Discrimination Based on Sex or Blindness: The federal government prohibited discrimination by schools on the basis of sex or blindness. Section 1681 of this statute reads:

> No person in the United States shall, on the basis of sex, be excluded from participation in, be denied the benefits of, or be subjected to discrimination under any education program or activity receiving Federal financial assistance, except that:

Descriptions of other title programs can be found at *http://www2.ed.gov/*. It should be noted that any school district accepting federal funding must comply with all rules and regulations pertaining to each title. Furthermore, money offered at the federal level is through competitive grants.

Breaking Down the Hierarchy

It is very important for teachers to understand the hierarchy when communicating with parents and children, and even with other teachers. Failure to go through the proper channels can cause many problems for the teacher, some of them legal in nature and very serious.

QUESTION
Can you define what the school superintendent does and what he is responsible for?
Can you define what the school board does and how it is chosen?

✦ Understand the roles of the school board and superintendent;

Many students do not understand the role of the local school board and the superintendent. Most preservice teachers have never been to a school board meeting. The local school board is elected by the people and is non-paid. This board, representing its constituents, officially hires the superintendent. The superintendent is not a member of the school board, and she or he does not get a vote on matters brought before the board. He or she, in fact, is an employee of the school board.

The superintendent sets the agenda for the school board and sees that school board members are trained in school policy. The superintendent's staff creates large, three-ring binders holding all the financial and legal data that the board will need to research and discuss before making decisions.

PUBLIC SCHOOL FINANCE

STUDENT QUESTION
Can you explain how public education in the State of Texas is financed?

This topic is very complicated and is often the source of much criticism from citizens and media alike across the nation. In 1994, it is estimated that twenty-eight states were in court over the financing of public schools. You may have heard the term "Robin Hood" attached to a 1993 Texas argument and subsequent law over funding but not be able to tell exactly who benefited and who did not benefit from this law's passage.

The simple answer is that the majority of public education in Texas is primarily funded through property taxes. Each district has the right to set its own tax rate within parameters set by the State. It is estimated that the majority of school districts get approximately 50 percent of their finances from local taxes. The rest of the funding comes from state sales taxes and the net proceeds from the Texas Lottery as well as earnings from the Permanent School Fund. The rest of it must be determined by the State Legislature.

To become better acquainted with public school finance in Texas go to this web site, which gives a "brief history of school funding in Texas": *http://www.investintexasschools.org/schoolfunding/history.php*.

State Proficiency #7 States That the teacher:

✦ Advocates for students and for the profession in various situations.

Teachers can and should be advocates for students. Remembering why one becomes a teacher pushes one in the right direction on advocacy. No matter how stressful the job or how arbitrary the student behaves, he deserves an advocate. Similarly, the teacher should be an advocate for the profession of teaching and promote teachers and teaching given the opportunity.

INDEPENDENT PRACTICE AND MODELING: (HOMEWORK)

1. **Scholar's Vocabulary**: Using the State-produced list of proficiencies preservice teachers should have related to Competency 13, highlight terms you wish to place in your interactive glossary. You should have a minimum of five terms from C1. (See the model in the Appendices.)

2. **Reflective Writing**: Using the eleven-sentence model in the Appendices, write a reflection on Competency 13.

3. **Assignment**: Paper on legal/ethical issues.

Access the Texas Classroom Teacher Association (TCTA) at *www.tcta.org* and find the latest "Teacher Survival Guide." Research at least ten problems that you would like to know the answer to (such as: Do I have to report child abuse? If so, to whom? Can teachers spank students? Etc.).

Write your ten questions using a question-and-answer format; that is, state the question (bolded and underlined) and then answer the question below.

Model

Question: Can teachers spank students legally?

Answer: Teachers must.....

The final two paragraphs of the paper should reflect upon:

✦ The web site: was it helpful? Did you find other helpful web sites that have similar information?

✦ What did you learn that surprised you?

CLOSURE/FOLLOWUP

The legal and ethical requirements for teachers can be both daunting and frightening especially for new teachers and special educators. By taking a careful look at the Code of Ethics and asking for advice before reacting, teachers can avoid troublesome events in the classroom and with parents.

ASSESSMENT

Ask yourself whether you have mastered these objectives.

- **Objective 1:** Draw a diagram of the hierarchy of the legal system/education in the United States.
- **Objective 2:** Draw a diagram of the hierarchy of public education administration in a Texas school district.
- **Objective 3:** Draw a diagram of the hierarchy of the educational structure in Texas.
  - ◇ Summarize the importance of following the chain of command.
- **Objective 4:** Can you define the roles of the school board and superintendent?
- **Objective 5:** Have you demonstrated the ability to use the Texas Education Agency and State Board of Education and The Coordinating Board web sites with assurance?
- **Objective 6:** Explain how public education in the State of Texas is financed.
- **Objective 7:** Can you find a Family Educational Rights and Privacy Act (FERPA) policy in an ISD's handbook?

PRACTICE QUESTIONS

Now assess your learning by answering these questions. Answers are given in the Appendices.

1. Ms. Stephenson calls on four students to stay and visit with her after class. The students all have declining grades and low motivation. Ms. Stephenson asks them why their grades are suffering this particular semester. All four students remain silent and look at the floor. She gets no response; therefore, the teacher immediately states in a loud voice that if there isn't any sign of improvement by next week, they will probably fail the class. The most INAPPROPRIATE action taken by Ms. Stephenson was:
    a. Holding the students to her expectations, NOT their own.
    b. Violating their confidentiality by reprimanding each student's grade in front of the others.
    c. Threatening they would fail if improvement was not shown.
    d. Placing emphasis on the final product and NOT enough on the learning process.

2. Little Timmy is in Mrs. Thompson's homeroom. Mrs. Thompson's room is decorated for the Christmas holidays. She has used Santa Claus and the manger scene as decorations. Little Timmy is excited and tells his mother about the decorations. Clearly disturbed, Timmy's mother asks for a teacher–parent conference immediately. While Mrs. Thompson's choices of decorations were probably not well thought out, she is within her rights to decorate the room this way. How should Mrs. Thompson prepare to answer Timmy's mother regarding the inevitable questions about Santa Claus and the manger scene in this case?
    a. Take down the decorations to please this one parent.
    b. Discuss her reasons for presenting the holiday in this fashion and see if she can get her point across to the parent.
    c. Simply tell the mother that this was her right to decorate this way and suggest that the mother be more tolerant.
    d. Add decorations that reflect the mother's culture.

3. Mrs. Jones teaches a seventh grade math class. One student, Kelsee, receives special education services because of severe physical impairments. Mrs. Jones should plan activities that:
   a. Focus on the main areas of Kelsee's developmental problems.
   b. Permit her to engage in class activities with teacher supervision.
   c. Are in compliance with her IEP (Individual Education Plan).
   d. Do not include her. She should leave the class during this time and tutor with an aide.

4. Students of a fifth grade Science class have decided to conduct a campus-wide recycling project. In a site-based management structure, who would most likely be included in decision-making regarding this issue?
   I. Superintendent
   II. Campus custodians/maintenance
   III. School board members
   IV. Principal
      a. II and III
      b. III and IV
      c. II, III and IV
      d. II and IV

5. Coach Jennings, the girls head basketball coach, notices considerable bruises and scratches on one of his best defensive player's, Gracie's, arms and legs. Gracie then comes to school one day with a swollen eye. The coach calls Gracie into her office and just casually mentions the wounds. She lets the girl know that she is only a concerned friend. The girl puts the wounds down to falls and the swollen eye as an allergy problem. The coach suspects physical abuse. What is the correct form of action for the coach to take next?
   a. Contact the Department of Human Services and report her suspicions.
   b. Contact the student's parents or guardian and discuss the situation.
   c. Continue to observe the student and record all incidents to help confirm her suspicions.
   d. All of the above.

6. Mrs. White has noticed that her teaching method of lecturing for the full period every day is not as effective with her current class. As a matter of fact, several students have confronted her with her boring class. In return, she has lost control of her emotions several times out of frustration and threatened to penalize the entire class for their rudeness. Ethically, what should she do?
   a. Apologize to the students and work toward creating new teaching methods.
   b. Not apologizing, but changing her teaching methods so the students will pick up on it and quit complaining.
   c. Apologize to the class; ask a coworker to come in to evaluate which aspects of her method are effective and which are not and develop a method based on this information.
   d. Apologize to the class by saying she is in the middle of a divorce and is having a hard time.

7. Tim's mother is taking him from school because today the teacher has a Christmas party scheduled. Does his mother have the right to impose her religious beliefs on her son? What should Tim's teacher do?
   a. Move the scheduled party to an earlier hour and have the party before Tim's mother arrives.
   b. Send Tim to the office until his mother arrives to pick him up from school.
   c. Respect Tim's mother's religious beliefs even though she thinks she is wrong to penalize her son in this way.
   d. Tim's teacher could put some of the Christmas goodies into a little bag for him and give it to him when he returns.

256 Competency 13 Legal and Ethical Requirements

8. Mr. Tibbs was teaching his sixth grade math class when suddenly he became ill. What school procedure must be followed?
    a. Mr. Tibbs can send a student to the office to request assistance.
    b. Mr. Tibbs can ask a teacher in his hall to cover for him until a substitute arrives.
    c. Mr. Tibbs can go to the restroom for a minute hoping he will feel better.
    d. Mr. Tibbs can just stick it out until class is dismissed.

9. For an administrator to be an effective leader, he must exhibit which of the following attributes?
    I. Vision of change
    II. Knowledge and skill in teaching
    III. Evaluation and planning skills
    IV. Creating individual and systematic change
        a. I, II
        b. I, II, III
        c. I, IV
        d. I, II, III, IV

10. Mr. Jones keeps records of each student's progress in his filing cabinet. In these folders are grades, tests, quizzes, homework, personal notes, and observations of the child. One of his student's parents comes to the school and demands to see Mr. Jones' personal filing cabinet so that she can look at her child's folder. Can the parent legally do this?
    a. Yes, preferably with the teacher' permission.
    b. Yes, she does not need permission; she can access the filing cabinet.
    c. No, access to the entire cabinet is denied.
    d. No, it is a personal filing cabinet for teacher use only.

11. At Smalltown High School with an enrollment of 150 students, a portable CD player was stolen from the music teacher's classroom. The principal had each teacher keep their students in their classrooms. The principal then started searching the lockers for the CD player. During the search the principal finds an illegal drug in Steve's locker. What can the principal do?
    a. Call Steve to the office and punish him for the drug.
    b. Dispose of the drug and do nothing to Steve.
    c. He cannot do anything about his find.
    d. Call Steve to the office and search him.

12. Phillip has been in trouble numerous times. Finally his parents just take him out of school and start to home school him. Is this within their rights?
    a. No, parents cannot take a student out of school because of disciplinary reasons.
    b. Yes, a parent can decide to home school a student at any time.
    c. No, parents cannot take their children out of school unless they enroll them at another school.
    d. No, they can only home school for religious reasons.

13. In a very Christian town, a student-led Satanic group has asked to be able to use a classroom, after school, to hold meetings. They say that since the Spanish club gets to, that so can they. When the community hears this, they become outraged. What can the school do?
    a. Refuse to allow the group to meet on school grounds.
    b. Allow the group to meet.
    c. Allow the group to meet as long as there is an adult in charge.
    d. Allow them to meet as long as there is a Christian group meeting at the same time.

14. Mr. Thomas allows a student-led bible study to take place in his classroom before school. Sometimes Mr. Thomas is in the classroom during the bible study but never says anything. Is this legal for the school to have?
    a. No, there can not be a religious club at a public school.
    b. No, since Mr. Thomas is in the room it is illegal.
    c. Yes, as long as Mr. Thomas is not involved with the group it is legal.
    d. Yes, Mr. Thomas can even lead the group if the students want.

15. Billy has Tourette's syndrome. He involuntarily yells out curse words. Mrs. Jones, a new teacher, hears Billy say a particularly bad word and sends him to the office. What option does the office have?
    a. The office can give him detention each time he says a cuss word.
    b. The office can suspend him until it is controlled by medication.
    c. The office can do nothing because the action is caused by his disability.
    d. Isolate Billy from the rest of the school so no one will hear him.

16. Mr. Luther has a problem following directions from his principal—primarily because the principal is a woman who got the job that he had applied for. The principal is a Methodist and a member of her church's women's group. She allows the women's group to meet in the library at the school one evening. This infuriates Mr. Luther, and he calls the Superintendent to complain. Why might this make Mr. Luther mad enough to complain?
    a. He is jealous of the principal because he did not get the job and hopes to get her fired.
    b. The Constitution states that there is a separation between church and state, and this meeting clearly violates that separation.
    c. Mr. Luther thinks of himself as a first-rate authority on school law.
    d. The school should not provide electricity and paper for this meeting.

17. The teacher is supposed to be a resource evaluator. What are some resources available to teachers in schools today?
    a. Newspapers
    b. People
    c. Maps
    d. Computers
    e. All of the above.

18. Ms. Kindfelter fancies herself a mainstream teacher with middle class values such as respect and honesty. She believes that everyone values those characteristics. Parents, however, might have a different set of values from the teacher. What does Ms. Kindfelter, or any other teacher for that matter, do to teach values to her students?
    a. Call the parents and ask them their values.
    b. Demonstrate in daily life and lead by example.
    c. Write the values on the board.
    d. Have the students vote on values they want to study.

19. Mr. George has been teaching for ten years in the same school and has been assigned to mentor a new teacher. Miss James is the new teacher at the school, but she has taught for twenty-five years in Mississippi. Mr. George shows her the required school curriculum and how the school divides the content into semesters, but she insists on sticking with her old way of doing things. What is wrong with this scenario?
    a. Mr. George is taking his job as mentor too seriously.
    b. The curriculum should relate to the TEKS, period.
    c. The curriculum should benefit students, so her methods may not be bad.
    d. Miss James has been teaching too long and resents the young man's interference.

Career Planning

Students who enjoy working with the legal aspects of education often become assistant principals. Other careers follow outside of the educational field but still involve kids: child advocates (particularly needed in special education), social workers who deal with adolescent probation, social workers working with Child Protective Services, or even lawyers specializing in school law. Some teachers nearing retirement may choose to go through *mediation* training and become mediators for school problems. Even though both of these careers take teachers out of the classroom, they are still connected in a rich way to their training. Every school administrator who hires new personnel hopes, however, that the new hires have a good conceptual understanding of the legal and ethical requirements of teaching and that they will always opt on the side of care.

Teachers who enjoy writing and budget issues might also consider becoming grant writers. A huge demand exists for grant writers. As noted, all ISDs must apply for grant money for any of the Title programs. In order to make budgets balance in years of recession particularly, school districts are actively working to apply for grants at the federal, state, and local levels.

MATERIALS NEEDED

Internet

SUGGESTIONS FOR ADDITIONAL ASSIGNMENTS

1. Code of Ethics Affadavit: Creating an Affidavit

   Turn the Texas "Code of Ethics and Standard Practices for Texas Educators" into an "affidavit." The affidavit should be a declaration of your intent to follow each of the Standards to the best of your ability. NOTE: YOU are the *deponent in this affidavit.* **You must get a Notary Public to sign your affidavit.**

   What is an affidavit? An affidavit is a statement a person makes under oath which attests to the truthfulness of the document.

   When are affidavits used? Affidavits are used to verify wills or to take a witness' statement to an accident or event.

   Who must sign the affidavit? The person who makes the statement (you) must sign the statement under oath. The person witnessing the *oath* is the notary (in your case).

   How are affidavits used? Affidavits carry great weight in courts; a judge will often accept an affidavit in place of the testimony of the witness.

   How to write your affidavit:

   1. Affidavit Title

      The title is at the top of the document stating the deponent's name or the reason for the affidavit: *Affidavit of Jane Doe, Affidavit of Publication,* or *Contract Affidavit.* In your case, the title is **Affidavit of Commitment.**

2. Affidavit fact statements. The first paragraph of the affidavit states the deponent's civil information (i.e., full name, age, occupation, complete address of residence).

   My name is *Jane Doe*. I am 29 years of age, work as a paraprofessional, and currently reside at 555 Sycamore Lane, Midland, Texas, 79709.

3. Subsequent Paragraphs: the next paragraphs constitute the deponent's statements of facts, with each paragraph being confined to one fact.

   I hereby state that….. (you will need one statement for each point in the Code)

   I hereby state that…..

4. Affidavit Signature: an affidavit must be signed by both the deponent and the person before whom it is sworn (the notary in your case) along with the date it was sworn. *Do not sign the affidavit until you are in the presence of the witness.*

5. You should include this statement at the end of your document:

   (your name) being sworn on oath, deposes and says that (he/she) has written the foregoing AFFIDAVIT OF COMMITMENT, and that the matters stated herein are true to the best of (his/her) knowledge and belief.

2. Legal/Ethical Critical Issues

   Access the Texas Classroom Teacher Association (TCTA) web site at *www.tcta.org* and locate the latest "Teacher Survival Guide." (There should be a shark on the cover.)

   Scroll down the index to the "Legal Issues" and "About Your Students" and research at least five topics that you know little about. (Examples: Do I have to report child abuse? If so, to whom? Can teachers spank students? Etc.).

   In a question-and-answer format, state the question (bolded) and then answer the question below.

Model

Question: **Can teachers spank students legally?**

Answer: Teachers must…..

Be sure to:

+ use correct grammar throughout the paper including complete sentences
+ make your answers complete, thorough

The final paragraph of the paper should reflect upon:

+ The web site: was it helpful? Did you find other helpful web sites that have similar information?
+ What did you learn that surprised you?

3. HIERARCHY: Perhaps one of the most difficult transitions to make in becoming a teacher is learning to operate well within a hierarchy. A hierarchy is defined as levels of power. In teaching, the hierarchy is like this:

- School Board
- Superintendent
- Principal
- Assistant Principal
- Teacher
- Student
- Parent

The teacher must remember that no matter what the problem, the school system has a prescribed way of approaching its solution. In other words, the teacher must follow the hierarchy of power. Often, the teacher can go straight to the principal, but the teacher would never go directly to the superintendent or to the school board.

Utilizing Microsoft tools, create a diagram that accurately reflects everyone in the hierarchy listed.

4. The School Board Meeting: Attend a local school board meeting in order to gain an understanding of the scope of the legal responsibilities and liabilities of the local school board in the political setting of a school board meeting.

Assignment: Attend a school board meeting to observe the superintendent, staff, board, media and other attendees and to report on the agenda.

Documentation: Date, time in-out, School District Superintendent, School Board members, others. Either the superintendent or a board member must sign the program or a verification sheet.

Answer the following questions after attending the meeting:

1. What is the role of the superintendent in this meeting?
2. What is the role of the school board?
3. What do you notice about individual board members during the meeting?
4. What is the agenda? Include official, dated agenda in an Appendix.
5. What is the role of the audience? Describe verbal/nonverbal communication.
6. What types of decisions are made? (Legal, curriculum, resources, policy, etc.)
7. Is conflict present? Describe how conflict is handled.
8. What types of communication are being utilized (i.e., verbal, nonverbal paralanguage)?
9. Are some attempting to persuade others to action? Example?
10. What is your opinion of school boards to govern education?
11. Reaction to the experience (your reflection).

5. Following are sample scenarios based on court cases:
   a. Ms. McCluskey is a new teacher of English Language Arts, and she decides to create a "packet" of materials that she downloads off the Internet and magazines and books. The students love this unit, so she decides to use it every year updating materials as necessary.
      1. What laws are involved with this decision to copy and create a packet of materials?
      2. What guidelines should Mrs. McCluskey follow?
      3. Evaluate Ms. McCluskey's decisions for curriculum.
   b. Mr. Brown decides the local curriculum guide for social studies does not investigate the Civil Rights Act of 1965 thoroughly enough nor present the minority views of Black Americans accurately; therefore, he decides to remedy the shortcomings of the departmental guide and tell "it like it was."
      1. Do Mr. Brown's First Amendment rights protect him? Why or why not?
      2. Review the 2006 Supreme Court decision, *Garcelli v. Ceballos*, to help you answer this question.
      3. Synthesize your research on a teacher's First Amendment rights with a statement of philosophy about the topic.
   c. Google *A Tale of Two Cities* and read the story of two very disparate school districts. Then, research the 1973 law case entitled: *San Antonio Independent School District, et al. v. Demetrio P. Rodriguez, et al.* This case formed the basis for the "Robin Hood" bill that went into effect in Texas in 1993. Gleaning as much information as possible from these resources, develop a philosophy statement about property taxes as a basis for funding schools.

Final Directions

The Field Experience Guide
How to Conduct a Classroom Observation
The Reflective Teacher
Writing an Educational Philosophy
Educator Standards Web Search
Web Searches
Benjamin Bloom's Cognitive Taxonomy
Scholar's Vocabulary Instructions
Scholar's Vocabulary
Answers to Practice Questions

Test Framework for Field 100, 110, 130: Pedagogy and Professional Responsibilities EC–6, 4–8, 8–12

Domain/Standard	Competency	EDUC
1: Designing Instruction and Assessment to Promote Student Learning	001: The teacher understands **human developmental processes** and applies this knowledge to plan instruction and ongoing assessment that motivate students and are responsive to their developmental characteristics and needs.	
	002: The teacher understands student **diversity** and knows how to plan learning experiences and design assessments that are responsive to differences among students and that promote all students' learning.	
	003: The teacher understands procedures for **designing effective and coherent instruction and assessment** based on appropriate learning goals and objectives.	
	004: The teacher understands **learning processes** and factors that impact student learning and demonstrates this knowledge by planning effective, **engaging instruction** and appropriate assessments.	
2: Creating a Positive, Productive Classroom Environment	005: The teacher knows how to establish a **classroom climate** that fosters learning, equity, and excellence and uses this knowledge to create a **physical and emotional environment** that is safe and productive.	
	006: The teacher understands strategies for creating an organized and productive learning environment and for **managing student behavior**.	
3: Implementing Effective, Responsive Instruction and Assessment	007: The teacher understands and applies principles and strategies for **communicating** effectively in varied teaching and learning contexts.	
	008: The teacher provides appropriate instruction that **actively engages** students in the learning process.	
	009: The teacher incorporates the effective use of **technology** to plan, organize, deliver, and evaluate instruction for all students.	
	010: The teacher **monitors student performance** and achievement; provides students with timely, high-quality **feedback**; and responds flexibly to promote learning for all students.	
4: Fulfilling Professional Roles and Responsibilities	011: The teacher understands the importance of **family involvement** in children's education and knows how to interact and communicate effectively with families.	
	012: The teacher enhances **professional knowledge** and skills by effectively interacting with other members of the educational community and participating in various types of professional activities.	
	013: The teacher understands and adheres to **legal and ethical requirements** for educators and is knowledgeable of the structure of education in Texas.	

The Field Experience Guide

DREAM OF TEACHING?

JOIN A COMMUNITY COLLEGE AAT PROGRAM

EDUC 1301
EDUC 2301

FIELDWORK GUIDELINES

For Early Field Experiences in the Schools

CONTENTS

Field Experience Guidelines
Student Contract
Observation Information Form/ Background Check Release
OISD Site Verification
Confidentiality Notice
Field Experience Log
Rules Governing Volunteer Work
Helpful Instructions

COMMUNITY COLLEGE
ASSOCIATE OF ARTS IN TEACHING

Field Experience

Field Experience Guidelines for Students Enrolled in Education Classes

All students enrolled in EDUC 1301 or EDUC 2301 are required to complete sixteen hours of observations in a K–12 public school setting. **You will NOT pass your course unless you complete the required observation hours and provide appropriate documentation for your professor. These records are STATE records and cannot be returned to the student.**

If you live in _____ ISD, you will be expected to complete your observations (FEX) in ___ISD. If you live outside _____ISD, you will complete the requirements for out-of-district schools (OISD Guidelines).

Guidelines for students who will complete their observation hours in the _____ Independent School District (___ISD):

1. Print and complete the Student Contract. Mail or deliver the contract to your professor or the AAT Program Director by date: _____. The mailing address is:

    AAT Program Director _____
    _____
    _____
    _____

2. Arrange to pick up a Permission to Obtain Criminal History Record form from your professor or the Associate of Arts in Teaching Director. Most Independent School Districts require background checks for all volunteers and non-employees who work with students.

3. Return the completed form to your professor or the Program Director within one week of the first day of class. Be aware that you may not schedule any observations until the form is completed and submitted! (Optional) You will receive a "yellow card" verifying that you have completed the background check form. Once background checks have been conducted, yellow cards will be distributed in class OR the yellow card must be picked up from the Director's office.

4. Print a copy of the "Field Experience Log." At every observation, complete the required information and ask the **teacher** to sign it. The original document must be turned in before a final grade for the course can be assigned.

5. Upon receipt of the "yellow card" you may begin making appointments for your observation visits. Select a school from the Approved Site List provided by your instructor. Establish communication with the Contact Person at that school via phone or email as prescribed and schedule appointments for observation visits.

6. Keep the following points in mind:
   - Be on time for all appointments. Punctuality is very important.
   - If an unavoidable situation arises that requires you to miss a scheduled observation, call the contact person and reschedule. Do everything you can to avoid canceling or rescheduling an observation.
   - When you go to the school, check in at the front office and sign in and out according to campus policy.
   - Take your "yellow card" with you to the campus. Be prepared to show the card to office personnel if they request to see it.
   - Be prepared to sign into the school if requested.
   - Wear your College ID.
   - Wear the "Visitor" badge provided by the school. **Keep the visitor badge and affix it to the back of your observation notes.**
   - Take your Field Experience Log with you for each observation, and have it initialed by the teacher or office personnel after your observation. Do NOT lose this piece of paper! At the end of the semester, you will turn in this form to verify that you have completed your observation hours. No log—no grade.
   - Dress in a manner that conforms to the ISD dress code and portrays your image as a future teacher. Remember—no tank tops, bare tummies, spaghetti straps, anything shorter than 3 inches above the knee; no chewing gum!
   - When observing classrooms, remain attentive to the teaching/learning process. Remain as unobtrusive as possible.
   - You must maintain confidentiality of student information. For this reason, no student should be identified by name in your field observation reports. You also must not talk about students with anyone other than the teacher, school administrator, or other pertinent school personnel. As a matter of professional courtesy, do not identify the teacher by name in your reports.

7. **During or immediately after your observation, type notes of what you observed.** These notes are informal and casual in nature. You do not need to worry about grammar, punctuation, or sentence structure. However, the following information should be included in your notes for each observation:
   - The date
   - The time the observation began, the time the observation ended, and the total number of minutes you spent in the observation.
   - The school
   - Grade level
   - Subject being taught (e.g., Math)
   - The content of the lesson—be specific. (e.g., Integers on a number line and plotting points on a grid)
   - What was the classroom environment—how was the room arranged; what was on the walls; was it orderly or cluttered; was it "relaxed" and welcoming; etc.
   - How student behavior was handled—what processes did the teacher use, etc. Pay particular attention to the teachers who seem to have no behavior problems in their classrooms. Identify what they are doing that is so effective.
   - How was the lesson taught—be descriptive and specific. What strategies did the teacher use? Group work; independent practice; lecture and note taking; etc.
   - What did you see relating to professionalism and ethical behavior on the part of the teacher? Did you see any legal issues?

8. Save your typed notes in individual files on your computer, disc, or memory stick. You will submit these notes to me as an assignment—approximately one month apart. These notes will also be the basis for your final field experience observation reports due at the time of the final examination.

9. Submit your field experience observation reports by the deadlines. Early completion of your required observations will help you successfully complete all of your courses this semester!

10. At the end of the course, you will mail or deliver your Field Experience Log documenting a minimum of sixteen hours of observations along with the Final Field Experience Essay. This essay will serve as part of the final exam.

STUDENT CONTRACT
EDUC 1301 AND EDUC 2301

Students enrolled in EDUC 1301 and/or EDUC 2301 must complete a field-based experience as part of their education studies. Each course requires a minimum of sixteen (16) hours of classroom observations in a public or charter school setting. You must fulfill the observation requirement(s) to receive a passing grade for either course.

Printed Student Name: _____

Course Title and Section: _____

Professor: _____

Please initial on the designated line after reading each statement:

_____ I understand that I am enrolled in a course that requires sixteen (16) hours of classroom observations in a public school setting.

_____ I understand that I am responsible for scheduling my classroom observations according to the guidelines established by my professor and the Program Director.

_____ I understand that failure to complete the required observations will result in a failing grade for the course.

_____ I understand that any forgery on the Field Experience Log will result in a failing grade for the course.

_____ I certify that what is recorded on the Field Experience Log is a true and accurate account of my observation hours.

_____ I understand that failure to turn in the Field Experience Log on the designated due date may result in a failing grade for the course.

Student Signature: _____ Date: _____

Complete and mail or deliver this form to your professor before the designated deadline.

STUDENT OBSERVER INFORMATION SHEET
AND CRIMINAL HISTORY RELEASE

Please Print

Name: _____   Birthdate: _____

Social Security #: _____   Driver's License #: _____

Home Address on your Driver's License:

_____
Street

_____
City   State   Zip

College: Midland College   Supervisor/Phone: Dr. Mary E. Braselton   685-6822

I, a student observer with the _____ Independent School District, hereby authorize the _____ Independent School District to obtain criminal history record information from any law enforcement agencies that may have criminal history record information on me, including but not limited to arrest, investigations, convictions, and other reports. I hereby release the _____ Independent School District and any law enforcement agencies receiving a copy of this authorization from any liability for the release of any information to the _____ Independent School District.

_____   _____
Signature   **Date**

OUT OF DISTRICT SITE VERIFICATION

If you are not able to do your field experiences/observations in Midland ISD, you must follow the guidelines on the next pages. You will still need to fill out the background check form, the confidentiality notice, and the student contract.

Be aware that ISDs are under no obligation to allow you to observe, so timeliness is of the essence as you must do all the groundwork to gain permission to observe in school districts outside of Midland. Please let me know if I can assist you in any way by making phone calls.

Student Name: _____ College ID#: _____
_____

To Whom It May Concern:

The student presenting this letter is enrolled in an online education course at Midland College. All of our education courses require students to complete a minimum of sixteen hours of classroom observations during the semester. The student is requesting to complete these observation hours in your school district.

This student will not disturb your students or teachers and will not be evaluating any teacher's performance or student behavior. The student is simply observing K–12 classrooms to gain a better understanding of procedures, routines, and environments as well as teaching techniques and curricular content.

If you wish to allow the student to observe classrooms in your school district, please do the following:

1. Print this letter on your school district letterhead.
2. Indicate your acknowledgment and approval of the following statements by initialing beside each one.
3. Designate a contact person.
4. Complete the information at the end of this document.
5. Give this completed document to the student. The student will be responsible for returning it to his or her professor.

Initials	
	The student presenting this letter has received approval to complete sixteen hours of classroom observations in K-12 classrooms.
	The school district assumes responsibility for conducting any required criminal history background check(s).
	The student has been advised of dress code requirements.
	The student has been advised of confidentiality requirements.
	The student has been advised of sign-in and sign-out procedures and any other procedures required by the school district.

Please provide the name, title, and contact information of the person in your district who will serve as the primary point of contact for the student's College professor. This person should be able to verify observation hours on a day-to-day basis and will confirm the number of classroom observation hours this student acquires at the end of the semester. You may wish to serve as the contact person or delegate that responsibility to another individual in the school system.

Name of Contact Person:	Title:	Phone:	E-mail:

272 Final Directions

The student's education professor is:

	Phone:	E-mail:

Thank you for allowing our student to observe classrooms in your school district. If you have any questions or concerns, do not hesitate to contact the student's professor or me.

Associate Professor and Program Director
Associate of Arts in Teaching Program
Address:

Phone:
Fax:
E-mail:

Please complete the following:

Printed Name of Approval Authority: _____

Signature of Approval Authority: _____

Title: _____

Phone: _____

E-mail: _____

Date: _____

CONFIDENTIALITY NOTICE

Please read and sign the following "Confidentiality Notice" along with your Background Check form and Student Contract.

School personnel should be extremely cautious about making student information available to non-school persons. Only when an "educational purpose" can be established should any information be shared.

The law is very clear that any information specific to a student is absolutely confidential. It is not a problem to share general information that does not identify a particular student. This means anything with a student's name or student ID number is absolutely private unless you can prove an "educational purpose."

If there is any question in your mind about whether to share student information or not, you probably should not.

When a student shares "questionable" information (e.g., disclosure of abuse, drug use) with a volunteer, the volunteer must advise the campus principal or counselor. They will guide you in making disclosure to the appropriate authorities. Child abuse must be reported by the person who hears the "cry for help" from the child.

I certify I have read and will abide by the Confidentiality Notice in the above paragraphs.

_____   _____
Signature   **Date**

STUDENT FIELD EXPERIENCE LOG—EDUC 1301/2301 (CIRCLE ONE)

Student Name:

College Education Class: *EDUC 1301/2301*   Professor:

Date	School	Grade Level	Subject	Teacher Name	Time (Minutes)	Signature

*The school representative's signature verifies that the student spent the specified amount of time observing the class.

IMPORTANT RULES GOVERNING VOLUNTEER WORK IN THE SCHOOLS
(College Policies and Procedures)

1. You need to be aware of liability issues in the schools. Neither _____ College or ____ISD has provided you with liability insurance. You may want to look into coverage offered by organizations such as ATPE or TSEA.

2. You should NOT be left alone in the classroom with a student(s). In addition, you should not be left alone on a playground or field trip with a group of students without a licensed teacher within "shouting distance." DO NOT volunteer to drive a vehicle for any school outing. These rules are for your own protection, and it is important to alert your professor immediately if they are being violated.

3. You may NOT serve as a substitute teacher unless you have been officially approved by the school district to do so. In order to apply to be a substitute teacher in the district, you must meet the criteria listed on the MISD web site.

4. Substitute time does not count toward observation time in the schools.

5. If you are a paraprofessional, you may not count your job hours as your observation time in the schools. The RULE is that anything you are paid to do cannot count as observation time.

6. IF APPLICABLE: Junior Achievement: You and your host teacher together determine the dates and times of your observation time in the classroom. Once the two of you have agreed upon dates and times, it is important that you are present and on time for your observations. Punctuality and professional dress make important positive impressions on the school and its faculty. If you find that you are ill or have car trouble, you should call your school immediately and leave a message for your host teacher. Then, call him or her later at home and reschedule your make-up appointment.

7. You will maintain an observation log that must be signed by the teacher you observe. There are no exceptions to this rule. This log will be turned in at your final examination and must be completed to complete the requirements of the course satisfactorily.

IMPORTANT THINGS TO KNOW BEFORE YOUR FIRST VISIT

1. Wear a college identification card clearly displayed on your collar or around your neck. Clearly identify yourself to the school secretary.

2. Ask for registration procedures you follow to **sign in and out** each time you visit the school.

3. Ask the secretary for her name and the school telephone number so that you will know who to call in the event of an emergency. A map of the school is also a useful guide.

4. When/If your host teacher introduces you to his/her students, stand up, smile, and tell the students you are looking forward to observing their class. It is best to be friendly, but not casual, in your relationships with students.

5. If your host teacher shares any confidential information about any student or other faculty members at your school with you, the information should remain confidential. Don't make the mistake of becoming entangled in school gossip or in belittling students. If you are placed with a teacher who makes a habit of this sort of behavior, you should finish your observation, but ask for another teacher. The college and the school district wants your classroom experience with another professional to be of the highest caliber.

6. If you are asked to prepare materials to use in working with a student(s), the school should provide whatever paper and copy services you may need. If you pay for any school materials or copying services yourself, be sure to keep copies of the receipts for income tax purposes.

7. The college recognizes that many students have relatives working in the public schools of Midland; however, we ask that you do not complete *any hours* of observation with a relative.

8. Dress appropriately. Avoid very casual, evening, or otherwise inappropriate clothing. Avoid flip flops, spaghetti straps, strapless dresses/tops, and mini skirts.

How to Conduct a Classroom Observation

Each student is required to spend sixteen clock hours (not partial hours, but actual clock hours) or more in public school classrooms. These hours must be documented on the Observation LOG as described elsewhere.

While you are observing, you must be aware of the Testing Framework for Pedagogy and Professional Responsibilities Standards (PPR) because the more you identify with the core content of this course, the better your learning.

During all observations, try to determine which behavior matches which Standard (as noted in the Observation Form), and then within that Standard, which Competency is involved. For example, if the teacher uses a graphic organizer, what Standard/Competency do you think that teaching strategy would fall under? (Standards 1 and 2, so your notes would go under that Standard; then, point out Competencies 3 and 6 specifically). If the teacher models writing a paragraph, which Standard/Competency would that strategy fall under? (Standards 2 and 3; Competencies 5, 7, and 8) Everything you are observing in a classroom can be identified under one of the Standards/Competencies in the chart that follows. The better you get at matching, the better your observations and your understanding of the interrelatedness of teaching skills.

Take the following chart of the 4 Standards/13 Competencies that comprise the PPR for all teachers with you to each observation to help you identify the proficiencies you should be gaining familiarity with.

Keep this competency chart handy for all of your future learning, because all your future preservice teacher activity will be designed around it.

INTERACTIVE FORM

Type your name here:

EDUC _____ Observation Report #_____

Fill in the following table with the information from your first four hours of observation time as recorded on your log:

Category	Date	School	Grade	Subject	Teacher	Time

Under each of the Pedagogy and Professional Responsibilities Standards listed below, type a thorough, detailed description of what you saw in your observations concerning these standards. Tell me why you liked or disliked what you saw and how you might do things differently. Tell me why you think some things worked (behavior management, teaching strategies, etc.) and other things did not.

This report should be at least three pages in length when you have completed it. Use correct sentence structure, punctuation, spelling, and grammar. Above all, be reflective—I want to know your thoughts and opinions!

I. The teacher designs instruction appropriate for all students that reflects an understanding of relevant content and is based on continuous and appropriate assessment.

II. The teacher creates a classroom environment of respect and rapport that fosters a positive climate for learning, equity, and excellence.

III. The teacher promotes student learning by providing responsive instruction that makes use of effective communication techniques, instructional strategies that actively engage students in the learning process, and timely, high-quality feedback.

IV. The teacher fulfills professional roles and responsibilities and adheres to legal and ethical requirements of the profession.

V. What is the most important thing you learned from your observations?

The Reflective Teacher

Paragraph Structure for Writing a Competency Reflection

The reflective practitioner is a teacher who has learned to think carefully about the process and act of teaching. Writing reflective statements is one way to create concrete evidence of personal philosophies and thought processes that otherwise might go unstated. Reflecting gives one the opportunity to refine or even change thinking as one matures into a practitioner.

Sentence	Content
1	In the topic sentence, restate in two or three words the general knowledge the competency requires of beginning teachers and three methods for demonstrating the knowledge to be discussed in the paragraph. In this sentence, add a specific feeling about what is being required of beginning teachers.
2	Introduce the first method for demonstrating required knowledge.
3	Present an opinion about the method. What is your reaction to or feeling about what is being required?
4	Provide an example or detailed support for the opinion. Clear, specific support must be provided.
5	Introduce the second method for demonstrating required knowledge.
6	Present an opinion about the method.
7	Provide support for the second opinion.
8	Introduce the third method for demonstrating required knowledge that you selected from this competency.
9	Present an opinion about the method.
10	Provide support for the third opinion.
11	The concluding sentence ties the paragraph together, repeating the ideas presented in the introductory sentence and a feeling about meeting all of these requirements.

Writing an Educational Philosophy

The following web sites may help you get started on your educational philosophy. The second web site stresses that an educational philosophy is a changing document—it matures as you mature as a teacher. Preservice teachers experience rapid learning curves each semester, so writing a philosophy early in the term will provide an opportunity for growth and revision.

http://www.edulink.org/portfolio/philosophies.htm

http://www.associatedcontent.com/article/462584/writing_your_philosophy_of_teaching.html

A beginning educational philosophy should be no more than one page, double-spaced, nor should it make reference to any education course.

Educator Standards Web Search

The Texas Educator Standards define the knowledge and behaviors that all teachers should have before they enter a classroom as a lead teacher. Although there are only four Standards, each standard is divided into sub-areas of competency which preservice teachers are expected to define, learn, and execute as a matter of habit.

1. Click on this link to find the State Board for Educator Certification (SBEC):

    http://www.sbec.state.tx.us

This is the home page for SBEC. This web site can be overwhelming, but your tenacity will enable you to find information which will help you understand who determines what classroom teachers should know, what they should know, and how individuals certify to be teachers among many other topics.

- In the left-hand column, click on "Testing/Accountability."
- Click on "Educator Testing."
- Click on "Study Guides & Preparation Manual."
- Click on "Approved New Educator Standards."
- SCROLL down to "Pedagogy and Professional Responsibilities."
- Select **one of the five** "Pedagogy and Professional Responsibilities Standards" categories and click on it.

Category Selected: _____

_____

Type Standard #1: _____

_____

_____

Type Standard #2: _____

_____

_____

Type Standard #3: _____

_____

_____

Type Standard #4: _____

_____

_____

After reading through the Standards, noting the columns below, "What Teachers Know" and "What Teachers Can Do," type one example of "What Teachers Know" and "What Teachers Can Do" from each of the four Standards.

	What Teachers Know	**What Teachers Can Do**
Standard #1		
Standard #2		
Standard #3		
Standard #4		

- Return to the SBEC home page and in the left-hand column, click "State Board for Educator Certification."
- Click on "Educator Certification."
- In the left-hand column, click on "Certification Information."
- Click on "Certification Information Home."
- Click on "Becoming a classroom teacher in Texas."

Type your answers to each of the following questions.

1. What are three basic requirements for becoming a teacher in Texas?

    1.
    2.
    3.

- Return to the home page and in the left-hand column, click on "Educator Certification."
- In the left-hand column, click on "Career and Technical Education."
- Click on "Specific Requirements for Standard Career and Technical Education Certificates Based on Experience and Preparation in Skill Areas."
- Click on "approved educator preparation program."

2. Name the five "Certification Routes."

    1.
    2.
    3.
    4.
    5.

3. Find the region these four universities are in:
   - Sul Ross University is in which region?   Answer: _____
   - Texas Tech University is in which region?   Answer: _____
   - UT Tyler is in which region?   Answer: _____
   - _____ is in which region?   Answer: _____
     (you choose)

4. Click on any college or university. Identify: _____

Write a brief paragraph discussing what you learned about the teacher certification program at that university. Pay particular attention to program entrance requirements.

WEB SEARCHES

Web Search: Why Teach?

In this web search, you will be introduced to the State Board for Educator Certification web site and several other web sites. These web sites contain information that is critical to your future planning as you work toward certification.

Access the State Board for Educator Certification (SBEC) at this web site:
http://www.sbec.state.tx.us/SBECOnline/default.asp

1. In the left-hand column, click "State Board for Educator Certification." Click "Educator Certification." In the left-hand column, click "Certification Information." Click "Certification Information Home." Then click "Becoming a classroom teacher in Texas." What are three basic requirements for becoming a teacher in Texas?

    1.

    2.

    3.

2. If you are already certified, how do you become certified in another area?

3. Click on "Resources to Help Pay for Educator Preparation" and research one area which might apply to you and describe how you might obtain funding under this program.

4. Return to the home page and in the left-hand column, click on the "Fingerprinting" link. Who will be required to undergo a national criminal history background check in Texas? What is the cost associated with this check? Who pays for fingerprinting?

5. Return to the home page and in the left-hand column, click on the "Certification Laws and Rules" link.

    Click on "State Board for Educator Certification—Administrative Rules."

    Click on "Texas Administrative Code—Currently in Effect."

    Click on Chapter 230 "Professional Educator Preparation and Certification."

    Click on Chapter S "Educational Aide Certificate."

    Click on each of these links—"230.553," "230.554," and "230.555"—to discover the rules for being a certified aide in public schools. Which one of these levels do you qualify for when you obtain the AAT? Describe your credentials here.

Final Directions 285

6. Click on the following link: http://www.usca.edu/essays/vol102004/thompson.pdf

   List the 12 characteristics of highly-qualified teachers.

   1.
   2.
   3.
   4.
   5.
   6.
   7.
   8.
   9.
   10.
   11.
   12.

7. Click on this link: http://www.tasanet.org/files/PDFs/gr/2008/08qualitystudy.pdf produced by the Association of Texas Professional Educators (ATPE). Page 5 of this report documents four important findings. What are they?

   1.
   2.
   3.
   4.

8. Google "Teacher Salaries in Texas 2008" and click on the top link: "Becoming a Teacher in Texas/Teacher Certification in Texas." How does the salary in the city you hope to teach in compare with the mean salary in Texas? For how many days do you work to get this salary?

9. Now that you have completed some general informational areas of the career in teaching, write a brief 11-sentence reflection based on the most important things you have learned.

   1.

   2.

   3.

4.

5.

6.

7.

8.

9.

10.

11.

Benjamin Bloom's Cognitive Taxonomy

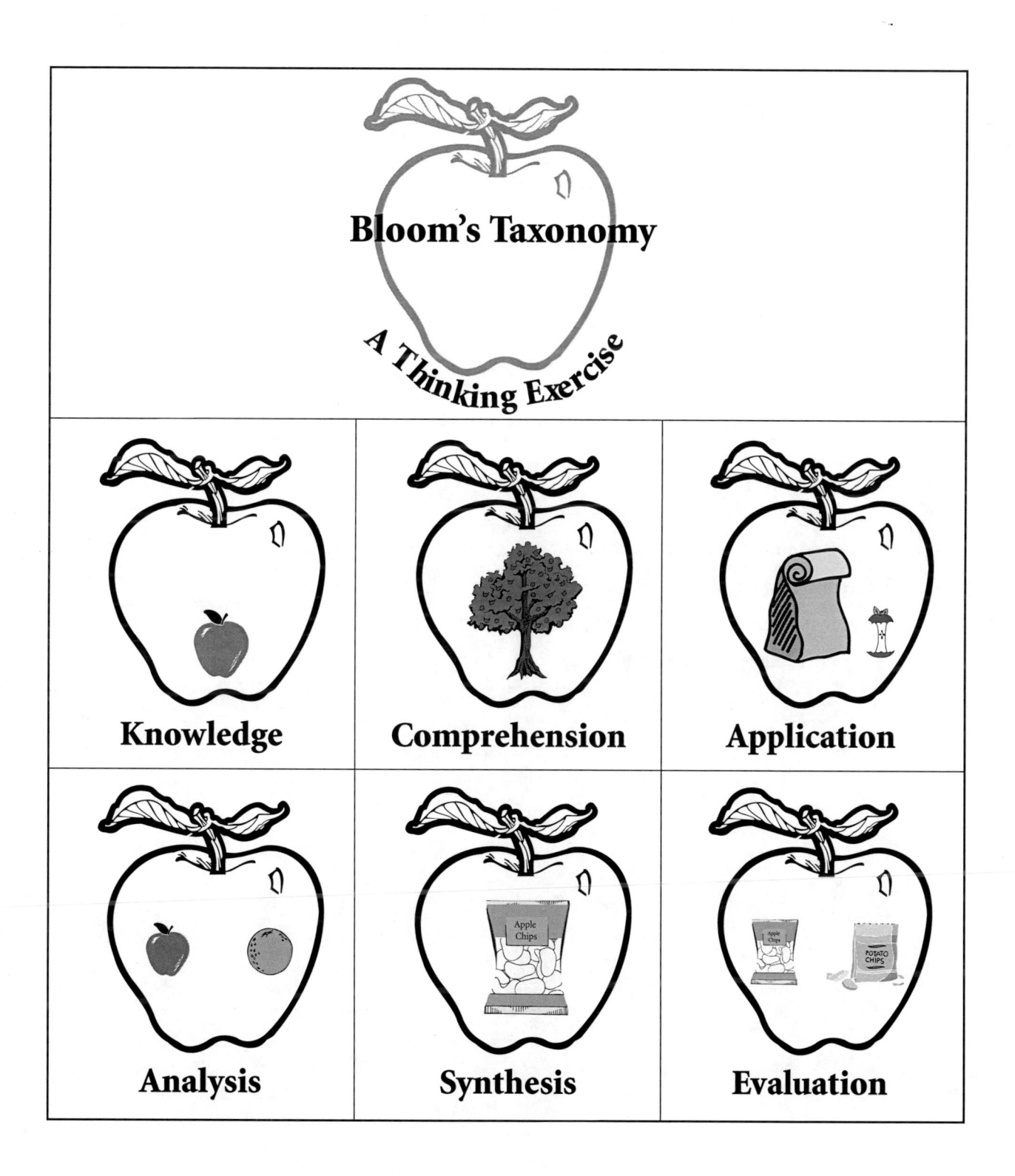

Bloom's Taxonomy

A Thinking Exercise

Knowledge	**Comprehension**	**Application**
Analysis	**Synthesis**	**Evaluation**

287

Scholar's Vocabulary Instructions

The Scholar's Vocabulary is composed of any educational terms that a student needs to know. One way to populate this vocabulary is to read through each of the Pedagogy and Professional Responsibilities (PPR) proficiencies provided at the beginning of each chapter and underline words that are critical to understanding in an educational context.

The first word is *cognitive* and demonstrates the procedure for completing this exercise for each competency.

DIRECTIONS

1. Do not use the term itself to define the word (this is called circular definition; i.e., a *dog* is a dog).
2. Define each word in an educational context.
3. The visualization is your "mind picture" of the word. You may/should use a word or two beneath the picture to make the connection clear.

The objectives for the preparation of the Scholar's Vocabulary are several. The scholar's vocabulary will:

1. place an emphasis on the proficiencies each teacher in Texas should accomplish before certification;
2. focus on the State's learning objectives for preservice teachers;
3. connect close reading with comprehension;
4. emphasize education jargon;
5. remind you that common words are sometimes hard to define without context;
6. create a personal study guide for competency exams; and
7. assess your ongoing learning.

Scholar's Vocabulary

An interactive glossary is a personal dictionary of terms that is constructed by the student for the express purpose of integrating with the term. Proper and consistent interaction with the jargon of education enriches your study and retention of key terms. The ultimate conclusion to this activity is to provide you with a study guide for your competency examinations.

Competency/ Page Reference	Word/Term	Dictionary Definition/ Context Sentence	Visualization
		Definition: Sentence:	
		Definition: Sentence:	
		Definition: Sentence:	
		Definition: Sentence:	

289

Competency/ Page Reference	Word/Term	Dictionary Definition/ Context Sentence	Visualization
		Definition: Sentence:	
		Definition: Sentence:	
		Definition: Sentence:	
		Definition: Sentence:	

Competency/ Page Reference	Word/Term	Dictionary Definition/ Context Sentence	Visualization
		Definition: Sentence:	
		Definition: Sentence:	
		Definition: Sentence:	
		Definition: Sentence:	

Competency/ Page Reference	Word/Term	Dictionary Definition/ Context Sentence	Visualization
		Definition: Sentence:	
		Definition: Sentence:	
		Definition: Sentence:	
		Definition: Sentence:	

Answers to Practice Questions

Competency 1
1. b
2. c
3. d
4. a
5. b
6. c
7. b
8. a
9. b
10. c

Competency 2
1. d
2. a
3. a
4. d
5. d
6. c
7. d
8. b
9. c
10. d

Competency 3
1. d
2. c
3. b
4. d
5. a
6. c
7. b
8. a
9. d
10. a

Competency 4
1. c
2. d
3. c
4. b
5. a
6. a
7. b
8. c
9. d
10. a

Competency 5
1. c
2. c
3. d
4. b
5. c
6. a
7. c
8. c
9. b
10. b

Competency 6
1. a
2. c
3. a
4. d
5. d
6. c
7. b
8. c
9. c
10. c

Competency 7
1. a
2. c
3. d
4. d
5. b
6. a
7. b
8. a
9. a
10. d

Competency 8
1. b
2. a
3. c
4. b
5. d
6. b
7. b
8. d
9. a
10. b

Competency 9
1. d
2. c
3. b
4. a
5. b
6. d
7. b
8. c
9. a
10. d

Competency 10

1. b
2. c
3. d
4. a
5. b
6. a
7. c
8. d
9. b
10. b
11. b
12. b
13. b
14. a
15. b
16. a
17. c

Competency 11

1. d
2. c
3. c
4. d
5. b
6. a
7. b
8. c
9. a
10. d
11. a
12. b
13. d
14. b
15. d

Competency 12

1. c
2. c
3. d
4. d
5. c
6. b
7. b
8. d
9. d
10. c

Competency 13

1. b
2. b
3. c
4. d
5. a
6. c
7. c
8. a
9. d
10. b
11. c
12. b
13. b
14. d
15. c
16. b
17. e
18. b
19. b